TWENTY YEARS

TWENTY
YEARS

Hope, War, and the Betrayal
of an Afghan Generation

SUNE ENGEL RASMUSSEN

Farrar, Straus and Giroux
New York

Farrar, Straus and Giroux
120 Broadway, New York 10271

Library of Congress Cataloging-in-Publication Data
Names: Rasmussen, Sune Engel, 1984– author.
Title: Twenty years : hope, war, and the betrayal of an Afghan generation /
    Sune Engel Rasmussen.
Other titles: Hope, war, and the betrayal of an Afghan generation
Description: First edition. | New York : Farrar, Straus and Giroux, 2024. |
    Includes bibliographical references.
Identifiers: LCCN 2024008247 | ISBN 9780374609948 (hardback)
Subjects: LCSH: Afghan War, 2001–2021—Personal narratives, Afghan. |
    Afghan War, 2001–2021—Youth. | Young adults—Afghanistan—Biography. |
    Afghanistan—Social conditions—21st century. | Afghanistan—Foreign
    relations—United States. | United States—Foreign relations—Afghanistan.
Classification: LCC DS371.413 .R376 2024 | DDC 958.104/70922—
    dc23/eng/20240315
LC record available at https://lccn.loc.gov/2024008247

Designed by Patrice Sheridan

Our books may be purchased in bulk for promotional, educational, or business use. Please
contact your local bookseller or the Macmillan Corporate and Premium Sales Department at
1-800-221-7945, extension 5442, or by email at MacmillanSpecialMarkets@macmillan.com.

www.fsgbooks.com
Follow us on social media at @fsgbooks

1   3   5   7   9   10   8   6   4   2

FOR DANIELLE

CONTENTS

TWENTY YEARS

PROLOGUE

The explosion hit around seven p.m. We couldn't hear the blast from the other side of Kabul, but we felt it: a deep, nauseating *whoomp* that rattled the windows and sent the street dogs into a barking fury. Then, the usual silence after an explosion, which always felt familiar and wholly wrong at the same time. Updates began rolling in on social media, where users pinned the location of the attack at the American University. I jumped into a car with Mokhtar, a trusted colleague and friend, and drove toward the university, racing the last part of the way on the wrong side of the road, Mokhtar with one hand on the horn and the other waving our press cards out of the window to get past police roadblocks. A car bomb had blown a hole in the outside wall of the university grounds, and inside, terrorists armed with machine guns and hand grenades were now hunting students around campus. Even the Taliban usually considered schools and universities off-limits in their war against the government and its foreign backers. Whoever was behind the attack wanted to send a message that things were about to change.

Outside the university, police, journalists, and onlookers stood in silence. Some flinched at the sporadic sound of explosions or rhythmic bursts of gunfire. On the other side of the walls, students were in a fight for their lives. Some survived by playing dead. In a classroom, a group of students barricaded the door, while the young women took off their headscarves and tied them together in a rope so they could flee through the window. When the gunmen threw a grenade at the door, the remaining students in the classroom jumped without a rope. One woman, Nargis, broke her leg in the fall and smashed her face into the ground, crushing most of her teeth. Her ears ringing, she crawled on her elbows to a row of bushes where she hid until she was able to make her way to a group of police officers still mustering the courage to enter the building.

Earlier that day I had met Rahmatullah Amiri for lunch. Fiercely smart, in his late twenties, Amiri was one of the bravest men I had ever met. During the day, he worked for a Western think tank producing reports on the Afghan war. In the evenings, he studied political science at the American University. For years he had sought to gain a deeper understanding of the Taliban: How was it organized, how could it be persuaded to lay down arms, how was it able to continue to recruit more young men than ever to its ranks, more than a decade after its regime was ousted? Born in the district of Musa Qala in Helmand, Amiri could pass for a Taliban fighter with his long scraggly beard and hair. His curiosity and easy temper won him the trust of many insurgents. While foreign journalists embedded with Western soldiers, Amiri hunkered down with the militants under bombardment, learned about their movements, and put himself through the visceral ordeal of heavy siege, a lived experience that had given impetus to the insurgents' holy war. Yet, at the same time, he was a product of modern Afghanistan. Engaged to a German woman, Amiri could often be found sitting in the sun dressed in the baggy garb of a villager, hunched over his laptop, doughnut and cappuccino in hand. Staunchly opposed to the Taliban's antiquated views of Islam, women, and law, he was equally critical of the abuse committed by Western countries against the Afghan population, which he thought was the main reason the Taliban could still mobilize.

That evening, shortly after the attack on the university, our lunch barely digested, I visited a hospital for war wounded in central Kabul. Throngs of relatives crowded the main entrance so the head of the hospital let me in through the back door. As soon as I entered, I locked eyes with Amiri. He was on a stretcher, wearing an oxygen mask and with his shirt ripped open to expose a deep wound in his stomach. I had met him for the first time less than twelve hours earlier, and by coincidence our paths crossed at the moment he was being rolled into the emergency ward. I noticed his hands trembling.

"They say I have internal bleeding," he said, visibly nervous. Amiri had seen enough gunshots to know which ones were dangerous and which ones only hurt. His did not look good.

He had been in class when the attack broke out. He had taken the lead in helping fellow students out a side entrance and down a set of stairs to an emergency exit, and had just stepped outside when a gunman appeared and shot him in the stomach. Amiri fell to the ground and pressed his backpack against the wound. He said he could feel his insides working their way out of the bullet hole. He waited two hours for an ambulance. Much longer and he wouldn't have made it. Two days after the university attack, I visited Amiri in the hospital again. His condition was stable, and now he was in pain and bored. He chuckled when I pointed out the irony of surviving years of embeds on the front lines only to be nearly killed in a classroom.

Seventeen people were killed in the attack on the American University, most of them students. More than fifty were injured. By Afghan standards, the casualty toll was tragically unremarkable. Bloodshed had been an everyday occurrence for forty years. Nevertheless, the attack shocked many—the callous targeting of teenagers marked a new chapter in the war.

During a decade of working in Afghanistan, I reported on countless explosions, mass shootings, and other attacks. Yet this one—in August 2016—was the one that defeated me. It was the first time I saw a young generation of Afghans—a generation with such promise and hope—turn so savagely on itself, with one side killing the other over competing visions of their country's future. The American University embodied ideals unattainable during the first Taliban regime from 1996 to 2001—equality, freedom of choice, human rights—and gave young Afghans, including women, the chance to pursue a secular education. And yet the young Taliban militants suspected of being behind the attack had also been empowered by the war: the university represented everything they resented about the US-led occupation and didn't want their country to become—and they were able to act on that belief. The perpetrators and their victims were from the same generation—and they had inherited an American war that had endured for so long that most of them likely didn't remember when it began.

No country has been changed more dramatically by the fallout of the 9/11 attacks than Afghanistan. This book is a story of war's astonishing transformative effect, and about the generation that tried to make sense and opportunity out of a superpower's twenty-year intervention in their country: Afghanistan's Generation 9/11. Some became dizzyingly wealthy or rose to the top echelons of government before the age of thirty-five. Others followed in their fathers' footsteps and became holy warriors. Most Afghans existed in the space in between, working daily to navigate society and find a way to fit in. All of them tried to build a life in the shadow of a war many in the United States and Europe had stopped following. The twenty-first century brought young Afghans new choices, and the choices they made is the story of what their country has become.

At the heart of the book are two characters whose conflicting experiences starkly indicate the broader divisions running through Afghanistan since 2001. Zahra led a personal war against the conservative norms of her society, a war every bit as brutal as an armed struggle. As a woman, and an ethnic Hazara, she belongs to the group that arguably gained the most from the intervention, and her struggle would not have succeeded without the fundamental changes Afghan society went through since 2001. Omari is among those for whom the new Afghanistan had no space. To Omari, who joined the Taliban at the age of fourteen, the US-led presence was a hostile occupation that had to be confronted violently, along with the Afghan government that assisted the Americans. Omari and his companions fought a battle for national self-determination, draped in religious cloaks. Aside from those two, the book tells the stories of other individuals I met and places I visited during a decade of reporting from Afghanistan, including three full years of living there. Among those I met were a young man who became so radicalized he chose to fight a holy war abroad, a young governor's son trapped in a veritable golden cage in a desert, and a young woman who ran a network of underground girls' schools.

For the majority of Afghans, twenty years of foreign occupation provided more opportunities in life: jobs, education, income, a measure of rights. Afghans today have more experience with democratic participation and state services and better living standards than they did before 2001, and that has created expectations that future rulers will have to reckon with. But millions of Afghans were also excluded from the post-2001 political order. The Taliban were a resistance movement that offered strongly pious young men a chance, and weapons, to vent their anger against invading foreign powers. If the longest war in American history left Afghanistan more developed, it also left it as bitterly divided as when it began. The failure to build the kind of fair, democratic system that Western nations promoted in words helped poison the ground upon which Afghans must build if they want to create a free and more prosperous society.

So this book is also a story of betrayal. The United States and its Western allies assured Afghans that the dark forces of fundamentalism would lose. They promised to help build a society where those who sought personal liberty, democracy, and a healthy partnership with the West were the future, and would be safe. They asked Afghans to believe in their vision. But if you topple a regime with military force, and promote an ideology on the back of an armed invasion, you implicitly ask the people who follow you to become soldiers, whether they realize it or not. That became brutally clear that evening at the American University, where young Afghans who sided with the Western coalition, even if only by seeking knowledge in an institution funded by American money, became targets. It became even more obvious in 2021, once the foreign troops had departed and the Taliban took control. It was not only those who had served the US-backed army, police force, or intelligence agency who faced immediate retribution. Lawyers, journalists, ex-government employees, civil society activists, and human rights defenders were hunted down and killed if they didn't manage to escape during the hectic weeks of evacuation. Once the protection of the US military evaporated, Afghans who had put their faith in the Western promises found themselves on the front line, alone.

Perhaps the American betrayal of a young Afghan generation was inevitable. Perhaps it was never possible to kill ideas and win over a population using military might. From the beginning, Western diplomats and politicians emphasized the necessity of forming an inclusive political order where all Afghans felt represented. And yet, the United States and its allies routinely rewarded chauvinism, political exclusion, corruption, and violent retribution.

After America left, Afghans were betrayed again. The Taliban promised the country would be freer and more just under their emirate. For the vast majority of Afghans, that has not been the case. The new rulers gave the impression that they had become more moderate since their first rule in the 1990s, but almost immediately set about imposing the same strict Islamic laws and restrictions, particularly on women. The arc of the past twenty years in Afghanistan has bent from fragile hope in the early days of the war through a bloody battle of values to the total collapse of the Western political project. Under the Taliban's authoritarian theocracy, the smallest claims to freedom—such as teaching girls to read—constitute courageous acts of resistance. And Afghans are resisting once again. The Taliban's victory marked the end of one story—America's war—but the beginning of another is already taking shape.

PART I
GROUND ZERO

1

ZAHRA

It was a hot, early summer day in early 2004, nearly three years after the planes hit the towers and changed the world, and Zahra was going home to a place she had no memory of. Surrounded by crowds of fellow Afghans, she stared down the highway that led across the Iranian border into her country of birth. She had been born on the road, literally. When her parents had fled Afghanistan twenty years earlier, her mother was heavily pregnant. During their escape, halfway between Bamiyan and Herat, her father suddenly ordered the beat-up taxi to pull over. In the back seat his wife gave birth to Zahra, their first daughter. Twelve days later they crossed the border into Iran.

Now, at the age of nineteen, Zahra was heading back into Afghanistan with her own children in tow, two of them, and her husband, Hussein. The family and about twenty other relatives, including Hussein's parents, had boarded a bus at the central terminal in Tehran. Zahra's mother and siblings had moved to Afghanistan a few months earlier, and her father stayed behind in Iran to work and support the family, planning to follow once they had built a stable life. The bus had carried them and the belongings they could carry through the suburban slums of the Iranian capital until the metropolis ceded and the mountains gave way to the melon country of Garmsar. They passed coffee-colored plains dotted with ancient mud fortresses and towns swept by fresh, chilly winds. It had taken them twelve hours to reach Mashhad near the Afghan border, home to the shrine of Imam Reza, the eighth of the twelve imams that Shias believe are the rightful successors to the Prophet Mohammad. The city's opulent mausoleum that attracted millions of pilgrims each year lit the night golden.

When they crossed the border the next day, surrounded by families who like hers were going home, Zahra burst into tears.

The twentieth century, with its wars and mass migration, was an era of displacement. But in the beginning of the twenty-first century, Afghanistan was, for a brief period, a place of homecoming. Afghans in Iran and Pakistan had in the 1980s, despite numbering less than twenty million people, constituted nearly half of the world's total population of refugees. Now, hundreds of thousands were crossing the border to partake in the regeneration of their country, promised by Western nations.

A life in exile is a life unrooted. A permanent feeling of not belonging, of perpetual loss of something left behind. Refugees who settle in new foreign places may be fortunate enough to escape physical danger and grow up in peace, as Zahra's family did in Iran. But they are often excluded from the native communities of that place, which emerge from culture, language, and shared experiences. The imagined bonds of national or tribal identity in which stable societies are rooted are directly opposed to the unmoored nature of exile.

"Exile is strangely compelling to think about but terrible to experience," the Palestinian American thinker Edward Said wrote. "It is the unhealable rift forced between a human being and a native place, between the self and its true home: its essential sadness can never be surmounted."

Despite having no recollection of Afghanistan whatsoever, Zahra's longing for the country of her birth was so strong it felt almost spiritual. Zahra's parents had fled Afghanistan during the war against the Soviet invasion in the 1980s. Along with tens of thousands of other

Afghan families, they had settled in Tehran where Zahra and her siblings had grown up with stories about Afghanistan that were mostly dreadful, tainted by her parents' trauma of war and displacement. Yet, her existence in Iran had always seemed temporary. As an Afghan, she grew up among Iranian classmates and friends in the street, but didn't have the same rights as them. Life in Iran had always had shades of fiction to it, as if she were the protagonist of one of the many novels she had devoured growing up. One of her favorite books was Victor Hugo's *Les Misérables*, about the good-hearted ex-convict Jean Valjean and the orphaned Cosette whom he adopts. Just like them, she had to go through trials and tribulations in order to break free from a troubled past and create a new life. Like theirs, Zahra's lifelong torment was surely temporary. It had to be.

To begin with, Zahra was only peripherally aware of the 9/11 attacks. The name al-Qaeda meant nothing to her. She knew little about the Taliban, the Islamist movement that ruled Afghanistan and sheltered al-Qaeda, beyond their reputation for brutally oppressing Afghans, women in particular. She heard from other refugees that under the Taliban's rule, some Afghans were so poor they had to boil and eat grass to survive. But even as a teenager, when the aftershock of the 9/11 attacks reached Afghans in Tehran, she sensed that something monumental was happening. Weeks later, an American-led coalition rained bombs over Afghanistan, invaded with ground troops, and toppled the Taliban regime, ushering in what was meant to be a new era of peace and prosperity. The country's new interim leader, Hamid Karzai, called on his countrymen and -women to be patriots and come home. Women, in particular, were needed to rebuild the nation, where they would find opportunities to study and work, Karzai said.

After the fall of the Taliban, Zahra began dreaming in earnest about returning to her country of birth. She often listened to the Afghan singer Dawood Sarkhosh, famous for his sentimental odes of feeling bereft of his motherland. One of them was called "Sarzamine Man," or "My Land": "I wander around aimlessly homeless / from one home to another, I move and move."

Zahra's younger brother, who like her husband was called Hussein, had been the first member of the family to return to Afghanistan, in 2003. Soon after his arrival in the western city of Herat, Hussein sent photos back in which he posed in front of a rented house and a clean white Toyota Corolla, which he said his new job had allowed him to buy. He described how peaceful their home country was. Zahra felt an unfamiliar rush of optimism. About a year later, the rest of the family followed.

At the border, the crowds slowly thinned as United Nations staff shepherded returnees into minibuses that took them to a reception camp near Herat. The physical distance from the Iranian border to Herat is about seventy-five miles but spans different worlds. Iran was modern and clean, with paved roads and new buildings. Zahra thought Afghanistan was grimy by comparison. This was partly a result of its location. Western Afghanistan is located in the path of the Wind of 120 Days, named so because it blows viciously for four months of the year, leaving all surfaces—tables, cars, teeth—covered in dust. Trash was strewn in the streets. Dirt seemed to crawl its way into all corners. Zahra's brother picked her, Hussein, and the children up from the camp. Driving through the center of Herat, Zahra was struck by a feeling that the city was changing rapidly, even if she had never seen it before. Apartment blocks and other concrete buildings shot up everywhere, several stories high, leaving the older houses, scarred by rockets and shrapnel, like vestiges of a bygone era.

Zahra's parents had fled Afghanistan in 1984. During the 1980s and 1990s, as many as six million Afghans lived as refugees abroad, most of them in neighboring Iran and Pakistan, where they settled in the cities and worked backbreaking and irregular jobs. Many from Afghanistan's Shia Muslim minority went to Iran, where the state religion was Shia Islam. At the time, Iran was undergoing its own historic upheaval. In 1979, a popular movement led by Ayatollah Ruhollah Khomeini, a fiery preacher with Hollywood charisma, had toppled the country's US-backed monarch, Shah Mohammad Reza Pahlavi, and established an Islamic republic. The Islamic Revolution catapulted

Ayatollah Khomeini into a Cold War pantheon of great Third World leaders, alongside Kwame Nkrumah, the overthrower of British rule in Ghana, and Egypt's Gamal Abdel Nasser who nationalized the Suez Canal. Like those leaders, Khomeini would come to uphold his rule with violently authoritarian means. But his anti-imperialist stance made him a hero to many, including leftists in the West. He cast Iran as a sanctuary for the world's oppressed Muslims and said it was a duty to welcome Iran's "homeless and disinherited" neighbors fleeing war, meaning Afghans. For most Afghans, life in Iran, despite an ongoing war against neighboring Iraq and growing repression of political dissent, provided more security than their own home country. The conflict with the Soviet Union killed as many as 1.5 million Afghans. Tens of thousands were killed in the subsequent civil war, before the Taliban took power and imposed a fundamentalist theocracy.

Growing up in the 1990s in Shahr-e Rey, a poor southern suburb of Tehran, Zahra was different not just from her Iranian classmates, but from her Afghan peers, too. From an early age, she found her own refuge in books, the heroes of which became her closest companions. Zahra's mother tried to teach her housekeeping skills to prepare her for a life as a homemaker and wife, but even as Zahra was cleaning or cooking, her mind spun alternate worlds. The written word seized her attention and got her into trouble. Zahra received her first thrashing one day when she absentmindedly tripped over one of the family's sheep and dropped a tray of glasses. Later, her mother slapped her because she had been so absorbed in *Les Misérables* that she burned the food. She beat her a second time when it happened again. The beatings, Zahra would later say, taught her to focus but also made her resilient to pain.

Plump, with delicate facial features, Zahra had angular eyes characteristic of her ethnic background—she was from a family of Hazaras, a Shiite Muslim minority. She got her narrow nose from her mother, Fatima, and her easy smile from her father, Eskandar, who also supplied her with her last name: Hosseini. She dreamed big. She inhaled magazine articles about women who rose up against difficult odds to become leaders. Like many other children, Zahra just wanted to be someone else. She idolized Benazir Bhutto, the elegant Pakistani prime minister who became the first female leader of a Muslim-majority nation. When she was around ten and Bhutto came on the television, Zahra's mother would change the channel and scold Zahra for admiring a woman who wore her headscarf so promiscuously. Zahra's mother valued education. If only Zahra had not been so distracted and clumsy. Those were flaws that, in her mother's eyes, needed to be exorcised from a young girl as quickly as possible.

At the time of her parents' escape from Afghanistan in 1984, the great global powers were carving up much of the world in spheres of influence, and Afghanistan was caught in the middle. Moscow had invaded Afghanistan in 1979 to prop up a feeble Communist government in Kabul, which had taken power in a coup the year before. The new government had launched social and land reforms, which it implemented through a campaign of violent repression that prompted Afghans across the country to rise up. Though fighting for national goals, the disjointed armed guerillas that sprang from the resistance, known collectively as the mujahideen, became part of the global Cold War struggle and soon found themselves flush with cash and weapons, including from the United States. The Soviet Union quickly discovered that it was impossible to hold all of Afghanistan. Months into the campaign, approximately one hundred thousand Soviet troops controlled the cities, while the mujahideen were able to roam more or less freely in the countryside and lob American-supplied antiaircraft missiles at Soviet planes. Soviet troops responded with bombings that displaced millions of Afghans. By 1982, 1.5 million Afghans had fled west to Iran, including Eskandar and Fatima, and nearly twice that number had crossed the southern and eastern borders into Pakistan.

Zahra's mother lived guided by the word of the Quran, which she interpreted strictly. Zahra's father, while also very religious, was less dogmatic. In Iran, he had found work as a cleaner and helping hand at a local businessman's company, but in Afghanistan he had been a farmer. Eskandar and Fatima both grew up in cultures worlds apart from the urban lifestyle of the Iranian capital they settled in, and which in the mid-1980s was home to five million people. Under the shah, Iran had undergone a rapid industrialization, fueled by a booming oil industry that belched out a thick smog over southern Tehran. The heavy, gray pollution blanketing the Shahr-e Rey suburb was Zahra's earliest childhood memory. Despite Iran's open-door policy to Afghans, many refugee families experienced discrimination and harassment. The influx of so many newcomers at a time when Iranians themselves were displaced in great numbers by the war with Iraq fueled mistrust of migrants. Zahra, immersed in her literature, didn't feel any of those tensions. She happily walked several miles to school every day. A supervisor at school, a woman in her thirties called Ms. Khorasani, was one of the few Iranians Zahra knew who treated Afghan kids as equals to their Iranian classmates. Ms. Khorasani took a liking to Zahra. Every morning she gave her a hug, against school rules. The supervisor had a large nose, which was shaped like an eagle's beak, and she was proud of it. She said it was a real Iranian nose.

"You Afghans have such small noses. How are you even able to breathe?" she teased Zahra. Whenever Zahra was sad or upset, Ms. Khorasani let her rest her head on her shoulder, something her mother never let her do. In Fatima's experience, tenderness got a woman nowhere in a life that could be utterly brutal. Marriage could be warfare, an actual battle to stay physically and mentally safe. A woman was best off making herself useful by raising a flock of children. Sentimentality was useless. By then, Fatima had given birth to three more children: a son, Hussein, and two daughters named Rokhaya and Tahera. Another son, Hassan, and daughter, Mohadesa, would follow, each spaced about two and a half years apart. The two boys would be all right, but Zahra and her three sisters needed to be bolstered against the cruelty of life and men. They needed to learn to read and cook, and to be raised in Islam. That's why Fatima hit Zahra if her daughter burned the food or broke glasses. At the age of nine, Zahra was able to cook a *ghorme sabzi* stew so delicious that the neighbors came to visit when the smell of slow-cooked herbs, beans, and meat wafted through the open windows into the street.

A good Muslim girl prays from the age of nine, so Zahra started when she was eight. She had already worn the Islamic headscarf, the hijab, from the age of four. Now, her parents would wake her up at dawn every morning and help her recite the Muslim declaration of faith and bow to God in the correct manner. Praying with her back to the door, facing Mecca, Zahra could often feel her parents tiptoe into the room to make sure she did it right. They didn't need to. Zahra enjoyed praying alone. The meditative surrender to God gave her a sense of privacy and peace, but her parents' eagle eyes felt coercive. When they were watching, she found herself praying fast. To get it over and done with.

One afternoon, Zahra heard music coming from the neighbors' yard. She dragged a plastic box over to the wall separating the two compounds and stood on her toes. The neighbors, who were Iranian, were celebrating a wedding in the garden. One man played a wooden flute called a *ney*, another beat a *daf*, a rattling drum made of goatskin. Men and women in colorful traditional dresses and baggy pants danced around in a circle. Zahra had never seen such a display of joy in her own house. The men formed a circle, taking turns to dance in the middle, each armed with a wooden stick that they clashed against each other like swords. The traditional dance, called *chubazi*, was particularly popular among the tribes of southern Iran. Suddenly, Zahra's mother came storming out of the house, grabbed a plastic hose off the ground, and whipped her daughter on the backside, knocking her off her perch. Zahra rushed inside. Music was sinful, and spying on your neighbors was even worse, her mother said. But Zahra had glimpsed a different world.

Zahra always sensed that they preferred her first brother, Hussein. Three years younger than her, Hussein was far more rebellious but, perhaps because he was their firstborn son, it seemed to Zahra that he could do anything he pleased. As the oldest in the family, Zahra became the target of her parents' scolding. She increasingly felt like a guest in her own family. Eskandar never laid a hand on his daughter, but he also didn't show her much love. He used to joke that Zahra wasn't his real daughter, that he had found her in a nearby Kuchi nomad camp. Fatima said he was just teasing, but it stung, and deepened Zahra's feeling that her presence was tolerated only temporarily until a suitable man came along. Shortly after she turned thirteen, he did.

Zahra met her future husband in a parking lot. She was at her uncle's wedding, and had taken her youngest brother outside to stop his crying, where she bumped into Hussein, who was about ten years older than her. He played with her brother and immediately calmed the boy down. A few days later, Zahra's parents told her that Hussein's family had asked for her hand in marriage, and that they had accepted. She was elated. Hussein seemed tender and thoughtful. He was a divorcee, but Zahra's family didn't mind as long as he could pay the dowry and would treat her well. Zahra's friends told her she was lucky to have found a good man. Hussein also appeared to be hardworking. For six months leading up to the wedding, Zahra barely saw him, and when she did, he was quiet. On the rare occasions when he would visit with his family, he only uttered a few words to her: "Hello. How are you?" He usually fell asleep on cushions on the floor shortly after arriving, and only woke up when his family shook him awake to go home.

"He works in the fields until late at night," his parents said. Zahra wished his visits would last longer.

The wedding was set for March 1998, on the last day of the year 1376 in the Persian calendar. As was tradition, Zahra's family shelled out for a wedding ring as a present for Hussein. To their surprise, his family didn't reciprocate. They didn't buy a ring or a dress for Zahra, even though all wedding expenses were the responsibility of the groom's family. Instead they bought Zahra a cheap white cotton shirt and matching skirt.

Hours before the wedding, Zahra sat reclined in a chair in a beauty parlor, head back and her eyes closed, wincing every time the beautician plucked a hair from one of her eyebrows. With every stroke of the makeup brush her face turned paler, until she looked like a marble figurine. The older ladies at the beauty salon fawned over her. "Doesn't she look beautiful for her wedding?" Zahra's grandmother crowed behind her. "She is a very lucky girl."

Zahra was excited. All her classmates were invited to her wedding. She knew most Iranians didn't approve of marriage at such a young age, but at least her Afghan friends would come. As the older women doted on her ahead of her big night, she felt ready to become a wife. Ready to fall in love.

"Is your fiancé good-looking?" the beauty assistant asked. Before Zahra could answer, her future mother-in-law, who also observed the preparations from a chair in the corner, burst in: "Yes, our groom is very handsome."

Afghan marriages almost always involved a financial exchange. Westerners tended to call this form of marriage arranged, or even forced, underscoring the lack of choice for the woman. For many Afghan families, free choice in marriage was an unknown luxury. For poor families, daughters were a sort of financial asset. That did not mean they were not loved. But life consisted of a series of logistical maneuvers aimed at securing the survival and safety of the family. While boys worked to feed the family, girls contributed their share by bringing in a onetime sum to the family in the form of a dowry, before becoming another's family's responsibility.

Ms. Khorasani likely knew that Zahra's family wasn't well off, but when the girl told her that she could no longer attend school because she had gotten engaged, the supervisor still broke into tears.

"Zahra, you are so young. Do you really want to get married?" she said. Ms. Khorasani stomped home with Zahra after school, demanding to see her mother. Through the door, Zahra could hear the two women argue. The supervisor begged Fatima to wait a few years so Zahra at least could finish school before getting married. Fatima did not relent. It was none of Ms. Khorasani's business how they did things in this family. Zahra, at thirteen, was already a woman and marriage would protect her against other men.

"She has spent enough time in school," Fatima said.

Zahra jumped out of the way when Ms. Khorasani burst out of the room, tears streaming down her face. She gave Zahra a brief hug, kissed her cheek, and slammed the door behind her.

Hours before the wedding, the reality that Zahra was leaving seemed to dawn on her family. Her father was dejected; her mother cried. Her younger brother Hussein held Zahra and wailed, begging her coming husband's family not to take her away. Nobody had told her much about the procedures of the wedding itself, or what was meant to happen on the wedding night.

"On your wedding night, you are meant to be together," Zahra's aunt had told her, but Zahra hadn't fully understood. After the ceremony was concluded and all the guests had been fed, the newlyweds were escorted to a room decked out with blankets and pillows on the floor. Hussein's demeanor was gentle. As a second-time groom, he knew what to do. Once alone, he asked Zahra to lie down. Before she noticed what was happening, he swiftly lifted up her skirt. It felt like she was being ripped open from the inside. Zahra bit down on her scarf to avoid screaming. Then she passed out.

She woke up the next day before dawn with a piercing pain in her abdomen. The bedsheet felt sticky. She felt scared and ashamed. Hussein lay next to her but did not stir.

"What on earth happened to me?" she thought. She started crying, and didn't stop until sunrise when the women of the house came and saw her, then took her to a clinic. Hussein's mother and her aunt and grandmother crowded in to hear what the Iranian doctor, a woman named Dr. Setayesh, said.

"What the hell have you done to her?" Dr. Setayesh shouted at the three women. She turned to address Mehtab, Hussein's mother.

"What in God's name is the matter with your son? Is he a donkey?" she said, invoking an offensive Persian slur. "How could he treat her like this?"

This couldn't have been the first time Dr. Setayesh witnessed a young Afghan girl after a marital rape, but Zahra remembered she looked shaken. After the examination, she told Zahra that the wound needed twenty stitches.

"I'm not going to charge you for this," Dr. Setayesh said when the older women had left the room. She fixed her gaze on Zahra.

"And in the future, don't come to any other doctor but me."

Zahra tried to settle into married life. She and Hussein moved into his parents' house. She forgot about Benazir Bhutto, her childhood idol. Burdened by new duties, she became a teenage housewife with no time for daydreaming or losing herself in books. She cooked for her in-laws and treated them respectfully. She spoke in the manner they expected from their son's wife, which meant not very much. She had been naive to think that she, an Afghan girl from an impoverished highland family, could be anything different than a satisfactory wife, and eventually a mother. A few days after the wedding, Zahra noticed that Hussein wasn't wearing his ring. He had sold it in order to pay for her wedding clothes.

There were carnal duties, too. In Hussein's family, according to their interpretation of Islamic scripture, God punished a woman who rejected her husband's request for sexual intercourse, the only exception being if she was ill or he was intoxicated. The angels would curse her until the day she returned to her obligation and satisfied him, and in the meantime, he was allowed to hit her if she refused. Dr. Setayesh had told Zahra not to have intercourse for three months to allow the wound to heal. After two weeks, Hussein was unable to wait any longer, and he convinced her to have sex again. It hurt again, but not as much as the first time, and this time she didn't bleed. Zahra found solace in the fact that he often worked in the fields outside Tehran at night, when temperatures were cooler. At home, he slept most of the day. One day Zahra returned home from the bazaar to find Hussein and a group of friends seated in a circle, shrouded in gray smoke that smelled pungent and sweet, passing a pipe between them. Opium use was widespread among Afghan day laborers in Iran, who were often offered the drug by their Iranian employers or colleagues as a way to help them work longer hours without feeling hunger. But Zahra had never seen anyone use drugs before.

That afternoon was the first time Hussein hit Zahra. He seemed embarrassed that she had seen him in such a state. Once he got going, he didn't stop. It was as if his first beating of her had knocked the lid off a vessel inside him full of bitterness and anger, now impossible to contain. These beatings were worse than what she had endured at the hands of her family members, and Zahra steeled her body against a new set of fists and feet. Hussein gradually paid less attention to his job. The opium consumed him. Yet he never seemed too tired to hit his wife. Zahra would come to think of the violence as the result of a deep-seated shame, combustible fuel in a man. Hussein must have been ashamed of his drug abuse, and of having disappointed his first wife, whom he divorced, Zahra thought. Still, while Zahra never doubted that her own family loved her, despite the lashings she received, it was different with Hussein. No matter how much she forced herself to smile in his company, or how often she told him she loved him, she never felt her love requited. Hussein's very existence seemed cloaked in a darkness that never let go.

Zahra could feel a darkness closing in on herself as well, embracing her until she could barely breathe. On a humid June afternoon in 1998, three months after her wedding, looking for an escape, she swallowed a handful of painkillers her doctor had prescribed her.

"In my family, divorce was as dishonorable as murder," she said. Her mother-in-law found her collapsed on the floor and rushed her to the emergency ward. When Zahra regained consciousness, her gut aching from having the pills pumped out of her, she saw Mehtab's face poised over her, throbbing with fury. How humiliating it was for her to stand here. Zahra had to get a grip, she said. Zahra replied that she didn't know what to do about a man who was meant to provide for her, but who was busy smoking his days away. She bit her tongue. She shouldn't have told on Hussein like that. She did not have to worry.

"We already know about that," Mehtab said, detecting Zahra's expression. Hussein had been smoking for the past four years, well before they got married. That explained why he had always been so tired when his family came to visit to court her.

"We thought he would get better once he got married to you. But instead here you are trying to kill yourself," Mehtab told Zahra. "Get yourself together. You could have killed the baby."

Zahra had no idea what the woman was talking about. Her words still hung in the air when the doctor entered the room.

"Has your mother taught you nothing?" Dr. Setayesh scolded Zahra. The tenderness returned to her voice. "There are a thousand ways to avoid something like this."

Zahra, not for the first time, felt like the only person in the room who didn't know what was going on. It took her a minute to work out what it was her mother hadn't taught her.

The pregnancy likely saved Zahra's life. In *Les Misérables*, the holy scripture of Zahra's childhood, the ex-prisoner Jean Valjean fought heroically to foster the orphaned Cosette. She had purpose now.

Zahra had been pregnant for about a month when she tried to kill herself. During her pregnancy she frequently consulted with Dr. Setayesh, who also prescribed medicine for Hussein to try to wean him off the drugs. It worked, periodically, but Hussein did not have the willpower to stay clean for long. Eight months later, when Zahra's water broke, Hussein was nowhere to be found, so it was his mother who accompanied her to the hospital. The birth went wrong from the beginning. Her young hips were too narrow to give birth, and the child's head got stuck. The midwife wanted to perform a caesarean but not without the consent of her husband. Even in Hussein's absence, as she was giving birth to their child, her body belonged to him. So Zahra pushed and pushed, for hours, until she passed out. At last, a little girl emerged, but she had suffered severe lack of oxygen and her temples had been squeezed during labor. The doctors said she had most likely suffered brain damage, as they wrapped up the child and let Zahra take her home. She was born on March 17, the same day as Imam Ali, one of the most important figures in Islam and, according to Shias, the rightful heir of the Prophet Mohammad. Hussein's mother named her Nargis, meaning daffodil, and Zahra didn't object. When she was younger, Zahra's mother had prohibited her from even carrying her little sisters, worried that she might drop them. For the first days with Nargis, Zahra was afraid to hold her. She was also slightly scared of her daughter, who cried incessantly, for months, until they took her to the doctor, who scanned the girl and found the brain damage they had feared. The condition would impede Nargis's development and they didn't think she had much more than a few years to live.

Looking back years later, those days bled together for Zahra in a haze of kicks and punches, in a ceaseless white noise of wailing and shouting, viewed through a shroud of tears. Her memory washed out. But she stayed loyal to Hussein. Love isn't always as love does, her grandmother had taught her, and a man can love you even if he isn't able to tell you. Perhaps Zahra's young age made her feel more connected to Hussein. Her universe was small and he was its center.

Darkness had followed Hussein since he was a child. His parents had been cousins and lived together with Hussein's grandparents. When they were old enough, his grandfather decided they should get married, a practical and cheap arrangement. When Hussein was four, his father eloped with another cousin, Mehtab. After losing her husband, Hussein's mother became plagued by violent migraines. One afternoon, the pain chased her out of the house and down to the river, where her body was found washed up on the bank. Hussein stayed in his grandparents' house for years until one day, his father came back and took him and his brother. There was a third child in the house, Hussein's youngest brother, but his father said he had been fathered by someone else, and left him behind. Hussein spent the rest of his upbringing with his emotionally distant father and aunt, Mehtab— the woman he would call mother.

Zahra tried to understand where his rage came from. She understood that he had been bruised by love. He told her how he as a young man in Iran had fallen in love with a beautiful girl who loved him back. He worked in the fields to make enough money for the dowry. When he had made what seemed like a healthy sum of money, he handed it over to his father, asking him to request the girl's hand. It did not go well. The girl's father disliked Hussein's family. He didn't say why. In a flash of cruelty, he agreed to marry off his daughter to Hussein for the equivalent of about $14,000, an astronomical sum he knew was unobtainable for Hussein's family. Hussein was crushed. When he asked his father for his proposed dowry back, his father told him he had spent it to pay off a debt. Hussein was never the same again. Men like him didn't get many chances. From that point on, when he toiled in the fields at late hours, he would often ease the night with opium given to him by other farmhands. Zahra realized her husband was not born a tyrant, even if he behaved like one.

Zahra had long felt suspicious of some medicine Hussein used to put in his tea. He said it was to help his back pain, but Zahra had never noticed him to have a bad back. With Hussein's sporadic salary, the couple had found their own place and invited his brother to live with them. One day Zahra brought the medicine to the brother, who knew more about that stuff than she did. Without telling him where she'd found it, she asked if she could use the brown powder as a painkiller. The brother immediately recognized the cumin-like powder as opium and, evidently upset, told her to stay away from it. Hussein had promised to stop using, and when Zahra later that day confronted him, he exploded. Their one-year-old daughter watched from her spot on the floor as Hussein thrashed Zahra so viciously that she wasn't able to stand afterward. There was a deliberateness in his violence that she hadn't noticed before.

"He wanted to make sure I never asked him about drugs again," Zahra remembered.

"This is who I am," Hussein hissed at her: "If you ever ask me such a thing again, you can go back and live with your father."

About a year later, Zahra gave birth to the couple's second daughter, whom she named Parisa, meaning someone who has the nature of a fairy. This time, the labor was easier and Parisa was a healthy child. But Nargis continued to wail, and one evening, Hussein couldn't take it any longer. It had been a while since his last fix and his daughter's screams made his throbbing head hurt. He grabbed a pillow and crawled on all fours over to Nargis.

"Can't you make her shut up?" he shouted at Zahra as he put the pillow over Nargis's face. Zahra jumped up and pushed Hussein's emaciated body aside and pulled Nargis close to her chest. Not yet two, Nargis seemed to instinctively understand what had happened. From then on, whenever Hussein entered the room, she would crawl toward her mother, and cry every time Zahra tried to leave her alone.

After Nargis turned three, her condition worsened. She was frequently struck by fever and what seemed like epileptic seizures that jolted her arms and legs straight into the air. Medicine prescribed by the family doctor brought the fever down, allowing Nargis to sleep for a few hours, and eventually the seizure subsided. The attacks hindered Nargis's development even more. At the age of four, she could say only two words: "mom" and "water."

One day, the fever wouldn't break. Zahra brought her daughter to the doctor, but this time there was nothing Dr. Setayesh could do. She told Zahra to bring Nargis to the house so she could spend her final hours at home.

Zahra didn't cry. She gave her daughter a bath, pouring water over her with a bucket. With every splash, Nargis breathed heavily and her eyelids fluttered almost imperceptibly. When Zahra stroked Nargis's head, a tuft of hair fell off as she removed her hand. She lifted Nargis out of the bath, dried her off, and put her on a mattress. She tried to feed her a bit of food from a spoon, but it dribbled out of her mouth. They sat like that for a few hours. Hussein worked in Karaj, an industrial city about an hour's drive from Shahr-e Rey, and he always came home later. That evening, he entered the door without a word and, not noticing his family, went straight to bed. Zahra didn't get up. After midnight, Nargis finally swallowed a bit of her own spit. Zahra gave her water, and she drank that, too. Shortly after, Nargis stopped breathing and her fingers relaxed their grip around Zahra's. Zahra went to Hussein and shook him awake. He listened to her and said nothing. He didn't touch Nargis, but went into the corner and sat cross-legged, weeping silently. Together in the room, they sat alone in grief.

They stayed like that until Hussein's brother came home after working through the evening. Zahra sent him to fetch his parents, who lived twenty minutes away. They arrived five hours later, at seven in the morning.

"Why haven't you tied her legs and closed her mouth?" Mehtab demanded.

"I have never seen a dead person before. How am I supposed to know what to do?" Zahra said, a new defiance singing in her throat. Her mother-in-law turned away from her and went to find a sheet and some string. She wrapped the sheet around Nargis's body as a shroud, then tied one string above her head and one below her feet. Zahra dried her eyes. She was eighteen, and she was done crying.

In the coming months, Zahra isolated herself. The loneliness was crushing, but Hussein was drifting deeper into an opiate fog. When he occasionally emerged, it was often in bursts of violence that Zahra didn't know how to stop. Their second daughter, Parisa, helped distract Zahra a bit from the loss of Nargis. It was good to stay occupied. When she wasn't looking after Parisa, she cleaned or cooked. She practiced the universal language of survival of the subjugated: silence. Only by staying silent was she able to set aside her own grief and focus on being a good mother and daughter-in-law, even if Mehtab continued to treat her as an intruder in the family.

Hussein eventually lost his job and gave Zahra permission to find work outside the home. Somewhat ironically, the job she found was as an assistant to a marriage counselor. She sat in on sessions with Iranian couples who had found each other spontaneously and fallen in love. Even those in arranged marriages had been asked for their consent before the wedding. It seemed love in marriage was possible. The counselor often reminded the couples that the husband had a responsibility to look after his wife's needs, too. It was all news to Zahra.

She met another counselor at the clinic who treated drug addicts, and who offered to help Hussein with his addiction. His fee was more than she could afford, so she went looking for work on the southern outskirts of Tehran, where hundreds of Afghan migrants labored in brick kilns to feed the seemingly insatiable hunger for construction in the Iranian capital. One of the kilns was owned by her father's boss. It was backbreaking work, but he hired her on the spot. Zahra brought Hussein and Parisa there, and the family settled in a one-room house offered to workers and their families. The kilns were located on the flat, arid plains that stretch into the semidesert of central Iran, and their long, slim chimneys protruding from the ground were recognizable from a distance. In the summer, the area shimmered with heat and dust; in the winter, it crackled with cold. When Zahra went to work in the morning, she brought Parisa along and put her in a homemade cot under a scarf to protect her from the sun. Sitting on the ground, resting on the side of one thigh, Zahra used her hands to tamp clay into molds before another worker placed them in the kiln. It was grinding work that left her with permanent pain in her fingers. The factory had about fifteen kilns, each of which occupied twenty-five to thirty families. In the first weeks there, Hussein was too weak to work but at least Zahra was making enough money for him to see the therapist four times a week. He had tried to kick the drugs twice before, but hadn't lasted long. Therapy seemed to help. After a few months, his face took on a bit of color and meat returned to his sunken cheeks. He slowly began helping out by carrying Zahra's molded bricks to the kiln. Soon, Zahra got pregnant again. She gave birth to a son, Jawad. After the birth she took a three-day break. Then she went back to work. Her mother would take care of Jawad while Zahra was at her job. They couldn't afford milk formula, so twice a day Fatima would walk from their home to the kiln so Zahra could breastfeed her son, then back home. When her mother had plans for the day, Zahra put Jawad in the cot next to Parisa and went back to work while trying to keep his face mostly free of dust.

It was too cold to work in the winter so most of the Afghan migrants at the factory returned to their houses in Tehran or in the surrounding villages. Zahra and Hussein stayed. The area was nearly

TWENTY YEARS

deserted, with the exception of a few Afghan and Iranian men who didn't have families to go home to. With Hussein sober, his mother out of sight, and some savings to tide them over during the lean winter, Zahra enjoyed the best period of their life together so far. She spent all day with the children. The sharp wind pierced the skin, and seemed to blow constantly, so they spent most of their time indoors. It had been three weeks since Hussein last saw the therapist, so he also suddenly had a lot of time on his hands. During the day he would saunter around the plains and chat up some of the other workers. He usually returned around dusk and settled in for the night.

One night, he hadn't returned by nine p.m., well after sunset. Zahra got worried. A kid on each arm, she left the house in the darkness and headed for a cluster of houses about half a mile away where the other men from the area often gathered. She saw lights in one of the houses as she approached. Before knocking on the door, she put the children down and got on her toes to peer through the grimy window. A group of men sat in a circle around a gas burner and smoked on long opium pipes. Among the dead-eyed faces she saw Hussein's.

"I have struggled for six months to help him get clean," she thought. "Three weeks is all he could manage to stay sober." An unusual anger boiled inside her, then erupted. She had learned to survive in a home full of explosive tempers by tempering her own. Now she was unable to. She grabbed a brick from the ground and tossed it through the window with a crash.

"How could you do this to me?" she screamed. Hussein was the first out of the door. The other men tried to restrain him but he wrested loose and started kicking Zahra. Parisa stood next to the house; Jawad was on a blanket on the ground. The first kick hit Zahra on the leg so she lost her balance. The next one landed in the stomach, and she fell to the ground.

"Shameless woman, how dare you interfere with my life like this," Hussein shouted. He kept going. Zahra tried to cover her face with her hands but a kick in the mouth split her lip open. Both children were crying. When he felt like he was done, or perhaps the men managed to

subdue him, Hussein went back inside. One of the other Afghan workers, a young man who had always been friendly toward Zahra, helped
her up and walked her home.

"I have seen how hard you've worked to make him sober," he said.
"It doesn't make any sense why he started smoking again. You have to
tell your parents."

At home, Zahra locked the door. There were no other families living nearby. She was frightened and had barely closed an eye by the
time Hussein returned in the morning. He pounded on the door, and
when she didn't open it, he smashed it open, breaking the hinge. He
came straight at her and gave her a slap that made her ears ring.

"Let this be the last time you meddle. I smoke, and I will continue
to smoke," he said. Hussein had given up. So Zahra gave up on him,
too. From then on, she would concentrate on herself and the children, and let Hussein do whatever he wanted. She was determined to
survive. A few months later, they packed up and left Iran, crossing the
border into Afghanistan to begin their new lives.

2

FAHIM

Fahim Hashimy could hear the Taliban the night the Islamists ran. For about four weeks before the Taliban government capitulated, Fahim's family's home had been trembling under American bombardments. This night, on November 12, 2001, he heard the sound of T-62 tanks rumbling past on the main road outside the house, which led from the airport to the western part of the capital, toward Wardak where the Taliban leaders would soon flee. Loud commotion continued through dawn, with the sound of gunfire and explosions and people screaming.

Fahim lived with his family near the airport, in an area with many key government buildings. The family's house shook from the pressure wave of American bombs targeting the city's electricity grid, the defense ministry, air defense systems, and command centers at the airport. The bombs were so close Fahim could see them drop from the sky, before sprinkling their street with shrapnel. One of them killed al-Qaeda's number three, a man named Mohammed Atef.

In the countryside, a newly developed American Predator drone hovered above the house where Taliban leader Mullah Muhammad Omar was hiding, but he narrowly escaped. Airstrikes obliterated Taliban training camps. Most of the targets the Americans planned to hit before the invasion were struck by the second week. The Taliban evacuated the capital the morning of November 13, sooner than many Afghans had expected them to.

In the morning, the capital was quiet. Fahim went for a walk through the town. There were no living Taliban in sight, only the bodies of fighters strewn across the central Shahr-e Naw Park. Within hours, shopkeepers pulled out speakers to play music and lined up CDs and VHS tapes for display, all stuff that until then had been sold surreptitiously. Within a day, people started dressing differently. Men donned jeans. Many women flung off their burqas and wore headscarves instead. Fahim even saw some women who walked around without a hijab.

"It was like being freed from prison," Fahim said. "We could shave, we could listen to music. You could talk to girls." At twenty-one, Fahim could only grow a patchy beard, which he immediately shaved off. Even before the fall of the Taliban, he had defied the government's ban on so-called Western hair fashion and repeatedly grew out his hair into a style known to Kabulians as "*Titanic* hair." Afghan men admired Leonardo DiCaprio's iconic mane in the movie they'd all watched in secret. Once as a teenager, Fahim had been browsing shops in the bazaar for a hat to cover his locks when a Talib grabbed his arm. The militant promptly led him upstairs to a barber, who was ordered to cut Fahim's hair off on the spot. The boy grew it back out as soon as possible. In 1990s Afghanistan, even small fashion choices were acts of rebellion.

For his entire life up until this point, his family had been at the mercy of others. They had fled wars, leaving everything behind—twice. In 1993, when Fahim was thirteen, the family fled the capital when it became engulfed in civil war and moved to Parwan, north of Kabul. Three years later, after the Taliban took power, fighting continued in Parwan, so they moved back to Kabul to escape the violence. The family-owned pharmacy was still there, and they owed the landlord three years' rent. All the medicine had expired, so his father, a trained pediatrician, had to go deeper into debt to buy new supplies. Though he turned the business around, even at its most successful, the pharmacy never became profitable enough for the family to move out of their mud house in northern Kabul and into something that could at least retain heat in the winter. For families like his, upward social mobility was rare.

Fahim soon discovered that in the new Afghanistan, people like him could take hold of their own fate. If you worked hard, had a few good contacts, and were willing to bend the rules, you could climb the social ladder quickly. That suited Fahim. At age seven, he had worked as a watchman at his father's pharmacy in Kabul. In Parwan, he worked full-time after school on a local farm, tending to two cows, a flock of sheep, and some chickens. When the family returned to Kabul, he was sixteen. He couldn't afford a bicycle, so he'd walk to school in the morning, then walk after class an hour to Khair Khana to buy wholesale medicine, then another hour to work at the counter at the pharmacy in Char Qala Wazirabad, carrying boxes of medicine on his shoulders. He even found time to teach private courses in English, which he excelled at in school. After six months, without consulting his father, he fired the middle-aged pharmacist who worked for them.

"He wasn't working hard, and he wasn't creative," Fahim said. The business was struggling and he saw no need to pay the man for something he thought he could do himself. The pharmacist complained to his father, but Fahim got his way and took the old man's place behind the counter. He knew nothing about medicine but was a natural with numbers. He was so fast with the calculator that customers would watch his dancing fingers and ask him if he was sure he wasn't making mistakes. He never did. After a year of hard work to cut their expenses, Fahim and his father had paid off their debts and had come to run the leading pharmacy in the neighborhood.

Fahim was behind the counter on September 9, 2001, when customers told him that the anti-Taliban commander Ahmad Massoud had been killed by al-Qaeda assassins. He was also there two days later when he heard about the al-Qaeda attacks on the United States. People who came into the shop were afraid. Those old enough to remember the first Iraq war worried that the United States would carpet-bomb civilian areas and destroy the city.

Weeks later, after the Taliban fled, the city was still standing. Fahim immediately began looking for opportunities. An old friend had already gotten a foot in the door of the newly established NATO mission called the International Security Assistance Force, or ISAF. The friend gave Fahim a slip of paper that granted him an interview for a position as translator. When he arrived at the NATO base in central Kabul, there were about two hundred people waiting before him in line. The coalition's early mandate was to secure Kabul and its surroundings while the US military conducted operations across the country. The international forces needed hundreds of Afghan translators to perform their daily tasks, and they needed them fast. Fahim breezed through the interview and the language test, and was assigned to accompany a unit of Scottish soldiers, who patrolled neighborhoods in western Kabul on foot alongside Afghan police officers. To please his father, he had enrolled in medical school, so he would go to class in the morning, swing by the pharmacy in the afternoon, and then join the unit after sunset. He carried schoolbooks with him everywhere and used any downtime to study.

In the beginning, the Scots and their Afghan partners mostly chased a few remaining pockets of Taliban militants. Soon, they became more of a quick reaction force against criminals. As they walked the streets of the poorer neighborhoods of Kampani and Dasht-e Barchi, the soldiers made an effort to speak to shopkeepers and reassure the local community that peace was coming. They frequently spent the night in the hills above Kampani.

Even with his proficient English, Fahim struggled at first to understand his Scottish superiors. Their dialect was nothing like the English he had studied in textbooks or the Afghan-accented pronunciation of his teachers.

They asked him to fetch them some "*wuh*-ah," which he learned meant that they were thirsty. He learned to swallow his *t*'s and *r*'s, and to exaggerate his "Hi, mate" in a way that amused his English-speaking Afghan friends. Still, the soldiers seemed to continue to make up their own language. "Ball and chain" meant someone's wife. "Dog and bone" was a phone, though he wasn't sure why.

In June 2002, Turkey took charge of ISAF from the British commander who had led it since the beginning of the invasion, and Fahim's assignment ended. He approached another old friend for help to secure an interview with the US Special Forces. Again, he was hired instantly. This job would take him to the provinces to hunt Taliban fighters, not thieves. He would get paid several hundred dollars per month. But he would have to spend weeks, if not months, away from Kabul and the family business.

"I'm not going to be a doctor," he told his father. For six years, they had run the pharmacy together and secured a stable livelihood for the family. They no longer had to worry about war. The family had never had it better.

"You know, people are making money everywhere," Fahim continued. "I need to go out and do something."

His father was furious.

"He almost kicked me out of the house," Fahim said. He kept the details of his new job to himself so as to not worry his parents. Fahim told his family that he was traveling to the provinces to help medical teams, when in fact he was traveling with American special forces. He went to Samangan and Bamiyan to help quell the last remnants of Taliban insurgency, then continued down south to the militants' heartland without returning to Kabul for months. They were ambushed, and the Humvee he was traveling in missed a bridge, dropped fifteen meters, and rolled over, leaving him with a long scar by his left eye. Fahim felt a fire in his belly. When he came back after months on the battlefield, he formally quit university. None of the other Afghans he knew of who worked with the international forces had any degrees.

"We learned on the job," he said. He asked his younger brother to take over for him at the pharmacy.

At first, the special forces only committed Fahim to one assignment of about eight months. With access to international military facilities, he sat around and waited for his luck. One blazing-hot morning at the Kabul Military Training Center, built on the eastern outskirts of Kabul to offer sixteen-week basic infantry training to Afghan soldiers, he sat with about two hundred other translators. Fahim watched as the well-connected among them received jobs. He knew no one. A door opened and a bulky American soldier in shorts entered. He said he needed a translator for a meeting with the Afghan commander of the training center. This wasn't the kind of assignment he was looking for, but Fahim was bored enough to raise his hand. The American took Fahim to see the Afghan commander. After the meeting, the American, still in his shorts, seemed impressed.

"When did you arrive from the US?" he asked. Fahim's many months with the American special forces had tuned his English with an American twang.

"I didn't come from the US."

"So where were you?"

"I was with the special forces."

"How come they never showed you to me?" the soldier asked. "I keep asking for very good quality translators and everyone they have given me has been crap. I had ten translators and none of them speak English. Come work for me."

The American colonel was in charge of the training center, but his tour finished a week later. When he left, he introduced Fahim to his friend who worked as a deputy to Gen. Karl Eikenberry, the head of the so-called Office of Military Cooperation who would later go on to become US ambassador to Afghanistan. Fahim was brought from the training academy to Camp Eggers in the center of Kabul, among all the big Western embassies. He noticed that the Afghans looked different from the brusque grunts he usually worked alongside. They were shaved, clean, and wore crisp suits. He was suddenly acutely aware of his unkempt beard and dusty boots. Muscle-bound after months of working out with the special forces, with the scar still fresh under his eye, he looked rough. An interpreter told him they went to the defense ministry every day and recommended that he clean up.

Fahim's first meeting was with Atiqullah Baryalai, the deputy to the defense minister, Marshal Mohammad Qasim Fahim. One of the country's most experienced military commanders, the defense minister had led the Western-backed rebel coalition known as the Northern Alliance into Kabul when they helped topple the Taliban. He was a household name, and a legend to his followers. Fahim was drenched in sweat before he met the deputy, who himself had been an aide to Ahmad Shah Massoud, the commander who had been killed by al-Qaeda. Despite his nerves, he did well enough to be asked to join meetings with the defense minister; the newly appointed interim president, Hamid Karzai; Eikenberry; and other senior personnel. Mild-mannered but with a tireless energy, Fahim was tasked with supervising the work of other translators, and read stacks of paperwork from meetings about proposed reforms, policies, and strategy for building an army. The work gave him a stake in the reconstruction of his country. He helped build the country's first post-Taliban infantry battalion, known as a *kandak*. Soon, he was accompanying senior leadership on trips across the country, to nearly thirty provinces.

"I had never thought about politics before," he said. "It was all really exciting. I was involved in everything."

He learned fast: policy issues and military terminology became part of his vocabulary. To clean up his military jargon, Fahim went back to his old school textbooks.

"I had to be professional," he said.

In 2003 and 2004, across Afghanistan, infrastructure sprang up to support the new Afghan security forces. To accommodate the growing need for supplies, and to prop up the local economy, the international coalition introduced a program to ensure that smaller items were purchased from Afghan companies. They dubbed the scheme "Afghan First," and asked Fahim to help out at the office that handled contracts for Afghan suppliers. He had been making about $700 per month doing translations, a decent salary for a young Afghan man with no university degree. But at the procurement office he saw young men supplying the new Afghan army raking in thousands of dollars per month. Fahim's friend Zahir had noticed the same. He had an idea.

One day, he handed Fahim two blue business cards, with each of their respective names on them.

"Look, I'm the CEO," Zahir said. Fahim was listed as principal, or co-owner, of a company called Arrow. The firm had no address and only two employees: Fahim and Zahir. They could use their cars as offices, Zahir said. He had already lined up a meeting with someone from the contracting unit.

The pair won their first bid: a contract to supply the Afghan army with bedsheets for six hundred dollars. They went to a shop downtown, bought the sheets, and delivered them to the base. It was that easy. Arrow General Supplies Company was off the ground. They won their second bid, too. This time, the contract was worth $200,000 to source ten thousand pairs of military boots. Their startup success was not unusual. Foreign military bases had created new supply chains, which young, entrepreneurial Afghans quickly tapped into, providing trucking services, sourcing local food and logistical items, and paying off insurgents on highways. But Fahim and Zahir were already in over their heads. Asking around in Fahim's local neighborhood, they found a baker who said he had contacts in China who could help. Weeks later, the baker delivered, but when Fahim and Zahir took a sample of the boots to the base, the American officer in charge rejected them because the quality was too poor. They eventually found another supplier but the baker still wanted his money, and their debt to him put the company in the red from the beginning.

This was a pattern they would repeat. For the next contract, they ended up with a massive stockpile of subpar cleaning kits for AK-47s bought in Pakistan. The first commission that went smoothly was when ISAF contracted them to print thousands of copies of a public relations magazine to be distributed to Afghan soldiers. The magazine was meant to boost morale and faith in the coalition. Printing the magazine earned Arrow revenue, but nowhere near what Fahim had his sights on. Things were not moving as fast as he had planned, and he thought about returning to the pharmacy and his studies. Then the pair struck gold.

3

OMARI

Omari was three days old when the village mullah leaned over him and whispered in his ear: "God is the greatest." As was custom in Pashtun villages, the cleric gently sang the *azan*, the Muslim call to prayer, for the boy. From the mullah's voice sprang the spirit of God, and from that moment, Omari came to believe, he was destined to live a life in the service of his creator. From a young age, Omari had an unshakeable faith that if he abided in God, he would always be protected. After the birth ceremony, his father ran outside and fired a machine gun into the air. A son was born.

It was 1995 in Sayedabad, a collection of villages shaded by green groves and nestled between barren hills two hours west of Kabul in a province called Wardak. At the time, the villages of Wardak were relatively peaceful, but the country had been at war for sixteen years. After the Soviet invasion in 1979, the United States intervened to prevent a Soviet expansion in Central Asia, by supporting groups of local rebels, known as the mujahideen, who had launched a holy war to repel the Soviets. The fighters, a motley bunch, were mostly Islamists, led by various commanders who had been exiled in Pakistan during the 1970s. Years later, Henry Kissinger, the former national security advisor and secretary of state, would argue that the United States had nothing in common with the guerrillas: "Yet they shared a common enemy, and in the world of national interest, that made them allies," he wrote. The Carter administration quietly supplied them with light arms to "harass" Soviet forces. President Reagan went into the conflict more forcefully to deal a blow to the overextended Soviet empire, while the new Communist leader Mikhail Gorbachev was distracted by a domestic power battle at home. In 1986, the United States boosted the mujahideen with Stinger antiaircraft missiles. In total, the United States, mostly through the CIA, funded the anti-Soviet resistance in Afghanistan with more than $2 billion in guns and money in the largest covert action program since World War II. Much of that aid went to radical Islamist groups that Washington saw as useful Cold War weapons against Moscow, and who also received vast sums from Pakistan and Saudi Arabia. More moderate groups were sidelined. The CIA even paid to have thousands of Qurans distributed among the fighters. The United States largely outsourced direct contact with the militants, including weapons distribution, to the Pakistani Inter-Services Intelligence, or ISI. Washington's partnership with Pakistan, and the sidelining of Afghanistan's other major neighbor, India, which was a firm ally of the Soviet Union, strengthened Islamabad's hand in the country in ways that would come to shape it for decades to come, and created fertile soil for radical Islamist groups to germinate and flourish.

Among the fighters who benefited from the American campaign in Afghanistan was Omari's father, who joined the holy war in the mountains. During Omari's childhood, his father regaled him with stories about battling infidel invaders. Still marked by his years in war, Omari's father was unsmiling and strict. He carried grudges and seemed perpetually angry, hardened, his son thought, by years in the mountains under bombardment and gunfire. But his stories were captivating, and in his telling, Afghanistan's history was a lament of oppression and heroic resistance, a symphony of suffering with few heroes, except the mujahideen. The best estimates suggest somewhere between one and two million Afghan civilians were killed, along with tens of thousands of mujahideen. Omari was drawn to the mountains and the echoes of the voices of the fallen.

By 1989, when the Afghan government signed a peace accord with the United States, Pakistan, and the Soviet Union, some one hundred thousand Russian troops had withdrawn. They left a divided and battered country, families depleted of men. They also left in place their proxy regime under Communist president Mohammad Najibullah, which the mujahideen continued to fight. After they toppled Najibullah in 1992, various rebel factions fought over spoils, pulling Afghanistan deeper into a bloody civil war that starved the country and sowed bitter discord among its ethnic groups. Warring mujahideen units shelled civilian areas of Kabul from the mountainsides. Their fighters raped and looted. Tens of thousands of civilians were killed. Hundreds of thousands were driven from their homes. Omari's father was part of an Islamic band of fighters who called themselves the Taliban, meaning "students" who promised to cleanse the country of corruption and root out abusive warlords. As internecine fighting among the rebels intensified, particularly around their southern, spiritual heartland of Kandahar, the Taliban remained cohesive and gained a reputation as righteous Muslims, winning new recruits with every slice of territory they won. Stories circulated of Taliban fighters freeing teenage girls who had been raped, and rescuing boys from sexual assault by warlords. Their leader, Mullah Muhammad Omar, was said to live a modest life, uninterested in financial gain. By 1996, the Taliban secured Kabul and declared Afghanistan an Islamic emirate.

After the Taliban took power, much of the violence that had plagued the country for nearly two decades was quelled. Some fighting continued in the northern provinces but most Afghans enjoyed a rare spell of peace. Omari's father moved his family from Wardak to Khair Khana, a suburb in Kabul. Afghanistan's economy was destroyed, but being a veteran of the anti-Soviet resistance helped him find work in the new administration.

The new rulers upheld peace with force. The price they exacted was absolute compliance with their ultraconservative interpretation of Islamic law, some of it rooted more in tribal culture than holy scripture. The Taliban banned music and coerced men to grow fist-long beards. They prohibited female education. Their Ministry for the Propagation of Virtue and the Prevention of Vice became feared for upholding rules with physical punishment. Courts penalized theft with prison or amputation of a hand for anything over fifty dollars. The Taliban stoned couples for alleged infidelity and extramarital encounters. They executed people accused of espionage in soccer stadiums. When a convicted murderer faced his executioner, he found himself in front of a relative of his victim, often a brother or father, and he would be killed by the same means that he had used for his crime, whether by gunshot or a knife to the throat. An eye for an eye.

Omari's family kept to themselves and had no major confrontations with the authorities. The family was poor, but so was everybody else, so Omari's parents didn't blame the Taliban for the hardship. The Islamist movement had inherited a nation in ruins and was now trying to govern while also being isolated by the international community, which imposed harsh economic sanctions and suspended diplomatic ties with Afghanistan. Only three countries—Pakistan, Saudi Arabia, and the United Arab Emirates—recognized the new Taliban regime.

Meanwhile, the Taliban's oppression fueled an armed resistance in the northern countryside where former rival Tajik and Uzbek forces formed the Northern Alliance. While the Taliban eventually forced the Uzbek commander, Abdul Rashid Dostum, into exile, the Tajik leader, Ahmad Shah Massoud, who became a key American ally, maintained control over portions of the north.

In 2001, Massoud, along with fellow Afghan leaders of other ethnicities, traveled to Brussels, where they took to the podium at the European Parliament to ask the international community for humanitarian assistance. He also warned European leaders that his group had intelligence that terrorists were plotting a large-scale attack on American soil. Massoud turned out to be right, but he did not live to see the attack himself. In his mountain hideout in Takhar province, Massoud sat down for an interview with two Tunisian men who had come to the commander claiming to be journalists. At the beginning of the interview, the two men detonated a bomb they had placed in their camera. The explosion wounded Massoud, who was later pronounced dead in the hospital. The Tunisians were in fact members of al-Qaeda. After his untimely death, Massoud became an icon for many Afghans, his ruggedly handsome face decorating billboards and car decals like a South Asian Che Guevara. The assassination robbed Afghanistan of its most obvious candidate to lead the country as an alternative to the Taliban, and the United States of its closest and most competent Afghan ally. Two days later, al-Qaeda terrorists struck again, this time by crashing two passenger planes into the World Trade Center in New York, and a third into the Pentagon.

In Omari's family, Massoud was no hero. They were Pashtuns, and although the Tajik commander had worked to improve ties with leaders of other ethnicities, many in Wardak distrusted him from the civil war days when he had led the fight against the Pashtuns. The Taliban belittled Massoud, who had learned French in school, as "the Frenchman" and cast him as an agent of Pakistan, which had supported him in an early rebellion in the 1970s and trained him in a military intelligence camp. Television was banned in Afghanistan, so Omari heard the news about the attack on the radio, although he didn't fully grasp the enormity of what had happened. His parents bundled him and his younger brother onto the back of a truck, wedged in among furniture and household items, and left Kabul, taking the highway west to their home district of Sayedabad, a Pashtun-dominated area of green hills, water canals, and orchards. Weeks later, American warplanes screamed across the sky above the capital, dropping bombs on people who once again heard the night air thunder with the sound of explosions.

The Taliban were not international terrorists. The group had never carried out an attack against a Western country, despite its anti-Western ideology. But they had given al-Qaeda a safe haven in Afghanistan and repeatedly rebuffed US demands to extradite the terrorist outfit's leader, Osama bin Laden, a wealthy Saudi citizen who had moved to Afghanistan from Sudan in 1996. At a time when the United States considered bin Laden a threat to its national security, Taliban leader Mullah Omar allowed him to run training camps in eastern Afghanistan and took his money, fighters, and ideological advice, ingesting ideas of global jihad. After bin Laden masterminded a bombing of the US embassies in Kenya and Tanzania in 1998, the Taliban still refused to give him up, claiming that the United States had not presented sufficient evidence against him. The Taliban and al-Qaeda were distinctly different organizations, and Taliban leaders at the time acknowledged that only a minority of Afghans, and of their own members, wanted bin Laden in the country. But the al-Qaeda leader was a popular figure in certain circles of the Muslim world. His Afghan sanctuary elevated the Taliban's status among anti-Western militants. His presence in Afghanistan deepened the Taliban's international isolation, but bin Laden also made hundreds of Arab militants available to the Taliban to assist in the fight against the Northern Alliance. Since bin Laden moved to Afghanistan in 1996, before the 9/11 attacks, US officials had requested his extradition more than two dozen times, saying that they believed he was plotting attacks on US interests. In 1999, the UN Security Council had passed a unanimous resolution calling for him to be handed over to a country where he could be brought to justice. Nine days after the terrorist attack in the United States, President Bush again demanded the Taliban hand over all al-Qaeda leaders hiding in Afghanistan and close terrorist training camps. The CIA tried to convince the Pakistani intelligence service, the ISI, to use its influence with the Taliban to syphon off moderates inside the movement to denounce Mullah Omar and deliver bin Laden. The CIA opened up a secret channel to the Taliban and sent its station chief in Pakistan, Robert Grenier, to Quetta to meet with the Taliban's senior military commander, Mullah Akhtar Mohammad Usmani, to persuade him to turn on Mullah Omar and hand over bin Laden. But Usmani remained loyal to Mullah Omar and did not deliver. Meanwhile, the CIA became convinced that its Pakistani counterpart was secretly advising the Taliban to hold firm against an American attack, rather than deliver bin

Laden. The Taliban were the ISI's only proxy inside Afghanistan, which it saw as a bulwark against its archnemesis, India. Even while some ISI officers were helping the American military identify Taliban targets for upcoming strikes, the CIA watched as the Pakistani agency also continued to send weapons, ammunition, and fuel to the Taliban, in breach of a UN Security Council resolution to ban arms sales to the Afghan movement. On October 7, when the Taliban hadn't complied, the first American bombs dropped on Afghanistan.

The US and NATO bombardments hit Kabul, Kandahar, and Jalalabad particularly hard. The invasion continued at a fast pace. The Taliban soon fled Kabul, leaving the capital to the Western coalition and the Northern Alliance, and retreated to the rural areas around Kandahar, the movement's birthplace, and to the Tora Bora mountains outside Jalalabad. Mullah Omar was hiding in Kandahar. On November 12, about a dozen Taliban leaders in Kabul decided to withdraw temporarily to Wardak. On November 13, the CIA reported that the Taliban had almost entirely evacuated the capital. By December, the Taliban had surrendered their stronghold in Kandahar and bin Laden had escaped.

For many Afghans, the arrival of the Americans and their NATO allies inspired hope of a return to a more liberal order of the past—in the 1970s—and reintegration of Afghanistan into the international community. Even people in Sayedabad who had worked in the Taliban government, like Omari's father, hoped that the Americans would bring jobs and money and pull Afghans out of poverty. Omari's father had originally joined the mujahideen, in the 1980s, because he believed in its anti-imperialist stance against the Soviet Union and its struggle for a sovereign Afghanistan. He was conservative in his faith, but picking up a gun had been a means to an end, not the goal itself. More than anything, he wanted to provide for his children and keep them safe. Since leaving the Taliban, he had supported his family as a construction worker, and if the Americans could bring peace and prosperity to Afghanistan, he had no issue with them.

After the Taliban leaders had passed through Wardak on their way to Kandahar, Sayedabad settled into a calm that seemed detached from the fighting that dominated foreign news headlines about Afghanistan at the time. Life in the village was quietly monotonous, punctuated by events such as childbirth—Omari's parents would over time be blessed with fourteen children—and the two religious highlights of the year. Eid al-Fitr marked the end of the fasting month of Ramadan, and Eid al-Adha commemorated the story of Ibrahim (also known as Abraham in the Bible): when God ordered him to slaughter his own son, he pressed the knife to the boy's throat only to see that his son had suddenly been swapped for a ram. To honor Ibrahim, Afghan families with sufficient means slaughtered a sheep, or even a cow if they were well off. Omari's family could usually afford a goat. Omari and his siblings woke up early in the morning and dressed in clothes bought for the occasion: white shalwar kameez, a white pillbox-shaped hat, and polished leather shoes. They took a thermos with tea to the mosque and swapped it for cookies and sponge cake. From the mosque, they went door-knocking in the village to collect almonds and walnuts from neighbors. Omari was allowed to help in the ritual of slaughter from the age of seven. Inside the yard of the family compound, he tied the goat's legs together before the village butcher uttered, "Bismillah, Allahu Akbar"—"In the name of God, God is great"—and slit the animal's throat in one swift movement. Once the blood had been drained from the goat's body, it was skinned and the meat was cut up and divided into three portions. One pile went to the poor in the village, another to relatives, and the third would feed Omari's family for three days.

Omari had begun attending mosque as soon as the family returned to Wardak from Kabul to escape the American bombings. In school, students learned not only about the tenets of Islam but also how to protect their faith. From teachers, Omari and his friends heard stories about the time of the Prophet Mohammad, which cast him in a pantheon of heroes to imitate. The villains were men like Abu Jahl, an archenemy of the Prophet who was killed in battle. Among the protagonists were Abdurrahman and Naeem, loyal acolytes of the Prophet who, as Omari learned the story, sent their children to fight a holy war at a young age. They studied the stories of Muhammad bin Qasim, a young general in the Ummayad Caliphate, which at its imperial height stretched from today's Pakistan to Spain and the Maghreb. The teachers sought to instill in the students an awareness of an Islamic golden age that long preceded Afghanistan's existence as a sovereign nation, and which could be revived.

Omari's family lived a modest life in accordance with village customs. In Afghan villages, girls were usually forbidden from leaving the house without a male guardian once they reached puberty. For Omari's five sisters, the only world available was the one unfolding inside the four walls of the compound. In the eyes of the family, they didn't need to go outside. Protected by the privacy of the compound, the girls acquired the same skills as they would have in school, only faster as there were no distractions. Omari would later say that his sisters had learned to read at age four and read Islamic literature their father brought home. The oldest sisters learned to recite the Quran by heart. When the girls occasionally left the house, they were enveloped in a body-covering burqa. The importance of the burqa was taught to the children with analogies: If you put two apples on a table, peel one of them, and return an hour later, which one would you rather eat? The unpeeled apple, of course. Another example: Would you rather eat a piece of candy that has been wrapped or one that has been tucked away in the pocket unwrapped? The burqa protected a woman's purity and her dignity, and was not only meant for her. Sullying a woman's honor was equal to violating the dignity of the family and the whole village.

But the US invasion didn't mark the end of the war, as Omari's father had hoped it would. The United States was bent on chasing down the last remnants of the Taliban and ensuring that al-Qaeda would never find a safe haven in Afghanistan again.

Early in the war, several high-ranking Taliban commanders offered to surrender and recognize President Hamid Karzai's new government in return for amnesty. Those making the offer included the movement's former defense minister, former interior minister, and Mullah Akhtar Mansour, who would go on to lead the movement more than a decade later. The Americans refused. President George W. Bush had declared, "Either you are with us, or you are with the terrorists," and that was still the standing order. The US government refused the offers of surrender, egged on by allied Afghan commanders seeking revenge over the Taliban. Instead, many Taliban fighters who had offered to surrender fled to Pakistan, where they would mobilize for a comeback.

When Omari first saw the Americans, they had been in-country for three years. To his nine-year-old eyes, the soldiers looked absurd as they descended from their Humvees weighed down by flak jackets and heavy backpacks. Waddling like slow armadillos among the villagers, the soldiers handed candy to children and spoke in a garbled language Omari didn't understand. He watched them curiously. Some of the soldiers were blond with pink skin. Some had hair so red it looked like it had been lit on fire. He saw Black soldiers and couldn't believe that the sun could burn someone's skin so dark. The strangest sight of all was soldiers who peed standing up. An Afghan would never do that. He would squat and pull his shalwar kameez aside, and be discreet about it. The soldiers, however, trudged over to a tree in their clunky uniforms, turned their backs to the watching crowd, whipped out their private parts, and let it gush. Omari thought it was hilarious.

In the early years of the war, the United States was focused on hunting al-Qaeda cells and groups of Taliban, primarily in the eastern Tora Bora mountains. After the opening salvo, many US military resources shifted to Iraq, where the United States was fighting to unseat Saddam Hussein, while Bush maintained that it was crucial "to build an Afghanistan that is free from evil." To expand the authority of the new government in Kabul, the United States created so-called Provincial Reconstruction Teams, or PRTs, which were eventually handed over to NATO states, which assumed control of the international security forces in 2003. Foreign military presence was slowly but steadily expanding into some of Afghanistan's remotest areas.

The outside world had arrived in Wardak. Omari had always yearned for adventures and travel, although he didn't necessarily want to go abroad. The hinterlands of Afghanistan were alluring enough.

The country's history, retold through generations, was adorned with tantalizing names of provinces, towns, and mountains: Kandahar, Helmand, Uruzgan—Omari wanted to see them all. Inside him burned the same desire to explore that has always driven young travelers to set out from their homes in search of new horizons. Paktia! Khost! From a young age Omari was fully aware that his village was nothing but a speck of dust in Afghanistan's mystical and wide-ranging expanses. Jalalabad! Perhaps that's why his first memory of speaking to a foreigner would stay so vividly with him, an American soldier with flaming-red, tousled hair peeking out from under his helmet. Omari's own curls were dark brown, as was the hair of all the other boys in the village, and he was intrigued by the soldier's ginger locks. The soldier was polite as he stopped Omari and searched his backpack. He pulled out Omari's Quran and recited a few lines from the holy book in Arabic. Omari was stunned.

"Are you Muslim?" he asked the soldier.

"Al-hamdulillah," the American replied. He had understood the word "Muslim" at least. "Thanks be to God."

"So why have you come to our country to kill Muslims?" Omari demanded to know, in Pashto. School had taught him what the Americans were here for. Even if the soldier had spoken Pashto, which he did not appear to do, he had no time to reply before another American interrupted them and told him to move on.

The second time Omari came into contact with the Americans, a group of soldiers climbed the roof of the school building to monitor the area, while others on the ground gave Omari a bottle of water and a pencil that was better than the ones given by their teachers. Excited, Omari returned home with his presents, but his father snatched them from him.

"Get those things out of here," he snapped.

When Omari later brought home a backpack that the Americans had given him, his father ordered that ejected from the home as well.

"No matter how many backpacks the Americans gave us, it didn't make any difference to the clerics and the elders," Omari said. "They all believed the Americans were enemies of Islam."

The friendly attitude of the Americans in Sayedabad soon changed. They were on the hunt for terrorists. Omari knew the old long-bearded men in black-and-white turbans who suddenly became suspicious in the eyes of the Americans, and as far as he knew, they weren't terrorists. Yet they were lined up, body-searched, and questioned by younger, clean-shaven Afghan men Omari hadn't seen before, who translated the words barked by brusque American soldiers. The Americans hit the old men, humiliating them in front of the villagers. Worse, the Americans frisked Afghan women. Omari remembered seeing a soldier facing down an older woman angrily asking him why they had detained her son, then pulling off her headscarf.

One early morning, a group of soldiers arrived at Omari's home. The women in the family were engrossed in the first prayer of the day. Omari was in the courtyard doing his ablutions in preparation for prayer—washing face, hands, and arms—when he heard a vehicle approach outside the gate. Emerging from the faint dawn light, a group of American soldiers climbed over the wall and pointed their guns at him. Inside the house, his mother and sisters screamed. The soldiers told Omari through a translator to fetch his father from the mosque.

"The Americans are at the house," Omari shouted when he found his dad. As they ran home, Omari saw that the soldiers were raiding the entire village. In his house, they only found a couple of hunting rifles and left again, but their neighbors were pushed into the street, the men's hands zip-tied behind their backs. The Americans gathered male villagers at the mosque, forcing them to kneel. Walking behind the bound men, the soldiers hit several of them with the butts of their guns, demanding to know where the "terrorists" were. They hadn't tied his father up, but still slapped him around, and threw water in his face. Omari felt humiliated and sorry for the men. Some men were released, others were taken away from the village, only to return months later with bruises and strange headaches and inexplicable insomnia. Omari had never heard that any of the men had been involved in armed struggle. Some of them were too old to even fight. One of the arrested men was a visitor from Kabul who could not possibly know who in the village was potentially connected to the Taliban. Years later that same man would be killed fighting for the Afghan police against the Taliban.

Such incidents occurred frequently across Afghanistan, often in even more violent fashion. The men taken from Omari's village added to a pool of detainees, which during the first three years swelled to more than fifty thousand. The raids bred resentment in Omari's village, where many at the outset of the war had viewed the arrival of the Americans with some optimism. Some, like Omari's father, openly hoped that the Americans would bring jobs. But with the trauma of 9/11 still fresh, the Americans soon found themselves in a conundrum: they were there to hunt every last terrorist in the country, but there were very few terrorists left to be found. Shortly after the invasion of Afghanistan, most Taliban fighters had either fled to Pakistan or melded into civil society, vanishing from sight. The Taliban were Afghans. The movement had emerged from the villages, and it could retreat back into the villages. Al-Qaeda had fled.

The American refusal of Taliban overtures early in the war reflected the impetus for the US intervention, which was to a large extent emotional, shaped by the shock of 9/11. American soil had been hit, and nearly three thousand Americans killed, their deaths monumentalized by live television. Decision-makers were gripped by a quest for vengeance and a desire to demonstrate, at home and abroad, the supremacy of American power. Waging war was politically more expedient than pursuing peace. The surprisingly quick ouster of the Taliban injected a sense of triumphalism into American policymaking, and within two years, the United States continued its military interventions in the Muslim world by invading Iraq.

This logic of revenge permeated politics and media across the spectrum. Expressing the prevailing position at the time, the Washington insider and *New York Times* columnist Thomas Friedman explained that the rationale behind US military intervention, first in

Afghanistan and then in Iraq, was that "after 9/11, America needed to hit someone in the Arab-Muslim world. Afghanistan wasn't enough. Because a terrorism bubble had built up over there—a bubble that posed a real threat to the open societies of the West and needed to be punctured." Iraq's leader, Saddam Hussein, had nothing to do with 9/11, yet Friedman argued that people and governments in the Muslim world writ large needed to be taught a lesson: "Smashing Saudi Arabia or Syria would have been fine. But we hit Saddam for one simple reason: because we could, and because he deserved it and because he was right in the heart of that world."

After invading Iraq, the US military shifted much of its focus there, diminishing the capability for strategic analysis and political recalibration involving Afghanistan, even as the quest to exert American dominance continued. While many Taliban members simply wanted to go home and lead peaceful lives, American soldiers in Afghanistan were ordered to capture or kill as many suspected terrorists as possible, regardless of the cost, targeting also Afghans who had never been in the Taliban, or who had left the movement and had no clear links to al-Qaeda. Australian commandos in 2012 joked about having to meet a "kill quota" during their operations in Uruzgan. US forces often acted on bad intelligence, sometimes provided by Afghan partners who tipped them off against their own rivals to settle local feuds. Killing a couple of people in the middle of the night could turn a whole subtribe against the United States, even as it was celebrated on a nearby base as a successful anti-Taliban raid. America viewed the Taliban almost as an external evil that had imposed itself on Afghanistan, and which could be purged from the country, instead of what it was: a movement sprung from conservative Afghan tribal culture and a decades-long history of resistance against foreign invaders.

The Taliban returned to Sayedabad in 2005, when Omari was ten years old. The fighters arrived on motorcycles, two persons on each, sleeping bags tied to the back. Young men in their early twenties, they wore sparkling skullcaps from Kandahar and crisp white tunics with baggy pants cropped above the ankle. They carried a pleasant scent of rose water, the smell of educated, pious men. Shortly after, they came to visit the children at the school with a clear message: The new government in Kabul was un-Islamic, propped up by imperialist powers, and served an American agenda. Holy war was the duty of any Muslim. Children made good fighters because they were too young to be punished by the government, which was restrained by its new commitments to uphold international law and human rights. The Taliban taught Omari and his classmates to drive motorbikes, their preferred means of transportation, and dig holes for roadside bombs. The boys took turns shoveling and looking out for government soldiers. In the village, many saw the Taliban as resistance fighters, as they had been during the time of the Soviet invasion. Some kids helped the Taliban transport explosives, and eventually the most courageous ones volunteered to place bombs. Once in a while a battery from a cell phone, used to detonate the bombs, would explode in a boy's face, leaving him with scorched eyebrows. Omari did not mind foreigners as such. But he felt in his gut, instinctively, that armed foreign soldiers shouldn't be in his country. Even his five-year-old younger brother, before he was able to lift a Kalashnikov, would point his finger at American soldiers patrolling the village and yell: "Kill them!" Omari could load a machine gun before he was strong enough to lift it. Although his father had retired from the armed struggle after the civil war, he still wanted his children to be able to handle weapons. Omari often wondered why his father had turned his back on the jihad, but never asked him. There are many things a young Afghan boy doesn't ask his father. As they learned the ways of resistance, Omari and his friends remembered their fathers' stories of the battles and bloodshed in the mountains. They found a heroism to emulate. They would discover that in another important aspect, their lives would mimic that of their parents. Omari and his friends would also not live in peace.

PART II
PROMISES

4

ZAHRA

Zahra and her family crossed into Afghanistan from Iran, surrounded by dozens of other families like theirs who hoped their motherland would offer them a fresh start. On the Afghan side of the border, they were met by United Nations workers in light blue vests who bundled them and their belongings into minibuses and drove them to a reception center on the road toward Herat. They were registered on clipboards, their names added to lists of hundreds of thousands of Afghans returning after the fall of the Taliban. Zahra's brother Hussein picked her and the family up in his white Corolla and drove them into town.

The city was imbued with a sense of renewal. New buildings were shooting up among bullet-holed ruins of vacated houses and store-fronts. Hussein brought them home, where they initially moved in with him and his wife, Amina. Their house was new but not big enough for two families. They all slept on blankets on the floor in the sitting room, separated by a curtain and a small fridge placed against the wall. With no job and no savings after the costly trip from Iran, Zahra and Hussein could barely feed their children, and the family often went to bed hungry. Her brother, it turned out, was far from wealthy. He and Zahra weren't close. As a child, he had been a tyrant who beat her until she left the house for marriage. His roughness had rubbed off on his wife, who seemed annoyed that Zahra and her family imposed on their lives. Frequently when Jawad woke up in the middle of the night crying, Amina snapped at Zahra through the curtain.

"Why does he cry so much?"

"Because he's hungry."

Amina picked up a dry loaf of bread and tossed it in Zahra's direction. It was humiliating. But Zahra wasn't too proud to break the loaf into pieces and feed her children.

Zahra's brother helped her find a house soon after their arrival and lent them money to pay the first installment of rent. Their new home was big enough for the four of them, and for Hussein's parents, who moved in, too. It was newly built and cheap. Local landowners looking to profit from the influx of new residents were rushing to build houses as quickly as possible, with little concern for quality. The family's new home had no water tank or taps inside. They collected water from a well in the garden so full that Zahra could dip a glass in it. The toilet was two wooden planks wobbling over a hole in the ground. In a way, the new houses were symbolic of the political order the Western coalition sought to implement in Afghanistan. The hastily constructed foundation under the new Afghan democracy was already being eaten away by rot, corruption, greed, and lust for power. At Zahra's house, they had a roof and four walls for shelter, but balanced on rickety floorboards with a full view of their own waste below their feet.

Zahra wandered the city looking for work, her senses alight with new impressions. In Iran, the family had lived among other Afghans who like them belonged to the ethnic Hazara minority. Their movements were limited to one socioeconomic rung: the bottom. In Herat, life was less segregated. Afghans who had never left the country immediately clocked her accent as Iranian, but the city was a hodge-podge of Afghanistan's various ethnic groups and social classes living among each other. Fellow Hazaras were easy to recognize by their Central Asian features, and now she learned to also distinguish between Tajiks and Pashtuns by their accents and sometimes the way they dressed. Afghanistan was much poorer than Iran, but certain markers of status were more available here than they had been there. In Iran, they hadn't had cell phones. Here, even fruit sellers had one.

"TV had only shown Afghanistan as a country of war and destruction, but once we saw what it actually looked like, it changed our perception completely," she said. The only people that unsettled her at first were the men who painted kohl around their eyes, like eyeliner.

"I thought they were Taliban," Zahra said. Kohl was a popular, traditional type of adornment that many men wore to emulate the Prophet Mohammad, whom they believed had done the same. Many Taliban wore kohl, but as she found out, you could not identify a Talib by looks alone.

The alleyways were buzzing with children playing tag and kicking punctured balls. There were plenty of women in public, but many of them still wore the all-enveloping blue burqas that had been mandated during the Taliban regime. Foreign soldiers populated the streets as well. First, they were mostly American, but Italians soon joined them after they were handed Herat as their area of responsibility in the NATO alliance.

Women who had come from Iran never wore the burqa, only a hijab or headscarf, often loosely wrapped around their shoulders to expose strands of hair. They walked with a different attitude, learned on the streets of Tehran. They earned a reputation among native Heratis for being loose, and men often catcalled Zahra. At the same time, returnees from Iran were also believed to be better educated, having had access to school, so it was easier for them to find work. Zahra wanted to work in a shopping mall, but Hussein wouldn't let her out of fear that men would go there to gawk at her. Instead she found work at an internet café. She had never touched a computer in her life, but claimed to the owner that she was a fantastic typist. The lie didn't matter. In the beginning, her job consisted mostly of two tasks: to serve tea and sugary instant coffee to customers, and to be present, in her capacity as a young woman, which the owner hoped would attract more clients. Zahra didn't mind. The work paid well and was safe.

Many of the young customers were local journalists working as string-
ers for international news agencies. Some of them spoke English and
helped her set up a profile in one of the many chat rooms that were
becoming increasingly popular among young Afghans. She gradually
learned her way around a keyboard and began typing for customers,
earning her an additional 3,500 to 4,500 afghanis a month—about
seventy to ninety dollars. Rent was only 1,000 afghanis, so she hoped
her salary would afford her family some level of comfort. When Zahra
was at work, Parisa mostly stayed at home with the other family members, while Zahra took Jawad to spend time with her mother. Even
before she started school, Parisa helped tidy up the house, washing
Jawad's cloth diapers and folding his clothes. Fatima doted on the
children, Jawad especially, in a way Zahra had never experienced during her own childhood. It pleased Zahra to see her children loved, but
it also stung to be reminded of the love she had been denied. Perhaps
because Zahra was the oldest daughter, Fatima had been intent on
raising her to be a housewife, and by the time Zahra turned thirteen,
she had left the house. There had been little time for tenderness. Zahra
also suspected her mother regretted marrying her off so young and
compensated by showering her grandchildren, of whom Parisa was the
first, with affection. Zahra never understood her mother's newfound
indulgence, and never summoned the courage to ask her about it.

Hussein's struggle to stay clean in Iran was nothing compared to
the temptations of Afghanistan. Closer to the source, the pull was so
much stronger. The country produced 87 percent of the world's opiates, a rate that would only grow as drug production exploded. No
country in the world offered cheaper opium than Afghanistan, and
nowhere was it more readily available. Before long, Hussein demanded
that Zahra hand over 1,000 to 2,000 afghanis at a time. He no longer
bothered concealing his drug use. Zahra watched as her income fueled
her husband's addiction, sapped his mind, and made his bursts of rage
even more erratic.

Life in Herat was unpredictable, too. Early steps of democratiza-
tion intertwined with violence. Zahra heard about two women who

worked at a local shopping mall and had been assaulted after work by men who ostensibly thought they were immodestly dressed. A local television station, high on the heralded winds of change, aired footage of women singing, sending Herat's governor, Ismail Khan, into a fit. A thickset, white-bearded veteran of the war against the Taliban, Khan was as calcified in his social views as the militants he was fighting. He would not tolerate such obscenities and ordered all audio and video recordings in town confiscated. When he discovered that was an impossible task, he backed down. Shortly after, the governor's son, Mirwais Sadiq, who had been appointed civil aviation minister, was killed by a rocket-propelled grenade in a shoot-out with a local rival of his father. It was a grim reminder that war could flare back up at any time. Khan himself was later deposed as governor and given a cabinet post, likely to get him out of Herat and within reach of the president in Kabul, prompting his supporters to flood the streets in protests and ransack the local UN offices. Seven people were killed in the unrest. It was the first time Zahra heard live gunfire. Tensions were never far below the surface. In the countryside, the waves of war were rising, threatening the uneasy peace.

Zahra felt suffocated. The polyester fit tightly around her skull, and straining to see clearly through the blue mesh made her nauseous. She clenched her jaw. She had never wanted to wear a burqa before but had bought one in the bazaar in an attempt to blend in a little better and avoid some of the catcalling. Her vision impaired, it took her three weeks to learn how to cross the street without being cursed by a choir of car horns. The attacks on the girls who worked at the mall, who like Zahra had returned to Afghanistan from Iran, had shocked many women in Herat. At the internet café, the customers were friendly and respectful. Getting there was the problem. In the streets, men hissed intimidatingly at her. The burqa offered her a measure of privacy, even if it felt oppressive. Afghan men who wanted their wives to wear a burqa often described the all-enveloping dress as a tool to shield female family members from the gaze of strangers, much like the four walls that surrounded any house with a garden protected their family. The burqa, which covered the body from head to toe, with a lattice in front of the eyes, was a way of taking that domestic seclusion into public space, allowing a woman to leave the house while protecting her dignity. Zahra saw the burqa as a purely practical device, a form of armor. But she discovered that hiding your body and face wasn't enough to deter all men. In Herat, the shoes gave you away if you were young and fashionable. A spot of nail polish, even more.

At home, Hussein was still threatening and often violent with her. Even if Zahra tried to work up compassion for him, knowing the life he had come to her from, she was frazzled and barely hanging on. The relationship had by now depleted her of love for her husband. In a sense, this was what she had been raised to expect from a marriage. Her parents' relationship had never been driven by romantic love. Their age difference was about fifteen years: her mother was about fourteen when she was married off to her father, who was in his late twenties. Theirs was not a violent marriage, but her parents fought a lot. Zahra always spoke of her parents with tenderness, even though she couldn't remember them ever treating her with affection. She was raised to be tough, not just for her own sake, but for the whole family's. In a country where the state was largely absent or seen as corrupt, the family was an important arbiter of justice and morality. Eskandar and Fatima raised Zahra to be a good Muslim, so she would be a moral citizen. Raising a child was not a private matter. They knew their relatives and neighbors were watching. If one family's honor was violated, it reflected badly on the whole community. This was partly why Zahra's parents had exerted sometimes authoritarian control over her. Fatima was the strictest. She had imposed, for example, a total ban on all music in the house. The only time she had wavered was for her husband's brother. Zahra's uncle was a gifted player of the *tanbur*, a long-necked, pear-shaped string instrument, and he could summon the whole family as soon as he strummed the strings. As a child, Zahra would sit at his feet, mesmerized. At times like these, when cracks showed in her parents' regime—or she peeked over the wall to the neighbors' wedding—she saw glimpses of another, more joyful life.

Zahra's father enjoyed listening to the radio and kept a small transistor that caught music from a radio station. Fatima reluctantly tolerated Eskandar's breach of her ban until one day when her husband refused to turn the radio off as the muezzin at the mosque began the call to prayer, a sin in her eyes. They fought so loudly that they drowned out both music and prayer call, until Fatima picked up the radio and threw it against the wall.

Later in life, their strict upbringing began nagging Zahra. She felt cheated. Why should she not be allowed to be loved? As the oldest daughter, she understood that she would bear the brunt of her parents' meticulous parenting yet never doubted their love. She saw it on her wedding night when her mother suddenly, and uncharacteristically, burst into tears when Zahra was driven off to her new home. She saw the anguish in her parents' faces when they learned how Hussein and his family were treating her. They allowed Zahra's oldest sister, Rayhana, five years her junior, to wait until the age of seventeen before marrying. She even helped choose her husband. While thrilled for her sister's happiness, Zahra felt a pang of self-pity.

Since his night of rage, Zahra expected nothing of Hussein. His drug use worsened; the beatings became more frequent. Cheap opium was everywhere, and often mixed in ways that exacerbated his mood swings. Zahra needed Hussein's permission to work, and he gave it as long as she financed his addiction. He had recently begun drinking cheap moonshine, too, also illegal. He suffered from chronic headaches, making him even more volatile. Any loud noise would set him off. He beat her when he didn't get his fix, usually by pulling her by the hair and knocking her head against the wall. He beat her when he had a bad fix, or when she got home from work twenty minutes later than expected. After he pulled out a knife and threatened to kill either himself or her if she didn't get him money for drugs, she hid all the knives in the house. The violence got so bad that when she avoided a beating once or twice a week, she would thank God for answering her prayers. Zahra once had to wear sunglasses outside the house, including at the internet café, for a week to hide a bruised eye. She pretended to wear them as a fashion statement, and no one asked questions. The couple still lived with Hussein's parents, until one day when Hussein beat Zahra so badly, kicking and hitting her entire body and face, that his father asked them to find another place to live. As long as they were living under their roof, his son's behavior toward Zahra was his responsibility. Zahra found a house close to her mother and siblings. Parisa had started school, and in the morning Zahra would walk her to class before starting work at the internet café, while Jawad spent the days with her mother as he had when she worked at the kiln in Iran.

One afternoon in late September 2007, Zahra's phone rang. It was Hussein.

"Remember to bring money home," he said. The family had been living in Afghanistan for nearly three years. Recently, Zahra had been forced to borrow money for rent, mostly from the owner of the internet café, who took pity on her. She had no money left now, and no one to borrow from on short notice.

"Of course, I will," she replied, knowing that she didn't have enough.

Zahra would often pray to God that she would come home and find Hussein sober. Today, she prayed to come home and find him too drunk or stoned to raise a hand against her. She went to her mother's house to fetch Parisa. Fatima had given Jawad a bath and asked Zahra to bring him fresh clothes. When she opened the front door at home, she found Hussein asleep on the floor of the sitting room. It was Ramadan, but Hussein didn't observe fasting. People who are pregnant or sick are exempt, and Hussein considered his addiction an illness. Zahra cooked them both a meal so she could break fast and then woke him up. He stirred and looked at her.

"Did you bring me money?"

She gave him 250 afghanis, about five dollars.

"What's this?" he barked at her.

"Don't worry, I will find more money for you tomorrow, this will get you through tonight." She could see the fury rising in him. He had once caught her hiding money from him and suspected she was doing it again. He was right. For weeks she had been squirreling away money from her salary to buy the kids new clothes for Eid, the end of Ramadan, as was tradition.

"It's okay," he said. "We'll talk about it later."

After their meal, Zahra took clothes to Jawad and returned an hour later.

"Dad has been drinking that stinky water again," Parisa said. He was drunk and passed out. Afraid that he would punish her if he came to and found her awake, Zahra bedded down quickly, resting on cushions on the floor with her arm around Parisa. She was so exhausted from work that she fell asleep immediately.

She woke up when Parisa shook her, to darkened windows and a room full of smoke. Hussein had placed piles of clothes around them and set fire to them. The door was locked. The bars in front of the windows, meant to keep burglars out, had turned the room into a cage. Through the window Zahra could see Hussein standing in the courtyard, looking at the fire inside. Parisa screamed. Zahra picked up a copper pestle from the floor and banged the door and the iron bars to wake the neighbors. Coughing, she could see people scaling the walls into her family's compound from the roof next door. Two of their neighbors entered the courtyard and grabbed Hussein's wrists to force him to hand over the keys. Parisa and Zahra got the door open and escaped. When they ran past Hussein, he tried to grab them, but more neighbors had now entered and restrained him, while others got the fire under control.

Zahra took Parisa by the arm and walked in the direction of her mother's house. She had always defended Hussein, insisting he was a good man, denying his drug abuse even when it was evident to everyone. The mask had come off. Hussein followed her, as did the neighbors, marching in a small procession through the night. As soon as the door opened, the words spilled out of her in an incoherent stream as she told her mother about the fire, Hussein's drug abuse, all the violence. Hussein interrupted. This was all Zahra's fault, he said.

"She walks around town all day like a prostitute. She is not a good girl. That's why I hit her," he said.

"Is that true, Zahra?" Fatima asked. Zahra was dumbfounded. She and her daughter had almost died in a fire instigated by her husband, and her own mother now doubted her story. Zahra cracked, and years of pent-up fear and anger erupted. She noticed she was shouting as she told her mother about the beatings and the humiliation she had suffered over the years. The neighbors chimed in. They had witnessed more than she had thought, and had just watched Hussein try to burn the house down. That worked. Zahra's mother turned to face Hussein, who stuttered that he wanted a divorce. He knew that Zahra's family saw divorce as something shameful. Zahra didn't care, and apparently, neither did her brother, who had been watching in silence but now squared off with Hussein, looking as if he was about to punch him.

"People only divorce someone if their spouse is useless. In your house, she works and makes all the money," her brother said. With their father still in Iran, the brother was head of the household, and he said he would no longer allow Zahra to go to Hussein's home, and that he would call the local mullah first thing in the morning to start divorce proceedings. Hussein left and slammed the door behind him.

It was three o'clock in the morning when the neighbors left, and the family sat down to discuss what to do. Divorce was usually taboo. Traditionally, a marriage was a form of contract between two families. The bride was married off in return for a dowry, and after her wedding, she was expected to obey her new family. There were strains of thought and activism in Afghanistan that challenged the traditional family structure. There had been previous governments that attempted to reform Afghanistan and promote a female identity unshackled from the family, and the autonomy of women to chart their own course in life, but they had never been strong enough to impose lasting change. Ultimately, divorce was unacceptable to most Afghan families, unless as a last resort.

"In my family, you couldn't even *talk* about divorce," Zahra said. "Divorce was as bad as murder. I had never considered getting a divorce. I didn't think I had any other option but to stay married."

But her family could see her desperation. Her life was in danger, and Fatima agreed that saving her daughter was more important than losing honor by breaking the marriage contract with Hussein's family, even if it meant that Zahra might never be able to marry again, as divorcees were widely regarded as damaged goods.

The next morning, as they waited for the mullah to come and start divorce consultations, Zahra's phone rang. She put the phone on speaker so the rest of her family could hear her mother-in-law. Mehtab, Hussein's mother, did not claim to be ignorant of the violence in their marriage. In fact, she said, she and her husband had asked Zahra and Hussein to move out of the house precisely because they realized how badly he was beating her and didn't want to take responsibility for anything that might happen.

"They were afraid that one day he might kill me, and they didn't want to be held responsible," Zahra said. Fatima made up her mind. Divorce was the only option. She called her husband in Iran, and he agreed. The cleric asked Hussein's father to find his son. When he finally appeared days later, he admitted to being a drug addict, but said he had never abused Zahra. When Zahra's family and the mullah visited him in the home where she and the children used to live, Hussein had changed the burned carpets so there was no trace of the fire.

Afghan law made it easier for men than women to break up a marriage. While it was often enough for a man to simply state that he wanted a divorce, a woman had to prove either that her husband could not financially support her, that he abused her without cause, or that he disappeared for long periods of time. She had to state a legal case, backed up by witnesses. This process, alongside cultural stigma, helped keep many Afghan women in abusive marriages, as many didn't have the financial means to hire a lawyer or have access to the limited number of local and international NGOs assisting women on divorce matters. Eighty-five percent of Afghan women were illiterate, making the demands for construing a legal argument insurmountable for most. Divorces were rare also when compared to other Islamic states. More than a decade after the ouster of the Taliban, Afghanistan saw about 2 divorces per 100,000 people. In Saudi Arabia, the divorce rate was 127 per 100,000 individuals, while Iranians got divorced at a rate of nearly 200 per 100,000 people.

Having only Zahra's words against Hussein's, the mullah gave Hussein three months to quit his addiction. In the meantime, Zahra and the kids were to live with her mother. The cleric hoped that the couple would find a way to stay together. For Zahra, temporary separation was an improvement, but she had no patience left. Her reputation was already tainted as a woman seeking to divorce her husband, and she was trapped. Three months later, in late 2007, the mullah reconvened the two families to negotiate a solution. Hussein appeared sober, though Zahra knew that he was able to stay off drugs for a short period of time if he had to. The cleric asked Zahra to present her conditions for staying in the marriage. Zahra had planned for this. First of all, she said, she no longer wanted to work. To any Afghan cleric, that was a more than fair ask. Second, she demanded to live with Hussein's parents, as she was afraid to live alone with him. Finally, she insisted that she could divorce Hussein if he didn't kick the drugs. Her ultimatum was reasonable to the mullah, as Zahra knew it would be, but she also knew her in-laws wouldn't agree. She had deliberately demanded not to work, because it would then fall to Hussein's father to support the couple, including his son's drug use.

"We will never accept this," Hussein's father said. "We don't care if you stay or leave."

The mullah didn't have time to mediate an argument. "This is not how it's going to work," he said. "Go home and decide."

They had barely entered Fatima's home before Mehtab agreed that divorce was probably the best option.

"I can't guarantee that my son won't hit her again, and I am not taking responsibility for it," she said.

"What about the children?" Fatima asked.

"Zahra has taken care of them until now, and she will continue to do so."

In a matter of minutes, the two matriarchs had come up with a verbal agreement. The next day, they all visited the cleric at the mosque to sign the divorce papers. Zahra felt a sense of relief wash over her. Then she heard Mehtab ask the cleric a question.

"How come you didn't mention anything about the children?"

Zahra's mother looked at her, puzzled.

"Yesterday you said Zahra could take care of them," she said.

Mehtab said she'd never said such a thing.

Zahra and her family had been tricked. Without a signed agreement stating otherwise, Afghan law gave the father's family custody of the children. Hussein was unable to take care of them, but responsibility then fell to his father. It was a shrewd move by Hussein's parents. This way, they could either coerce Zahra to give up her demands and return to the marriage, or they could at least avoid losing their grandchildren, the only good thing to have emerged from their son's failed and dishonorable marriage. Mehtab said Zahra was welcome to come visit the kids as often as she wanted. Zahra stood her ground. She wanted a divorce, and she wanted guarantees in writing that she could see her children at least once a week. She had no faith in her mother-in-law's promises. That, Mehtab agreed to.

On the sixth day of Muharram, when Shia Muslims mourn the martyrdom of Imam Hussein, the third descendant of the Prophet, Herat was seized by ferocious cold, and snow fell lightly on the ground. Zahra hadn't cried since Nargis's death, but when the taxi pulled over by her in-laws' house, she couldn't hold back her tears. Parisa was eight, Jawad was five. Both hugged her legs and would not let go. Zahra watched as Hussein's mother pried their fingers free and led them into the house. Zahra's mother was devastated, hitting herself in the face with both hands and crying uncontrollably.

The next few weeks passed in a daze. Zahra had lost three children, and her mind was about to go, too. She went to a doctor, who prescribed her antidepressants, which she wolfed down absentmindedly. She slept all day long. She was so frail that for months, she never once claimed her right to see her children.

5

PARASTO

"If only you had been a boy." Parasto's grandmother's words stalked her through her childhood. A family needed sons to survive, but Parasto's mother, Sofia, had so far only given birth to five daughters: Gul, Parasto, and Forozan, plus two twins who had died young. Parasto's father, Abdulhakim, was almost twenty years older than his wife, and the grandmother, knowing that the need for a son was pressing, took her frustration out on Parasto. Aunts and neighbors chimed in, lamenting the burden that a large girl flock put on a family.

Parasto Hakim was born in 1997 in Pakistan, where her parents had settled for a brief stint after the Taliban swept to power in 1996. Abdulhakim and Sofia never felt at home in a Pakistani refugee camp, and returned to Afghanistan after only a year, two young daughters in tow. Abdulhakim had been a commander in the Soviet-backed government army and had taken a four-year tank engineering degree in the USSR in the 1980s, but hoped that the Taliban would leave them in peace despite his past loyalties. The family settled in the Western city of Herat, where Abdulhakim comanaged a radio mechanics store. From a distance they watched violence engulf Sheberghan, the main city in their home province of Jowzjan, where Abdul Rashid Dostum,

an Uzbek former plumber turned feared war commander with a pro-
clivity for vodka, was fighting to retake the province from the Taliban.

In 1999, after Dostum had fled to Turkey, Abdulhakim arranged
to move his family to Jowzjan, where they'd lived before fleeing to
Pakistan. The family set out from Herat at dawn on a Soviet-built
highway going four hundred miles east to the town of Aqcha, in a barren landscape with little to distract the eye but some mountains in the
distance. The family's new home had a small, empty pool out back, and
clusters of opium poppy growing in the garden, which bloomed in the
late spring. Abdulhakim lanced the bulbs of the plants when they had
matured to extract the sticky resin inside and sold it to pharmacies to
turn into opiates. At the end of the growing season, the poppy pods
turned brown and developed a hard carapace, which Parasto and her
sister Gul cracked open to eat the seeds.

"They were really yummy," she remembered.

The family was struggling financially. Selling vegetables from a
street cart, Abdulhakim made just enough to put two meals on the
table a day. Rarely meat. The mud house had two bedrooms, one for
Parasto and her growing number of siblings, and one for Abdulhakim and Sofia. Parasto was a stubborn child. Her mother said she had
"anger issues." When she didn't get her way, she turned to face the
wall, where she drew pencil sketches of flowers, cars, and matchstick
men. Her angry drawings decorated the walls of the home, next to a
few pictures that Abdulhakim had brought back from his time studying at a military academy in the Soviet Union, where he had been one
of about twelve thousand officers from Afghanistan sent for training
in the 1970s and 1980s. One of the pictures showed a green-domed Islamic building in Uzbekistan. Another portrayed a Caucasian-looking
baby with blue eyes and chubby cheeks. Sofia was perpetually pregnant, and Abdulhakim said that if a woman looked at a beautiful baby
while expecting, her child, too, would be born beautiful.

The Hakims were a decidedly modest family. Pashtuns originally from Kandahar, now living in a multiethnic province among
mostly Uzbeks and Turkmen, Parasto's parents were religious, but not

overly so. They raised Parasto and her siblings to pray five times a day, but not to care very much whether others did the same. They told them stories about heaven and angels, and about a merciful God. Parasto remembered the story of the river Zam Zam, a holy source of water that appeared after the angel Jibril struck the ground with his wing, and which nourished Hajar and Ismail, the wife and son of the Prophet Ibrahim, as they were thirsting in the barren lands of Mecca. As a child, she imagined God as kind, forgiving, and motivated by love. It was the opposite image of the one propagated by the Taliban. Parasto learned that one's relationship to God was private. God tested your patience and rewarded you accordingly. Most sins could be forgiven by muttering a repentant "Astaghfirullah." The Taliban, however, primarily saw God as vengeful.

"They see mostly the dark side of Allah," she reflected. "They will ask a man, have you prayed this morning? No? To hell with him, burn him." In prayer, Parasto found space for contemplation. As she got older, during dark times, praying reminded her that someone was watching over her, and gave her space to dwell on reasons to be happy.

True to character, the family had a tempered reaction to the 9/11 attacks. Though Abdulhakim had fought American-backed militias in his youth, Parasto's parents saw the terrorist attack as a crime and condemned the killing of civilians. Not everyone shared their views. They heard from people in their old camp in Pakistan, even some of their own relatives, who celebrated al-Qaeda's assault on America, vindicated that, for once, the United States felt some of the pain Afghans had suffered for decades.

The US invasion transformed the north. The defeat of the Taliban opened the way for a return of warlords who had been forced into exile, including the notorious General Dostum. In November, when Kabul fell to the US-led coalition, the Taliban were still putting up fierce resistance in the northern city of Kunduz. Dostum moved his men there to take part in a three-day siege by the Northern Alliance on the city, and eventually helped force the Taliban defending it to defect or capitulate. Dostum's men packed thousands of surrendered

Taliban militants into shipping containers to drive them from Kunduz to Sheberghan. Three days after Kunduz fell, another group of about four hundred foreign prisoners, most of them Arabs, rose up against their Afghan and Western guards at Qala-i-Jangi, or the "Fort of War," a fortress turned jail outside Mazar-e Sharif, the biggest city in the north. During the six-day uprising, more than two hundred prisoners and a CIA officer—the first American to die in combat in the war—were killed. Hundreds of prisoners surrendered after Dostum ordered their cells flooded with ice-cold irrigation water. Some of them were added to the shipping-container convoy as it passed through Mazar. On the way to Sheberghan, scores of prisoners died from asphyxiation. Dostum's soldiers opened fire on prisoners in at least three of the containers. As many as two thousand prisoners were buried in mass graves in the Dasht-e Laili desert. Despite Afghan and international calls for Dostum to be prosecuted for war crimes, he was never held accountable. His status as the undisputed leader of the Uzbek minority in the north made him a guarantor of millions of Uzbek votes for any president willing to grant him influence, and a dangerous source of political rivalry and potential ethnic conflict for those who weren't. Sheberghan became one of two major power centers in the north, and Dostum one of the country's main power brokers.

After the Taliban were toppled in 2001, life for the Hakims changed immediately. Parents in Sheberghan sent their girls to school in droves. Within four years, about 1.7 million Afghan girls enrolled in education, equaling one in three of Afghan schoolchildren, fewer than international donors had hoped for but a big leap from anything Afghanistan had ever seen. Parasto started first grade in 2003. Sofia was literate but had only completed tenth grade. She wanted her daughters to make more of themselves. As a small child, Parasto had been mostly quiet, subdued perhaps by the feeling that she was a disappointment to her family. Now, a waterfall of words flowed from her. In the north, most people did not speak Pashto, her family's language, but Dari, the Afghan dialect of Persian. Both sisters quickly began conversing in both. The girls enrolled in a school in the town of Aqcha, built by

General Dostum. Known for his bloodlust, the general also splashed personal wealth on welfare and services to constituents, in return for one of the most loyal power bases in the country. Every morning Parasto walked fifteen minutes to school, where teachers would inspect the students' school uniforms—black leggings and long jacket with a white headscarf—to ensure they were clean and presentable. Parasto was a fast learner, and she adored one teacher in particular. One day, she complained to the teacher that she had wanted to bring her a present but didn't have anything to give.

"You're my gift," the teacher said.

After school, Parasto and her siblings would change into their daily clothes and jump into the empty pool in the garden to play with other children from the neighborhood. They played tag and football with balls made from rolled-up scarves. On weekends they got ice cream from a shop one street over from their house. As Afghanistan opened up to foreign soldiers, journalists swarmed over the country. Parasto's first meeting with a foreigner was with a reporter who took a picture of her giggling among her friends.

The Taliban regime had banned television, but now screens lit up the living room every night in the Hakim household. The family watched the evening news from the national broadcaster, and foreign movies, picking up short sentences in Indian, English, and Russian. Abdulhakim found a job at the Ministry of Public Works as a bureaucrat, making around $90 a month, and moved part-time to Kabul. Sharing a small room with other workers, returning home one weekend every eight weeks, he was able to support the family.

On the morning of October 9, 2004, Parasto grabbed hold of her mother's blue burqa, followed her out the door, and walked with her to school. Mothers and daughters, fathers and sons, across the country did the same. It was a historic day, the first Afghan election in decades. Afghans turned out in the millions. Parasto's school had been turned into an election center, and as they entered the wave of blue burqas at the women's section, seven-year-old Parasto sensed that something exciting and new was happening. Hamid Karzai had been the country's interim leader since December 2001, three months after September 11, when an international conference in Bonn, Germany, picked him. The Bonn Conference was a US-organized gathering of Afghan leaders and international powers. The only major faction not invited was the Taliban. Excluding the Taliban from the Bonn Conference seemed a natural choice to many at the time, but it would have grave consequences and help prolong the war for decades. By including the Taliban, the United States could have shown the Afghan people that it was serious about building a democracy with space for anyone who wished to take part. Instead, it marginalized from Afghan political life an influential group that, due to the historic role of its members in fighting the Soviet occupation in the 1980s and ending the civil war, had earned respect among many Afghans. However, much of the West, and many Afghans, resented the Taliban regime and wanted to see the Islamists banished from influence. Barring them from Bonn was an early sign that the new supposedly democratic order in Afghanistan was not open to everyone. For decades to come, the Taliban's propaganda and armed struggle would center around the claim that the country had been occupied by imperialist invaders. Lakhdar Brahimi, the Algerian diplomat who oversaw the Bonn Conference, later said the failure to include the Taliban at Bonn was Afghanistan's "original sin."

Karzai was also not present at the conference. At the time, two months into the American campaign in Afghanistan, the forty-three-year-old Pashtun tribal leader was in Uruzgan with a team of CIA operatives battling one of the last pockets of Taliban fighters. Karzai was not the most obvious choice to lead Afghanistan, and when he gave a speech to the delegates over a CIA-supplied satellite phone from a mud house in Kandahar, he apparently didn't expect to be chosen. "We are one nation, one culture, we are united and not divided," Karzai told the conference. "We all believe in Islam but in an Islam of tolerance." Yet Karzai emerged as the consensus candidate. He didn't have military experience or a militia under his command, which also meant he had no track record of war crimes from the brutal years of civil conflict. He descended from traditional chiefs of the Popalzai clan in

Kandahar, was the son of a former deputy speaker of Parliament, and had strong tribal links. He was a consummate diplomat. The fact that he was Pashtun, like the majority of the Taliban, meant that picking him would help quell notions that the new administration was waging ethnic war. Furthermore, he had ties to the West, particularly the United States, where some of his brothers lived, spoke English fluently, and had the charisma to charm foreign leaders making major decisions about Afghanistan's future.

On December 5, 2001, as the conference was underway, an errant American airstrike confused its target and mistakenly struck near the compound in Kandahar where Karzai was staying with the CIA team. Fifty of Karzai's men were killed. Years later, as president, Karzai would come to resent these kinds of indiscriminate airstrikes, and the attitude behind them, as the heart of what was wrong with the US war in his country. Fifteen minutes after he had nearly been killed, Karzai's satellite phone rang. It was the BBC's Lyse Doucet calling from Bonn to congratulate him.

"Am I the new leader?" he replied. She assured him that he was. Two years later, Karzai ran for president without a serious challenger, and with wholehearted support from the United States. Articulate and fluent in the ways of the East and the West (he claimed to love Starbucks and country music), Karzai wanted to create a new image for Afghanistan and cast himself as a man who could bridge the country's ethnic differences and create new opportunities for women (although his own wife was never seen in public and gave up her work as a doctor after marriage).

It was illustrative of the new era of supposed political plurality in Afghanistan that when Sofia entered the ballot booth with Parasto to cast the first vote of her life, she did so in a high school named after Abdul Rashid Dostum, who himself was a candidate in the election, and voted for his election rival: Karzai. Among the eighteen competing candidates on the ballot, there was even a woman, Massouda Jalal. Like most other contenders, she received less than one percent of the vote. More than half of all the Afghans who turned out did like Sofia and voted for Karzai. Though his reputation would come to suffer, as would his relationship with the United States, Afghanistan's first president in the twenty-first century was initially known as an extraordinary statesman. He welded together a coalition of strongmen, until recently mortal rivals. His choice of clothing signaled this ambition to unite the nation: In public he wore a green-and-blue-striped *chapan* cape traditional among Uzbeks, and the triangular lamb's-wool karakul cap of the Tajiks. His shalwar kameez tunic was collarless and cut in a southern Afghan style. Among Pashtuns, he wore a turban. The striking outfit made Karzai globally recognizable. Designer Tom Ford called him "the chicest man on the planet today." Every day, dozens of villagers from around the country would visit him at the palace to request everything from mediation in land disputes to help in getting supposedly innocent relatives freed from prison. Karzai relished the role, and welcomed everyone with a ceremoniously vigorous handshake, a smile, and full concentration for the duration of their audience. He was said to be able to make anyone feel like a king for fifteen minutes. In those years, he embodied the hope that the country could start anew.

Buoyed by this fresh start, Abdulhakim moved the whole family to Kabul when Parasto was about to start fourth grade. The air carried a farrago of scents: of burning rubber, exhaust fumes imbued with cheap petrol, sizzling frying oil in pots on street carts, and rose bushes. Pillowy clouds of dust surrounded the feet of beggars, farmers, amputees, and conmen, wagon-pulling donkeys and street dogs. Deep-fried samosas and *bolani*—a pancake folded around potato—lay sweating in the sun on rickety wooden carts. Ragged-looking chickens stood squeezed in cages. Before 2001, some six million Afghans had lived outside the country. Now, they returned in the hundreds of thousands, waves of returnees crashing onto the shores of Kabul along with throngs of Afghans moving to the city from the countryside, like the Hakims. Kabul was hopelessly ill-equipped to handle all the new arrivals, and on its periphery, shantytowns expanded way beyond the city's limits. Built to accommodate less than a million people, Kabul's population swelled in a few years to six million. The Hakims' first house was located, as many other homes of the newly arrived, on a hillside in the southern part of town. Mud houses spread upward above the center of the city whose buildings lay like marbles in a bowl amid the softly curved slopes. The informal houses on the hills lacked access to water and electricity grids, but amid the dust and reek of open sewers there was a smell in the air of promise, of new beginnings.

While setting up a new life in Kabul, Sofia conceived a son, in her sixth attempt. They named him Inayat. In total, Sofia carried nine children, six of whom survived past infancy. For most of Parasto's childhood, Inayat—and Milad, a second son three years younger— was too little to be useful around the house, and she worked hard to show everyone in her family that she could do anything as well as any boy. She ran toward her father when he came home to help him carry the heavy grocery bags. In sixth grade, on the cusp of puberty, she went alone to fetch water for the house, which had no running water. Balancing a plank with two plastic buckets like a yoke, she scaled the slopes of the mountainside. She went to the bakery every day for bread and walked with her siblings to the mosque for religious studies.

"I was the only girl walking to the bakery like that," she said. She quickly became an attraction. Boys stared at her in the street and told her they were in love with her.

"Why are you looking at me?" she shouted at them.

"Because we like you."

"Shut up!"

She hated the attention.

"I felt really uncomfortable because I was so young." One boy was particularly persistent and accosted her when she walked to and from the mosque. One day, she told the mullah about it, and never saw the boy again. The rumor in the girls' section of the mosque was that the mullah had gotten some other boys to beat the kid up.

She was reaching a dangerous age. Her father brought home a large dog from his base in one of the provinces, and she started bringing him along whenever she left the house. Max was a large, muscular mutt who lived in a shed in the family's courtyard. Many Afghans disliked dogs, but the Hakims loved Max. According to local superstition, if you regularly fed your dog meat and suddenly stopped, he was going to eat you. So Max was kept on a strictly vegetarian diet. Trained in the military, Max would walk alongside Parasto, off leash, and wait for her outside when she went inside a shop or the mosque. Mostly the boys left her alone.

Abdulhakim had leveraged his military training and experience to find work in the national police, where he rose quickly in the ranks. He was appointed chief of police first in Wardak, then Khost, a province near the Pakistani border with a heavy presence of Taliban militants. The position put him on the front line of the American war, working alongside US Special Forces, and took him out of Kabul for long stretches of time. Khost was a tribal borderland that no administration in Kabul had ever fully controlled. Osama bin Laden was spotted there shortly after September 11, 2001. Rebuilding the Afghan security forces was meant to strengthen Afghanistan's own ability to deny terrorists a safe haven, and to bolster the capability and the legitimacy of the central government in Kabul. This was part of a counterinsurgency doctrine promoted by Western warrior-intellectuals for decades, from British commanders putting down colonial insurgencies in Africa and Northern Ireland to US general David Petraeus in Iraq. According to this school of thought, it wasn't enough to suppress an insurrection. To make sustainable peace, a warring party needed to win the hearts and minds of the people. Persuading the Afghan population to throw their support behind the new government was meant to erode support for the Taliban and other militants and allow the United States and its allies to leave as soon as possible.

The Afghan army grew sixfold, from 1,750 troops in March 2003 to more than 10,000 a year later. By 2009, there would be 92,000 army soldiers and nearly 70,000 police personnel who were also tasked with fighting the Taliban. But the stated ambitions were not matched by sufficient cash. By 2002, the Bush administration had spent $4.5 billion in Afghanistan, but the vast majority of that went to fighting the war. Less than 10 percent went to recovery or even to building the new Afghan forces.

The fighting in Khost made Abdulhakim a regular fixture on national television. Whenever Parasto and Gul saw him on TV, strapping in black wool jacket, stiff police cap, and a dense black beard, explaining the latest operation against Taliban or al-Qaeda militants, they beamed with pride. Their father made good money now, ensuring that his family back in Kabul ate meat and beans on the regular, and fresh vegetables daily. They moved from the shantytown on the slopes down into Chehel Sotoun, a crowded residential area closer to the city center named after a garden with a nineteenth-century pavilion built by the Iron Emir. The area was poor but the family now had access to government services and lived close to the girls' school.

Abdulhakim was becoming a well-known face. When the fighting in the east heated up, he received threats and the army sent armored vehicles to take Parasto and Gul to and from school. They weren't permitted to give their friends a ride. It was an uncomfortable solution. The Hakims had always tried not to draw attention to themselves, which in Afghanistan was a liability, and Chehel Sotoun was a poor neighborhood where an expensive government vehicle turned heads.

The girls thrived in school. Parasto returned home every day brimming with questions for her parents: Who was Dr. Najib, and how was he killed? What were the Taliban about? What happened to the Communists? She spent a fraction of the time Gul did studying for exams and still got top grades. She had an almost photographic memory.

"How do you do this?" Gul asked her one day, before turning to their mother and saying, "I have to study something a hundred times, but she doesn't even read it!"

Parasto did read. She tore through Persian translations of books about Winston Churchill and Hillary Clinton, Gandhi and Mandela. She read Jane Austen and the Turkish novelists Orhan Pamuk and Elif Shafak. A few years later she read *Dreams from My Father* and came to idolize Barack Obama. Parasto thought Obama was asking some of the same questions that she was, from the perspective of race instead of gender. Why don't Black people have the same facilities available to them as white people? If life for her would have been easier had she been a boy, Obama's life would have been easier had he been white.

She devoured documentaries about Adolf Hitler, the two World Wars, and Fidel Castro. She loved *The Motorcycle Diaries*, the 2004 feature film starring Gael García Bernal as Che Guevara. The Argentine revolutionary had been a hero of the Afghan rebel leader Ahmad Shah Massoud, and the two men carried a similar battlefield chicness in photos. She was obsessed with movies about war, whether documentaries, feature films, or even her father's appearances on television. Parasto aspired to be at the center of important world events. She dreamed of representing Afghanistan at the United Nations in New York. At home, she and her siblings entertained each other by doing role-plays. Parasto pretended to be a CEO going to an office, or a surgeon treating her sisters as patients. She even entertained the idea of joining the actual military to become an air force pilot.

"My whole life I wanted to be in a place like the front lines. Just to prove to myself that I was capable," Parasto said.

In the house, they listened to pop tunes by the great Afghan singer Ahmad Zahir, who blended Afghan traditional styles and instruments with a Western pop tradition, and lent his croon to soulful love songs and, occasionally, somewhat steamy lyrics. They listened to Naghma and Mangal, an Afghan couple who since the 1970s had been popular with Afghan exiles for their patriotic songs, including some dedicated to the military.

Parasto's manners were not considered befitting for a young girl. She crossed her legs sitting on a couch. She spoke loudly, shoulders back and chest forward. She had no wish to be desirable to boys, and had been told that she wasn't. Parasto and her sisters had inherited relatively dark skin from their father, compared to their cousins who were fairer and green-eyed, and whom Parasto had always found beautiful. She had confidence in herself yet craved her family's acceptance for who she was.

"I wanted to be enough. I wanted them to look at me and say, 'Parasto, she is enough. She is perfect the way she is.' I wanted them to see what I was able to do," she said.

In fact, she was her father's favorite, even though she gave him grief.

"As a child, she was very clever," Abdulhakim remembered. "She would say, 'I wish I was in the military with you,'" he said. "If she was a boy, she could have done anything. But we worried about her."

Parasto saw women around her suffer for no other apparent reason than being female. Her secondary school history teacher was always immaculately dressed, pretty, and carried herself with calm dignity. A model of the kind of woman Parasto imagined her family would have wanted her to be. More than once, the teacher arrived at school with bruises on her face. She kept her private affairs to herself, but it was not hard to guess what had happened to her at home. If the teacher had to suffer like this, Parasto thought, then no woman could expect to live an easy life. The teacher fulfilled all society's norms, yet she had clearly not found happiness in marriage. Parasto wondered what a woman was supposed to do. It seemed to her that the only time a man was ever judged was when he asked for a woman's hand and her family inquired about his family, background, and wealth. A man was not asked about his personality, or to guarantee that he would treat the woman right. He wasn't questioned on his faith or his commitment to the vows of marriage. Forget about his looks. Parasto had never heard of a woman who had been asked if she found her suitor attractive.

The odds were stacked against Afghan women, yet Parasto didn't think women in the West necessarily had it much better. She resented the way Western movies portrayed women as free only if they were willing to use their body as currency.

"From movies, I got the idea that men and women had to pay their bills separately, then they would sleep together, and even then, it wasn't even clear that they were committed to each other," she said. "If someone only wants you for your body, that can make a woman hate herself."

She didn't accept that claiming sexual pleasure, although it might be a woman's right, was a valid way to achieve self-determination.

"Just because you can doesn't mean you have to," she said. "The last thing a woman can give up is her body," she said. "Not everyone deserves to touch it."

Women were not men, and shouldn't act like them.

"God created men and women very different," she said. They were capable of doing the same things, and should have the opportunity to do so, but at the same time, they had different roles in society.

Increasingly, she had to agree with what her family members had told her growing up: she wished she had been a boy. As far as she could tell, even the most accomplished and powerful women in the world wished they had, too. One of the most popular songs at the time among her and her friends was Beyoncé's "If I Were a Boy," a guitar-driven ballad about how life, even for one of the world's biggest female pop stars, who had grown up in the world's most admired democracy, was hindered by her gender: "If I were a boy / Even just for a day / I'd roll out of bed in the morning /And throw on what I wanted then go."

Parasto exchanged songs with friends and listened to them on YouTube. The local hero was the London-based Afghan pop star Aryana Sayeed, who set Dari and Pashto lyrics to arrangements of traditional Afghan strings and percussion, wrapped in slick Western-style pop production. They listened to Iranian singers and the Lebanese pop star Nancy Ajram. Every evening, a local radio station called Radio Jawanan aired an hour of foreign pop music. Jennifer Lopez's Latin pop songs were everywhere, as was four-to-the-floor dance pop, like "Rain over Me" by the Cuban American rapper Pitbull. Parasto wrote down lyrics so she could recite them line by line in school as a way of practicing her English. It was Beyoncé, though, who made Parasto feel seen: "If only I were a boy . . . I'd put myself first and make the rules as I go."

Parasto recognized her ambition to do something extraordinary in the heroes of history but also in its villains. She thought she understood at least part of what drove Osama bin Laden. The son of a billionaire construction magnate with ties to the Saudi royal family, bin Laden had been raised to think that he was special. He wanted to make history. Parasto thought she could decipher some twisted logic in bin Laden's thinking. He claimed that he was perpetrating attacks against the West to protect the security of the worldwide Muslim community, the *ummah*, whose blood he said had been spilled at the hands of Westerners for centuries. Civilian casualties were a necessary evil in a greater battle for justice. A year after the US invasion of Afghanistan, bin Laden had written: "Whoever has destroyed our villages and towns, then we have the right to destroy their villages and towns. Whoever has stolen our wealth, then we have the right to destroy their economy. And whoever has killed our civilians, then we have the right to kill theirs."

It was a morally abhorrent argument, Parasto thought, but not so different from what the United States said. She remembered a television clip of the *60 Minutes* correspondent Lesley Stahl, in 1996, asking US secretary of state Madeleine Albright about the suffering caused by US sanctions in Iraq following the 1991 Gulf War.

"We have heard that half a million [Iraqi] children have died. I mean, that is more children than died in Hiroshima. And, you know, is the price worth it?" Stahl asked Albright.

"I think this is a very hard choice," Albright answered, "but the price, we think, the price is worth it."

In Afghanistan, the United States had framed the invasion as an act of self-defense, and defended it as a way to bring democracy to the Muslim world and counter a growing threat of terrorism. It was an ideologically motivated war. Weeks before the US invasion of Afghanistan, President George W. Bush had said: "The advance of human freedom—the great achievement of our time, and the great hope of every time—now depends on us."

His successor, Barack Obama, a liberal law professor, had campaigned against the torture used in Iraq, Afghanistan, and Guantánamo, and pledged to end America's wars so convincingly that he received the Nobel Peace Prize in 2009. In his acceptance speech,

Obama explained how sometimes war is "not only necessary but morally justified." When Obama inherited the war, he ordered a surge of tens of thousands of American troops and initiated an air campaign using drones that killed at least nine hundred civilians. Parasto sympathized with the ideals that the Americans claimed to promote. But like al-Qaeda, America justified the killing of civilians—even if unintentional—in pursuit of a bigger cause. To her, these were two shades of the same ugly hypocrisy.

Her career ambitions might have been in sync with the new political order in Afghanistan, but she faced staunch resistance from relatives who held more conservative values than her parents. While Abdulhakim and Sofia had become exposed to more liberal values and other ways of life when they moved to the north, their relatives had remained in Kandahar and were still shaped by the traditional ideas of women's roles in the family and society. They exerted pressure on Abdulhakim to take his daughters out of school. He wanted them to do well and had no ideological qualms about girls going to school, but as a survivor of several authoritarian regimes, foreign occupation, and civil war, he knew that the best way to stay out of harm's way was to not stick your neck out. His relatives from Kandahar were all telling him that it wasn't proper for his daughters to study.

"What made us different from our relatives was that all of them were either in southern or northern Afghanistan, but we were in Kabul," Parasto said. "Our mentality was different. We were trying to make our own destiny. Everybody has a future, and we knew we had to decide our own."

Their relatives were not in the minority with their conservative views. Girls still made up only a third of Afghan schoolchildren, and just 5 percent of eligible girls enrolled in secondary school. Decades of war had left many rural districts without functioning schools. Transportation was poor and teachers scarce. Many Afghan families still refused to send their daughters to school. Islamic fundamentalists were threatening girls' education and repeatedly attacked schools, including in Wardak—where Omari grew up—where they torched girls'

schools. Sofia worried and would occasionally side with her conservative Kandahari relatives. Parasto, Gul, and Forozan, the third of four
sisters, who by now had also started school, argued with their mother
over breakfast, lunch, and dinner. Sometimes they got up early in the
morning to do their domestic duties and pray and then slipped out of
the house to walk to school before Sofia woke up in time to stop them.
They knew that, when it came down to it, their mother wanted to raise
her daughters to have more opportunities in life than she had had.
When Abdulhakim's job took him out of Kabul, Sofia found it easier to
persist and make sure the girls went to school every day. But the family nagging never ceased. Whenever relatives from Kandahar came to
visit, they would argue constantly about their schooling. When Abdulhakim's family thought his girls were getting ahead of themselves, or
worried they might get into trouble, relatives would invoke a Pashto
saying: "A woman belongs inside the house, or in the grave."

6

OMARI

In Sayedabad, Omari spent more and more time with the bearded Taliban warriors, but not everyone in the village was as unhappy about the American presence as he was. One of his oldest friends was the neighbor's son Rahimullah. As boys, the two had giddily thrown stones at American soldiers and narrowly escaped their wrath. Rahimullah tried before Omari to join a local Taliban unit but was told he was too young. As he grew older, Rahimullah's view of the foreigners changed. Rahimullah's father had not fought in the jihad against the Soviet Union and had been killed during the civil war of the 1990s, so Rahimullah had not been raised on the same stories of holy war as Omari had. He didn't approach the Taliban again. Instead, Rahimullah was lured off the path of jihad by the smell of money.

The war was escalating. By 2009, the Taliban were growing in strength across the country, and President Obama ordered an additional seventeen thousand American troops to Afghanistan in an attempt to turn the tide. Less than a year later, under pressure from the military, he committed another thirty thousand soldiers, bringing the total number of US forces in Afghanistan to almost one hundred thousand. To have a stronger presence in the provinces, the

Americans strengthened their web of bases across the country. A new world of contracts for security and logistics work opened up and became a source of wealth for many young Afghans. Still a teenager, Rahimullah found work with an Afghan logistics company contracted by the US military to transport equipment and fuel to Bagram Air Base north of Kabul. Like Omari's work for the Taliban, the job allowed him to carry a weapon and ride a motorcycle, but the pay was much better. Even before Obama's troop surge, the United States had been drenching the Afghan economy in fresh dollars, fueling corruption that drove support for the Taliban. In 2006, the US National Security Council had written a strategic review of the Afghan war, which recommended to President Bush that America should spend more money, put more American boots on the ground, and build more schools, roads, and electricity grids. The aim was to tie the Afghan people closer to the government in Kabul, improve security, and undermine the drug economy. At the time, President Bush had just authorized a surge of 150,000 troops to Iraq, so no extra soldiers were sent Afghanistan. But the money was available, and as it tried to kickstart the Afghan economy, the US military became heavily dependent on Afghan partners for nearly every task in the country.

One main challenge was securing the highways, in order to supply American bases with equipment and fuel and to boost the economy by persuading Afghans that it was becoming safer to move around the country. It was cheaper and more secure for businessmen in Kandahar, Helmand, and Herat to import goods from Pakistan or Iran than it was to receive them from Kabul or the north. That needed to change to build a self-sufficient economy.

Considering how crucial these companies were to the overall American strategy in Afghanistan, their vetting process for new hires was shoddy. Often, contractors directly undermined the security they were responsible for upholding. Many highly paid Afghan security contractors had no more local knowledge of a particular area than did foreign troops because they weren't from there. They had only superficial understanding of the Taliban. Contractors drove up and down highways, firing blindly at hamlets, from where villagers naturally shot back, confirming to the contractors that they were insurgents, even if they were merely regular civilians trying to defend themselves in a country awash with guns. At times, security deteriorated so badly that massive construction projects were abandoned. USAID gave $270 million starting in 2009 to a company owned by the Afghan entrepreneur Ajmal Hasas to build 1,200 miles of gravel road. The project was canceled three years later after more than 125 people had been killed in insurgent attacks against its workers. Only a hundred miles of road were completed.

The money poured into logistics and security fed corruption that benefited the Taliban. One security contractor, Watan Risk Management, was run by two brothers, Rashed and Rateb Popal, who happened to be cousins of President Karzai. The Popals had lived for years in the United States, where they had been found guilty of heroin smuggling. Rateb has spent nearly a decade in prison. Despite this, after returning to Afghanistan, their company became one of eight firms found fit to share a $2.2 billion contract to supply American bases around the country with everything from chocolate, toilet paper, and fuel to muffins and lobster meat. The contract was worth more than one-tenth of Afghanistan's gross domestic product at the time. Several contractors working for Watan were caught shooting at civilians while traveling with US military convoys. One of the mercenaries working for Watan was Ruhollah Popalzai, also known as the Butcher, who in 2009 claimed to be protecting 3,500 American trucks per month, demanding $1,500 in payment per vehicle, an astronomical sum in Afghanistan. Popalzai was efficient partly because he paid off the Taliban not to attack. Similar schemes took place across the country, indirectly funneling American taxpayer dollars meant to rebuild Afghanistan and quell the growing insurgency into the coffers of militants the United States was fighting. Popalzai was later convicted of heroin smuggling in Afghanistan but released at the request of the president's half brother, Ahmed Wali Karzai.

If Rahimullah was tempted by such riches, Omari was not. He

tried to talk his friend out of taking the job, not least because it would mean that Rahimullah had to leave Sayedabad, which would no longer be safe. He failed to persuade him, but the two stayed in touch, even when a rumor spread in the village that Rahimullah had been taken under the wing of an Afghan army commander who had offered him bigger guns, access to a car, and money. In return, Rahimullah had apparently agreed to become the commander's *bacha birish*, a term for young boys who danced and sometimes performed sexual favors for older men, often for protection and money. The practice, called *bacha bazi*, was so shameful that it didn't matter whether the rumors were true. This was now the story of Rahimullah in the village.

"It was so bad. I couldn't let anyone know that we were friends, because everybody knew that he was a *bacha birish*," Omari said. Months later, Rahimullah's unit ran into a group of Taliban on the highway, and he was killed in the ensuing shootout. Omari's family mourned him, as they would any other friend of the family. He might have been persona non grata in the village but to them he was still the neighbor's son.

The Taliban's insurgency was more than a village-based rebellion. It was transnational, bolstered by fighters traveling across the Pakistani border. Wardak, which outside the provincial capital was dominated by pro-Taliban elders, landlords, and clerics, was a crucial node in the insurgency. A contiguous band of insurrection ran from Wardak through Logar province to Pakistan, whose support for the Taliban was hardly a secret, although Pakistani officials always denied it. The Afghan government and American officials had taken issue with it for years. The Taliban used Pakistani soil as a safe haven, benefiting from Pakistani military intelligence to escape Afghan and American capture-or-kill missions. Taliban leaders relied on Pakistan for identity papers, residency, and subsidies, including for family members living there in exile. Islamabad wanted Kabul to curb the influence of India, which had boosted its defense budget on the back of a booming economy and which Pakistan worried might use the presence of thousands of its nationals in Afghanistan as launching pads for attacks on

Pakistani soil. In 2008, the Taliban carried out a suicide attack against the Indian embassy in Kabul, killing fifty-three people, including the Indian defense attaché. According to the United States, the attack relied on assistance from the powerful Pakistani military spy agency Inter-Services Intelligence (ISI).

Alongside the troop surge, a new counterinsurgency doctrine was becoming gospel. Gen. David Petraeus, after commanding the surge of 150,000 soldiers in Iraq, had emerged as the dominant scholar-warrior in Washington, promoting the idea that to win the war, the coalition had to win the hearts and minds of Afghans. The surge of troops was meant to help the coalition seize territory and hold it temporarily, buying space and time for the central government in Kabul to establish its own presence and legitimacy. Petraeus and his acolytes believed the way to winning the war was to entice Taliban fighters on the battlefield to defect. They had little faith in the strategy favored by some at the State Department of finding a diplomatic solution. As long as Taliban commanders enjoyed protection in Pakistan, they would not have reason to negotiate in earnest, they thought. Petraeus, who took the helm of the international combat mission in Afghanistan in 2010 before becoming CIA director in 2011, had become so powerful and popular that even figures inside the Obama administration who opposed his ideas didn't openly challenge them. The dissenters included Richard Holbrooke, the top US diplomat for Afghanistan and Pakistan from 2009 until he died in 2010, who did not believe the war could be won militarily.

But waging counterinsurgency against the Taliban was different from anything the CIA or the US military had done in Iraq. The purpose of the American intervention in Afghanistan was to defeat al-Qaeda, but al-Qaeda was primarily in Pakistan. The Taliban were an Afghan movement, deeply rooted in local communities and drawing on conservative values that were closer aligned with many Afghans—particularly Pashtuns living in the southern heartlands—than the ideals promoted by the West. To try to bring the central government closer to Afghans in the villages, the United States and the United

Kingdom in 2010 formed the Afghan Local Police. Modeled on similar militias in Iraq, the ALP was formed as a tool to extend Kabul's authority into villages through local leaders whose men were paid and armed in return. But the strategy often backfired, as many ALP commanders used their newfound power to strengthen their own position through extortion. Pouring American troops into Afghanistan to defeat an insurgency with safe havens in Pakistan, without devoting enough diplomatic firepower to pressure Pakistan to change course, was unpredictable at best, and possibly counterproductive.

The commitment of troops wasn't backed up by sufficiently strong analysis of the Afghan insurgency. Some top-level insiders admitted as much. In 2010, Maj. Gen. Michael T. Flynn—then a respected soldier who would later serve as Donald Trump's national security advisor and peddler of conspiracy theories—wrote a scathing criticism of the US intelligence community. Eight years into the war, he wrote, intelligence officers in Afghanistan were "ignorant of local economics and landowners, hazy about who the powerbrokers are and how they might be influenced." When decision-makers sought knowledge about how to wage a successful counterinsurgency, "U.S. intelligence officers and analysts can do little but shrug in response," Flynn wrote.

One of the starkest examples of the flaws in the surge occurred in Marjah, in the southern Helmand province, in 2010 when about 15,000 foreign troops, including 3,500 US Marines, descended on an area the size of Saratoga Springs, Florida. The operation, called Moshtarak, was the largest of the entire war. Marjah, population eighty thousand, was underdeveloped and strategically insignificant, but home to a grand bazaar of opium smugglers and about four hundred Taliban militants. President Karzai was dead set against the operation. He couldn't see why the dirt-poor, virtually unknown town of Marjah warranted an operation of that size. The international shine had long since worn off his presidency, and American goodwill toward him had evaporated. Karzai routinely clashed with American ambassadors and commanders over indiscriminate airstrikes and night raids in Afghan villages and the resulting civilian casualties, which he said helped fuel the Taliban insurgency. The United States increasingly saw Karzai as an obstacle. They accused him of allowing corruption to flourish in the ranks of government officials and his own family members, and of micromanaging the country by using his personal authority over Afghanistan's budget to reward powerful loyalists and allow governors to create their own militias. They said he harbored harebrained anti-American conspiracy theories about their intentions in the country. Karzai's supporters said the American political establishment hated him because he acted as the president of an independent nation and not the manager of a franchise of the United States of America. Such allegations had gained steam during the 2009 elections, when it became clear to the public how badly the Obama administration wanted Karzai gone. Holbrooke, Obama's envoy, went searching for a candidate to stand against Karzai. Some voices in the West advocated for reducing the power of the presidency, pushing Karzai into a more ceremonial role and installing experienced technocrats to run the government. When Karzai won the election, the result was marred by widespread allegations of fraud. Western powers tried to arrange a second rote vote, but the effort collapsed, and Karzai was inaugurated. The election conflict soured relations with Karzai and damaged Western attempts to win public support for the central government. It's hard to do effective counterinsurgency if you're actively undermining the government meant to serve as an alternative to the insurgents. It was hard to sell Afghans the idea of an Afghan-led, Afghan-owned process when the US intervened at will.

The Americans partly wanted Karzai's approval for the Marjah operation as a public relations boost for the troop surge. Scores of journalists had flown in from Washington, DC, just for this. It took a personal evening visit by US commander Stanley McChrystal to the president's residence, and the persuasive powers of Karzai's half brother Ahmed Wali in Kandahar, a good friend of a US-allied police chief in Helmand, before the president gave his blessing. When thousands of foreign troops on February 13 stormed Marjah, accompanied by airstrikes from Predator drones and Apache helicopters, the Taliban fled. At least it appeared that way. Many of the few hundred insurgents in the district center simply tossed away their weapons and blended into the civilian population. The Taliban, always in civilian clothes, continued their guerilla warfare for months in the streets where Western armies had next to no intelligence. The coalition did eventually secure Marjah, temporarily. McChrystal had famously promised the residents of Marjah that Washington had a "government in a box, ready to roll in." But America's own government was intent on wrapping up the Afghan war as quickly as possible. Building strong local governance was not a priority. In Marjah, McChrystal handpicked and installed the civilian representative of the Kabul government, Abdul Zahir Aryan, a member of the powerful Alizai tribe who had spent fifteen years in Germany working in laundromats and hotels. He also served four years in a German prison after stabbing his stepson, who intervened when Aryan was beating his mother. Aryan lasted six months in the job before he was pushed out by local pressure. He was later assassinated. Absent a strong presence from the Kabul administration, the Taliban returned. By 2017, they controlled 80 percent of Marjah.

A direct impact of the Taliban's growing strength was a surge in American deaths. One metric: By 2009, militants in Afghanistan conducted more than two hundred attacks every month with improvised explosive devices, and the number of killed Americans doubled from the year before, to 310. In 2010, it spiked further to 496. The deadliest incident of the entire war for American soldiers happened in 2011 down the road from Omari's home. Two American Chinook helicopters were on a mission to capture or kill a senior Taliban commander in the Tangi Valley when the heavens opened and a massive torrent of rain washed over Wardak. In the downpour, a Taliban militant took aim at one of the helicopters with a rocket-propelled grenade as it was about to land. The helicopter went down, killing everyone on board: thirty Americans, including twenty-two Navy SEALs, and eight Afghans. Omari gathered with other villagers to watch the fire from their homes as it lit up the night. It wasn't until the morning that it became clear what had happened. The helicopter crash was evidence of how central Wardak had become in the war, and it became part of Taliban lore. To Omari, the incident was divine intervention. God had taken revenge on the Americans for their assault on Islam.

While Rahimullah was working the highways, Omari spent more and more time with the Taliban. One of his trainers was a middle-aged man called Haji Muhib who strutted around the village with an intimidating air of seriousness. He carried himself with the discipline of a soldier and the gravity of a scholar. Haji Muhib had made a fair bit of money during the jihad against the Soviet Union and now paid the local mullah to preach to the kids and tell them stories about the jihad. Haji Muhib himself also taught at the village mosque where he took on a role as moral and spiritual guide for Omari and his friends. When they found out their new teacher was a commander in the notorious Haqqani network, which had a reputation for being stealthy warriors, they were awestruck.

The Haqqani network, named after the hard-line Islamist family controlling it, was an especially brutal and violent wing of the Taliban with links to al-Qaeda. The network was headed by the patriarch, Jalaluddin Haqqani, who founded a string of madrassas in the Afghan-Pakistani border regions—where Parasto's father served as police commander—some of which became the region's most important academies for indoctrinating suicide bombers. The Haqqanis were responsible for some of the most ruthless attacks on foreign forces of the war. Having emerged as an independent entity in the 1970s, the network was now a semiautonomous but integrated part of the Taliban with an estimated ten to fifteen thousand fighters. Part of its power came from the privileged support it received from the Pakistani military and intelligence agencies, which used the group to exert influence in Afghanistan and mediate disputes in the border areas where the Haqqanis had roots. As opposed to the mainstream Taliban, which was almost exclusively concerned with matters in Afghanistan, the Haqqani network had a firm belief in global, transnational jihad. Coupled with its close links to the Pakistani intelligence agency, the ISI, the Haqqanis were natural partners for other international terrorist groups, notably al-Qaeda. When the Taliban leadership under international pressure in the 1990s put restrictions on the movement of al-Qaeda members in Afghanistan, placing senior leaders under virtual house arrest, the Haqqanis allowed al-Qaeda to maneuver in areas under their control.

The Haqqani family's founding of Quran schools had given them religious authority, even if senior Haqqani family members themselves were far better versed in the gun than Islamic scripture. More important were their impeccable military credentials. Being in the presence of Haji Muhib stoked Omari's dreams of waging holy war against the Americans, even taking the fight to foreign lands such as Palestine. Haji Muhib told the other boys to cool their heels. The "near jihad," he said, was the important thing to focus on. Protect the honor of the women in the family. Make sure God's word is respected and followed in the village. And behave when using the Taliban's good name. There were people in the area, he said, who misused the movement by committing crimes in the name of the Taliban. They erected illegal checkpoints to extort people and break into private homes. Haji Muhib asked Omari to report if he ever saw the Taliban's good name tarnished in this way. One day Haji Muhib himself set an example after the Taliban arrested a gang of alleged kidnappers. They tied them up, painted their faces black with charcoal, and paraded them around the whole district on the back of a truck to instill fear in others.

The Taliban gradually allowed Omari to take part in training. The young recruits were given basic weapons training, but no physical drills. The older Taliban had the sinewy muscles of people who carried heavy weapons every day. When they passed checkpoints, unarmed, government soldiers would feel up their shoulder and neck muscles and inspect their skin for gun strap marks. Omari learned how to pad the inside of his shirt around the shoulder area with a bit of extra fabric so the AK-47 wouldn't leave any marks. He knew his parents wouldn't approve of him hanging out with Taliban fighters every day. While they were both sympathetic to the Taliban's struggle, they did not want their son risking his life for the resistance. But neither of them ever asked Omari what he did during his spare time outside the home. Perhaps, he thought, they preferred not to know.

Haji Muhib had told them to focus on near jihad, but soon the armed struggle came to them. The United States was increasingly using drones to surveil and strike targets in Wardak. The sound of the remote-controlled killer robots that circled above Sayedabad every night, humming menacingly like lethal lawn mowers in the sky, penetrated Omari's mind. They left everyone living under their flight path clueless but fearful about where they would strike next and leave their signature of death, destruction, and loss. Omari didn't know what a drone was before he heard the sound of one, but they soon became a regular fixture of life in the village. Gliding airborne assassins named Predators and Reapers, carrying missiles called Hellfire. Names colored with American bravado but operated by an enemy so far away that you couldn't even fight back. Conceived by the American mind of war and now lodged in his.

The drones left Omari unable to sleep. When he did drift off, they appeared in his dreams, where they annihilated his father and his younger brothers in balls of fire. The buzzing of the drones ground away at his nerves. The helicopters were a source of anxiety, too. Their metallic flutter could be heard first around midnight, like a distant tinnitus, and continued until morning prayer. It foretold of night raids, of foreign soldiers who descended on ropes from the dark night sky and marched through fields toward unsuspecting villages where they would enter bedrooms and private chambers and haul away men. Some men were shot in their houses or on the outskirts of villages. Some never returned. Those who did come back, months later, quivered like children. Nobody knew which village would be the next, or who would be tied up and dragged off to one of the twenty-five American detention sites across the country. Several of them were so-called black sites—secret prisons where the Americans were accused of torturing prisoners, including civilians accused of being terrorists.

The experience of incessant American harassment of his village hardened Omari's resolve to fight the invaders. In some of his dreams, his family was killed, but in the more heroic ones, he saw himself standing on a hilltop, fatally injured by gunshot wounds to the chest, but with enough strength to turn his machine gun on the American soldier who shot him and place a bullet in his head. He was dead, yet living, just like the martyrs in his father's stories.

"People think martyrs are dead, but they are alive among us," his father had told him. Haji Muhib had taught him that a martyr's sacrifice for God would be rewarded in the afterlife with an abundance of food and virgins and inner peace.

At fourteen, having gained Haji Muhib's trust, that was the fate Omari decided to pursue. Haji Muhib arranged for Omari and a couple of friends to travel from Wardak through Logar and Gardez to Khost near the Pakistani border. They traveled in a rural belt of Afghanistan that was fully under Haqqani control. It was here in the southeast where the network had its roots, and where much of its power inside the Taliban sprang from. It was a strategically and culturally important area of the country for the insurgency, and the Taliban depended on the Haqqanis to manage the local provision of justice and services so the movement could present itself as a viable alternative to the central government. Afghanistan was being watched by American surveillance technology, but it was far inferior to the equipment they had deployed in Iraq, where US commanders by 2008 had developed a system that gave them, in Gen. Stanley McChrystal's words, an "unblinking stare" at insurgent activities. That system included drones, surveillance blimps carrying digital cameras, and reconnaissance aircraft, which allowed commanders to watch as insurgents buried roadside bombs or moved around the landscape in preparation for attacks or ambushes. In Afghanistan, where the battlefield was larger and harder to delineate, only one blimp hovered ominously over Kabul at the time, and there was a shortage of drones. Traveling through the barren countryside of Logar and the mountainous Khost-Gardez Pass where the mujahideen had routinely ambushed Soviet convoys, the teenagers drew little attention.

They arrived in Khost, a city of about one hundred thousand, in spring, as the city turned leafy and green on its plateau amid the mountains. They met their guides on the outskirts of the city, nominally under government control. Their destination was Miranshah in the tribal areas of North Waziristan district in Pakistan, one of the best-known centers for training of teenage suicide bombers in the world, where the Haqqani clan had built a rogue ministate. They ran courts and tax offices, built religious seminaries and madrassas, and trained a ready supply of fighters. In the Haqqani family's gangster-like empire of kidnapping, smuggling, and racketeering, Miranshah was the administrative center. The group's reclusive founder and chief, the wizened Jalaluddin Haqqani, was believed to live here.

From Khost, the escorts took Omari and his friends off the road, through the mountains that rose steeply above them. The slopes were already so overgrown that at times, all Omari could see of the sky were dots in the canopy, a patchwork of stars. His entire life he had dreamed of traveling to far corners of his own country. Going abroad surpassed that. He didn't even notice when they crossed the border. After days of hiking, they reached a checkpoint demarcating the beginning of a camp. The guards spoke Urdu, which Omari didn't understand. So did the guards at the next checkpoint. But at the third, the guards spoke to him in Pashto. Omari remembered crossing eight checkpoints in total. He looked around. They had made it to the foothills of Miranshah.

7

FAHIM

Fahim had gotten a tenuous foothold in the world of military contracting, but his business was expanding much more slowly than he had hoped for. During the first decade of the Afghan war—before violence peaked, and before the surge of more than one hundred thousand US soldiers—construction was booming, but he and Zahir were only getting piecemeal contracts for boots and bedsheets. They knew they were missing out. Then they had an idea. The ever-expanding web of military bases that was sprouting across the country created an insatiable need for one thing in particular: fuel, to power everything from generators to trucks and construction work. Fuel deals were bigger and far more complex than anything Fahim and Zahir had handled so far. To even be considered, they had to convince the contracting office that they were a larger and more capable outfit than they actually were. They began cobbling together a bid. One acquaintance who had a massive fuel storage facility took photos of his stock. His fuel was of poor quality, so they took a sample from someone else, hoping that no one from the contracting office would check if the fuel in the photos and the sample matched. A third friend helped Fahim write a proposal, and Fahim and Zahir submitted it. To their own surprise, they won. They had hit the right balance of quality and price, and now had a blanket purchase agreement for up to $120 million, a fortune. They had no idea how to deliver.

"Everywhere we went with this piece of paper, people laughed at us," Fahim said about the contract. "Don't be funny, don't waste our time, they said."

They had almost given up when Fahim met an Afghan man at the badging office at Camp Eggers, a small-time petrol station owner named Haji Mal, who said he could help. He only owned two pump stations and had a very small storage but said he could buy enough fuel on credit from other traders to fulfill the contract. Like Fahim and Zahir, Haji Mal recognized the smell of opportunity.

"Had we not found this guy, we would have thrown it away, because no one else trusted us," Fahim said. "We had this in our hands, and we almost messed it up."

Haji Mal came through. From then on, he became a subcontractor to Arrow. Fahim and Zahir never saw any fuel, they just processed contracts on their computer. When the fuel was delivered, they turned the receipts into invoices to the military. They never exchanged paperwork with Haji Mal, working solely on trust. At one point, the fuel trader had $35 million in receivables with Fahim and Zahir, but they always managed to pay. At the time, the US military paid contractors in the local currency to support the national economy. Every Wednesday, dozens of SUVs gathered around Camp Eggers to pick up large black bags full of cash. Most contractors employed bodyguards, but many still got robbed on their way home or to the bank. To minimize the risk, Fahim paid his subcontractors in front of the gate. Now in his midtwenties, Fahim bought a couple of nice cars and rented several properties for himself and his family, spread around Kabul for security purposes. Members of Kabul's nouveau riche were fast becoming juicy targets for kidnappers. Most of the money, Fahim and Zahir invested back into their company. They had found a better supplier in China for boots and sold hundreds of thousands of them, $35 a pair. They expanded into uniforms, duffle bags, raincoats. Once they had enough capital, they cut out the middlemen and built factories employing hundreds of tailors to produce and supply uniforms directly to the Afghan army and built massive storage facilities for their fuel. Fahim became a full-time proposal writer and won nearly everything he bid on, which the company then promptly subcontracted to others.

In 2008, Fahim married, and two years later he became a father for the first time. He was studying accounting on the side and had met his wife in class. He had courted her through one of his employees, who was her friend and could vouch for him.

"It was love from my side. I don't know how much she was in love with me," he later recounted, laughing. But he felt certain that she later fell in love with him. Their family grew, and seven years into their marriage, they had three children.

While Fahim and Zahir were not alone in building startups that tapped into foreign aid money, most of their peers were spending what they earned, on cars or villas either in Kabul or Dubai. Instead the pair invested their profits back into their business. By 2010, Arrow employed about two thousand people. At its peak, it boasted an annual revenue of about $300 million. Fahim and Zahir had built an empire founded mostly on hustle and luck.

Torrents of money were flowing through Afghanistan, but people like Fahim and Zahir, who were able to dip their toes in it, were a small minority. Afghan GDP grew by 21.4 percent in 2009 and 14.4 percent in 2010, but the money was poorly distributed. Historically, Afghanistan's primary source of government revenue had been foreign assistance, leaving the country's economy exposed to dictates by donors or patrons, often ideologically driven. The Afghan government's first strategy document, the 2002 National Development Framework, wasn't even officially translated into local languages, published only in English. US money flows were designed to support a particular kind of neoliberal economic ideal—the idea was to slim down the public sector, promote privatization, and entice foreign investment. The result was a free-market economy, hastily implemented before the country's political and legal institutions were ready for it. Academic studies suggest that in underdeveloped economies in transition, aid levels exceeding 15–20 percent of the country's GDP become counterproductive. The state cannot absorb an excess of aid, which instead feeds corruption and risks turning the country into a rentier state that will eventually collapse because it cannot sustain itself. From 2002 to 2004, aid levels to Afghanistan were low, but the country's output was so small—less than $4 billion—that aid accounted for between 30 and 60 percent of GDP. A decade into the war, although GDP grew to $20 billion, aid levels had surged to an equivalent of 100 percent of GDP.

The market-driven economy rewarded young entrepreneurs with capital to invest. It accelerated the growth of essential infrastructure, such as mobile phones, media, and air travel. But it also sent corruption spiraling out of control. Social and economic inequality grew, widening the gulf between not just rich and poor, but between supporters of the government who benefited from the wealth and political privilege, and those who did not. From the early years of the war, policymakers in Washington were not sufficiently alert to how US aid directly contributed to exorbitant corruption in Afghanistan. While Afghan strongmen allied with the United States got rich and powerful, the Bush administration believed it had more pressing priorities in Iraq. By the time the United States woke up to the problem, it was too invested in its allies, and the power structure in the country too consolidated, to start tearing out corruption by the root.

Economic inequality carved a deeper wedge between city and countryside. State institutions were privatized, undermining the public sector's ability to create jobs for a struggling population at a time when success for the entire political project after the fall of the Taliban depended on building legitimacy around the central government. A huge share of US funds allocated for either the Afghan war effort or reconstruction never directly reached the Afghan population. Much of it ended up back in the US economy without ever touching Afghan hands as a result of Pentagon outsourcing to American contractors. As much as half of all the money spent on the wars in Afghanistan and Iraq went to US defense contractors, whose employees through most of the Afghan war outnumbered actual troops on the ground. In December 2008, 69 percent of the Department of Defense's workforce in Afghanistan were private contractors. The share prices of the five companies that dominated the field—Lockheed Martin, Raytheon, General Dynamics, Boeing, and Northrop Grumman—outperformed the stock market overall by 58 percent during the Afghanistan War. The money that did reach Afghans created an economic system based less on fair competition and merit than on corruption, nepotism, and the strong grip of old-time power brokers. Afghan citizens saw the state hollowed out by predatory capitalism, waste, fraud, price gouging, and profiteering. The new system and its poor vetting processes allowed men like Fahim to amass huge personal wealth. He learned quickly how to navigate the new economy, and was rewarded for it.

Like many wealthy men before him, Fahim did not settle for riches that would have allowed him and his entire family to live very comfortably for the rest of their lives. He wanted to help shape the nation. There was an element of vanity to that desire. Working with the army, he had felt the rush of change. Now, he wanted to have an impact on the field of ideas in the country his children would grow up in.

Afghanistan's emerging media landscape was a battlefield of values. There had been no independent media under the Taliban. Now, commercial television stations backed by American aid money promoted an explicit agenda to liberalize a majority illiterate and overwhelmingly conservative country. They showed Indian soap operas and challenged power brokers in live interviews. Female anchors wore loose headscarves alongside men. Presenters became celebrities. On Tolo TV, the country's largest private television network, famous for its breaking news coverage, men and women competed on *Afghan Star*, a show similar to *American Idol*. The biggest channels were largely independent, in conflict with the Taliban by virtue of their pro-democracy agenda, but also exposed government corruption and civilian casualties caused by American airstrikes. The largest independent radio network, Salam Watandar, ran sixty-seven stations with programming including shows about women's issues and good governance. The largest independent news agency, Pajhwok, launched with the help of $5.2 million in USAID money, exposed corruption among officials involving fuel imports, which got a provincial governor fired. Even if the roads weren't safe enough to transport people, information could be carried along the electricity grid being drawn across the country and through the rapidly expanding mobile phone network. As much as half of the population watched the presidential debate live on Tolo during the 2009 election. Most self-respecting warlords had a TV station or radio channel. Twenty years after the war began, the number of media outlets in the country would grow to nearly five hundred. Fahim was on a trip to power and influence, and media was the ticket.

"I didn't want to just be another haji with a lot of fuel. I wanted to do something cultural, something political. Something more important that wasn't purely about money," he said. "I was always interested in changing people's minds," he added. "Or else we won't move forward."

In 2010, Fahim launched 1TV as part of his newly minted Hashimy Group, which specifically targeted educated, younger middle-class Afghans. It quickly became one of the country's leading networks with its news and entertainment programs. The channel was the first in Afghanistan to televise live debates in front of a studio audience. It launched a program called *The Mask*, in which women, wearing masks to hide their identity, recounted stories of domestic abuse and forced marriages. Fahim's new line of work was risky. The Taliban and various warlords who didn't appreciate being challenged publicly had it in for new media outlets like 1TV. Fahim set up office in a compound behind thick blast walls in Kabul's Wazir Akbar Khan neighborhood, next to a government intelligence headquarters and opposite the German embassy. Other networks, particularly Tolo, were attacked more often, but 1TV also became a target.

On a Monday morning in April 2018, a young man on a motorcycle slipped into the morning rush hour in central Kabul. Near the

NATO headquarters and dozens of foreign embassies, he detonated the explosives strapped to his body. Forty minutes later, as crowds of medics and onlookers had gathered around the scene, another man, carrying a camera and pretending to be a journalist, sidled up next to a group of reporters and blew himself up. Nine journalists died in the double-tap bombing, including two of Fahim's employees: the reporter Ghazi Rasooli and the cameraman Nawroz Ali Rajabi, both in their early twenties. After the bombing, Fahim went to the four-hundred-bed Sardar Mohammad Daud Khan Hospital to identify the bodies. When he opened the freezers in the morgue, Rajabi's blood was still fresh, his face peppered with shrapnel. The young cameraman had just gotten married, and Fahim helped bring his body to the suburb where his wife lived. Rajabi's father had recently died, and there were few family members at the funeral, so Fahim helped carry the casket on his shoulder. Rajabi's wife later gave birth to a child she was carrying when her husband died. Fahim continued to pay her husband's salary.

"We had expected something to happen, but to see it in real life, and smell the blood, carry their bodies, that was totally different from just being scared," Fahim remembered. "I realized then what was required of us to defend people's rights and the freedom of expression."

He started vanity projects, too. He was appointed chairman of Afghanistan's Olympic Committee and got a seat on the Chamber of Commerce. He bought an airline.

"Everyone sold fuel," he said. "Airlines are sexy."

East Horizon Airlines began operations in 2013 and immediately became a drain on his finances. He bought CASA planes from Spain and MD-11s from the United States, and rented a Boeing from a Sri Lankan businessman; all of them turned out to be either old or of poor quality.

"We got cheated all the time," he said.

Eventually, he managed to open a route from Kabul to Bamiyan, the peaceful and unlikely skiing destination where Afghans and a limited number of foreign tourists could enjoy the central highlands without fear of violence. But in 2015, his fleet was grounded due to safety concerns. Fahim said he hadn't been aware of regulations that banned airlines from operating planes that were more than fifteen years old. He was also accused of tax evasion, which he denied. After most of his old fleet was scrapped and the rest stood idle in a corner of the Kabul airport, he bought two new planes, an Avro jet and a Bombardier, but the civil aviation authorities required him to recertify his airline. He accused rivals and political forces of monopolizing the aviation industry. Once again Fahim had waded into unknown territory he had little knowledge of. This time he face-planted into a thicket of bureaucracy that he couldn't disentangle from. A couple of years later, he sought to get involved in mining. After paying local teams to do initial surveys of the mines and getting verbal consent from the ministry of mines that he would receive a permit to dig, the government kept him waiting indefinitely for his license. The two sites, a coal mine in Baghlan and a chromite mine in Logar, were both in Taliban-controlled areas and out of reach for the local authorities. While he was waiting for his permit, Fahim said he employed between three hundred and four hundred locals on each site to protect the mine—who likely paid the Taliban protection money. The new government under President Ashraf Ghani had pledged to reform the public sector and create accountability, but for Fahim, adding more layers to the bureaucracy bogged down any moves to further expand his business. He was never told why he wasn't given a license, and claimed that the government was targeting businesses that could rival its own control over state resources. If the government found as much as a grammatical error in an application, they would delay it, he said.

"And they can't even go to the site themselves," he said, frustrated. He had hoped Afghanistan would eventually be home to an actual financial market, even a stock exchange. He had pictured himself becoming Afghanistan's version of Al-Futtaim, the massive Emirati-based conglomerate that operates in everything from automotive to electronics and insurance and has built a string of supermalls across the Middle East. Now, he wasn't so sure.

"Are you going to stop the whole economy for violating one regulation?" he asked—a man who had built an empire by tap-dancing around regulations.

"They call it reform, but I think this was really a big roadblock against economic development."

8

ZAHRA

One day bled into the next. Zahra had left Hussein and moved into her mother's house in a different part of Herat, where her sisters vacated a room for her to sleep in. Sedated by medicine and grief, she was barely aware of her surroundings. It had been three months since Parisa and Jawad moved in with Hussein's parents, and it had taken her until now to find the composure to visit them once a week. In early 2007, she was twenty-three, and so miserable that even her oldest sister, Rokhaya, by now married and with children of her own, had stopped visiting because she couldn't stand to see her younger sister this way. If Hussein's parents had hoped the divorce would jolt their son into action, they were disappointed. On the contrary, he had paid them 5,000 afghanis—about a hundred dollars—from the money Zahra had given him to look after the children. Then suddenly, he disappeared. After four months, the money he had given his parents long spent, his mother allowed Zahra to see her children a few times a week.

Fatima was pleased to have her grandchildren around, and Parisa and Jawad were happy, too, but she missed Iran and its holy shrines. "I wish I had a passport so I could go back and visit," she said one day when the family sat together. Jawad chimed in, "I wish I had a passport too, so I could go somewhere far away." Jawad was five and didn't grasp the consequences of what he was suggesting. "Dad left, so maybe we can, too."

Months earlier, Zahra would have never entertained the thought. But she had recently met a woman who had opened her mind to new ideas. Zahra had gone to the city council for an errand where a friend introduced her to Adela Mohseni, a women's rights activist visiting from Kabul to hold a workshop in Herat. Warm and talkative, Adela seemed to immediately take a liking to Zahra. In their first, short conversation, Adela spoke to Zahra about equality between genders and a woman's right to determine her own life. These were concepts that Zahra, despite her reading about empowered women of history and literature, had never thought would be available to her. She spoke with such force, Zahra thought. They stayed in touch after Adela returned to Kabul, and over time Zahra told her new friend about her abusive marriage, the divorce, and the suffocating life with Hussein's family. Adela often called to check up on Zahra, and it was Adela whom Zahra called for advice after Jawad suggested they could just leave Herat. As Zahra said it out loud, the idea of a divorced woman fleeing with two children to Kabul sounded insane. But Kabul was different from Herat, Adela assured her. The capital was big enough for her to hide.

Shortly after, Hussein's mother called Zahra. She had things to do, she said. Would Zahra like to take Parisa and Jawad for a full week? Zahra decided it was time. She had made only one trip in her life, when her family traveled from Tehran to Herat. Afghanistan was mostly unknown territory, the roads risky. The main highway from Herat to Kabul was one of the most dangerous stretches of road in the country, dotted with Taliban checkpoints. Where crossfire between militants and coalition forces didn't pose an immediate danger, kidnappers and robbers stalked the roads. The only safe option was to fly. The Herat airport had been destroyed during the invasion but had since been rebuilt for domestic flights.

Zahra planned her escape meticulously. By law, fleeing with her children without Hussein's family's consent amounted to kidnapping.

She couldn't even risk telling her own family about her plans, as they might try to stop her. Any legal action could impact them as well and taint their reputation. After the divorce, she had managed to work for about a month and bought two gold rings and a necklace with her salary. Fighting to calm her nerves, she took one ring and the necklace and sold them at the bazaar for about four hundred dollars. She bought three one-way tickets to Kabul and kept the second ring and the remaining 1,200 afghanis, about twenty dollars, in her purse. She packed a bag of clothes that she stowed away in a shop where her brother Hassan worked, without telling him. In the morning, Zahra told her mother she was going to spend the day at the park and then drop the children off at Hussein's family's house while she'd spend the night at an aunt's house nearby. She wanted her mother to not expect her until the next morning. She called the taxi driver that the women in her family regularly used, who usually took her to her in-laws, and went to the shop to pick up her bag. It was still early, and Hassan hadn't begun work yet. To throw her family off her trail, she had left a letter to her mother explaining that she had gone back to Iran. She asked the driver to take her and the children to the international bus terminal. She expected the driver to divulge everything about their trip to her mother, and she wanted to make it look like she was in fact heading to Iran. After the driver had dropped them off and turned a corner, she hailed another cab to the airport. As she boarded the plane to leave a whole life behind, she felt trepidation and a twinge of relief. She settled into her seat with Parisa and Jawad on each side of her. Then the plane took off.

Kabul formed a spectacular view from above. To the north of the capital, the snowcapped dragon's tail of the Hindu Kush mountain range stretched from central Afghanistan into Central Asia and northwest Pakistan. East, beyond the urban concrete buildup of Soviet-era apartment blocks and warehouse complexes, the road surrendered to the unrepentant Tora Bora mountains where the Americans were still searching for Osama bin Laden. South of Kabul, the clusters of houses scattered and the capital dissolved into the dusty plains surrounding Kandahar and Helmand where the Taliban were reviving their movement, the latest insurrection in the country's long history of violence. Babur, the sixteenth-century ruler of the Mughal Empire, is believed to have said that, in a single day, you could travel from lowlands that had never seen snow to mountains where the snow never melted. Zahra's thoughts were absorbed in her own personal struggle, but once the plane touched down on the tarmac, she became part of a throng of people before her who had opened new chapters of their lives here. Few of them, however, had done it as single mothers. With a bit of luck and courage, she felt it was possible to start afresh.

She arrived in Kabul in early July 2007 as a fugitive, carrying with her property that legally belonged to her in-laws: her children. It was her in-laws, not law enforcement, that she feared. The cultural conservatism many Afghan women faced within their families was so strong that it could topple political leaders. In the 1920s, the reform-ist king Amanullah Khan sought to implement a series of bills to pro-mote gender equality and the emancipation of women. He introduced compulsory education and sent a group of female students to enroll in university in Turkey. He advocated against polygamy and the Islamic hijab. A hundred years later, Afghan liberals still praised his wife, Queen Soraya, who at the end of one of the king's speeches pulled off her headscarf in front of a large crowd. Amanullah's efforts drew se-vere backlash, and in 1929, the king was forced to abdicate and go into exile. A later ruler, King Mohammad Zahir, continued the moderniza-tion of Afghanistan, though at a slower pace. In the 1960s and '70s, Afghanistan was a secular-minded monarchy where women in the cit-ies had the freedom to wear miniskirts at university if they chose to, at least in Kabul. But four decades of war, beginning with the Soviet invasion, torpedoed any modernization efforts, and the personal free-doms of the 1970s had never been reestablished.

Following 2001, proponents of gender equality made significant strides in the form of legal reforms. Men and women became more equal in the eyes of the law, even as the Western-backed government made concessions to more conservative forces in the country. The minimum legal age for marriage was set at sixteen for girls and eighteen for men, in breach of the UN Convention on the Rights of the Child, which Afghanistan had signed on to. If a man caught a close female relative—wife, sister, daughter, cousin—being unfaithful to her husband and killed her, his sentence could be limited to two years in prison if the murder was found to be committed as a crime of passion. One of the most prominent disputes was over the Elimination of Violence Against Women law, or EVAW, which criminalized twenty-two acts of abuse toward women, including rape, forced marriage, battery, and prohibiting women or girls from going to school. Though the law was never fully ratified in Parliament due to opposition among conservatives, President Karzai enacted it by decree in 2009. The law led to an increase in reporting and investigation of abuse of women, and the establishment of specialized police units, prosecution offices, and special courts. Still, the new measures did not change the fact that male family members often pressured women not to report abuse, or to accept mediation outside the courtroom.

When she traveled to Kabul, Zahra was unwittingly putting her own body and life at stake in this cultural war. The Kabul she arrived in was vibrant with new ideas about women's roles in society. The country's conservative norms were often defended as ways to protect women's honor. Liberal Afghans who debated the country's future in teahouses and at dinner parties were, like conservative Afghans, preoccupied with women's dignity, but thought women would be safer if they had more agency. Traditionally, a woman's honor was inextricably tied to that of her husband and family, making any violation against her a matter of shame for a whole community, and the woman was seen as culpable for crimes made against her, such as sexual abuse. The battle for women's emancipation had ebbed and flowed for decades. Now, taking the side of liberal Afghans was a coalition of Western states and their soldiers with guns. There was a well-intentioned arrogance to the way Western countries co-opted the Afghan rights struggle and appeared to think that any activist or cause would benefit from their support. In reality, while Western countries boosted the struggle for women's rights by elevating it on the political agenda and bankrolling it with cash, they also often put Afghan women's rights activists at a disadvantage. Western involvement helped undermine the push for reform in Afghan society at large by confirming, to some Afghans, that it was the work of foreign occupiers. Imagine if the fight for legal abortion in the United States was bankrolled by Russian oligarchs or the Chinese state as part of those countries' foreign policies. Tying the fight for women's freedom to a military occupation made an already fraught cultural question even more explosive.

Zahra's diversion back in Herat had worked. Fatima, her mother, was still frantically calling her father and other relatives in Tehran as Zahra slipped into the crowds of Kabul and disappeared. After a few days, she broke her silence and called her sister Tahera to tell her where she had gone. Before long, Hussein's family knew which city she was in and swore they would come find her and take the children back. In Herat, rumors had begun circulating, Tahera said. The neighbors claimed Zahra had gone to Kabul to be with a boyfriend, and that he was the reason she wanted a divorce. The rumors filled Zahra with shame, but most of all, she knew how devastating they would be for her mother. For months, she was too mortified to call Fatima directly.

For the first three months in Kabul, she and the kids lived with Adela Mohseni. A divorced woman with two children would draw attention, so Adela and her friend, another activist called Palwasha Hassan, suggested that she tell everyone who asked that her husband was in Iran earning money to send home. Adela was newly married, and before long, Zahra sensed that they were an imposition on the young couple. She found a small one-bedroom flat that shared a wall with an office in the Hazara-dominated Dasht-e Barchi suburb. Their new neighbor was also a single mother with children of around the same age as Parisa and Jawad. Mice scurried along the walls at night, keeping her and the children awake. She had no money for new clothes, cutlery, or plates, or even electricity. At night, they passed the time talking, their faces lit by the glow of candlelight. The children had spent their entire lives in some kind of flux, Jawad staying mostly with his grandmother and Parisa living amid the cyclonic relationship of her parents. It was just the three of them now, and Zahra savored the precious moments alone with her children. Jawad was a calming presence. Parisa was scarred by living under the constant threat of violence. She was more on edge, a bit like Zahra. Physically, they were strikingly similar as well. Zahra had once found a photograph of herself at Fatima's house and thought it depicted Parisa. During the day, they walked the streets freely, going to the zoo and some of the large Shia mosques the city had to offer. Zahra would don only a headscarf, not the burqa, and gradually she allowed a couple of inches of her sideswept chestnut hair to be visible. She loved wandering the streets, soaking up the city to make it home. Kabul was growing rapidly. In 2007, the war was intensifying in the countryside but had yet to seriously threaten life in the capital. Aid workers and UN agencies were still flocking to the country in growing numbers. After toppling the Taliban and snuffing out the international terrorists that used the country as a safe haven, Western nations had turned their focus to rebuilding Afghanistan. Problem was, the country they sought to rebuild had never existed. Western nations were attempting to mold an entirely new political order built on democratic principles and a flourishing economy that, most importantly, served Western national security interests. Part of that agenda was to raise living standards, promote human rights, and alleviate everyday suffering of Afghans. For many Western nations, Afghanistan had become the largest single recipient of foreign aid. But for the United States, development work was always secondary to broader national security interests. Of the estimated $2.3 trillion the United States spent on the war in Afghanistan through 2020, about $131 billion, or less than 6 percent, went to reconstruction projects. More than half of those reconstruction funds were managed not by civilian agencies but by the Department of Defense.

Through Adela and Palwasha, Zahra found employment at a United Nations compound in the center of the city. She was hired part-time to teach guards, cooks, and female cleaners how to make homemade marmalade that they could sell after working hours. When she was at work, her neighbor looked after Parisa and Jawad. She found a second job as an administrator for a local NGO near her apartment. With no formal education, she felt insecure working in the office and overcorrected by meticulously reading NGO proposals and legal documents to prove that she was up to the task. Soon she was making close to a hundred dollars a month and was able to move into a better one-bedroom flat.

As she stitched together the fabric of a new life, the threat from Hussein's family in Herat still loomed. Hussein's parents called her family in Herat from Iran to say he'd been sentenced to eight years in jail for drug smuggling. Since he disappeared, Parisa and Jawad had gotten used to the thought of not seeing him again and were adjusting to life in Kabul, growing closer with Zahra as she slowly got better. But Hussein's parents still wanted their grandchildren back. If they did manage to seize the children, a court would likely rule in their favor. Zahra's sister told her that Hussein's brother, also an opium addict, was planning to travel to Kabul with his uncle and search for her. The night before they were to set off, a stroke of tragedy—could divine intervention be this cruel?—hit the uncle's house when a perilously placed pot of boiling water dropped on his young son. The family rushed the toddler to the hospital with severe burns but couldn't save him. The death consumed the family, who had to spend their meager savings on the funeral. A trip to Kabul was suddenly unaffordable, and no one's immediate priority. Zahra appeared to be safe now but was so disturbed when she heard about the accident that she couldn't relax. She also couldn't be sure that Hussein's parents wouldn't find another way to get to her. Again it was Adela who helped Zahra focus on the future. Having worked for several human rights organizations that had sprouted in Afghanistan since 2001, Adela specialized in legal assistance to divorced women and told Zahra that as soon as Parisa and Jawad turned twelve, they were legally entitled to choose which parent they wanted to live with. If she couldn't afford a lawyer, Adela's

NGO could help with the cost. Parisa was eight, and Jawad five. Safety was still a few years away, but if Zahra could look after herself and make sure the kids felt safe, Adela said, it would come.

Both children were mature for their age. Afghan children needed "to learn how to walk on their own," Zahra said, and Parisa and Jawad "grew up fast because of all the hurt around them." Parisa was now old enough for Zahra to trust her to look after herself and Jawad when they got home from school in the afternoon. About a month after she started work at the UN compound, Zahra heard that a local television station was auditioning hosts for a cooking show and thought she'd try out. At the taping, Zahra cooked Afghan macaroni, a dish of short pasta turned in tomato sauce, topped with garlicky yogurt with herbs. Fixing her eyes on the camera, Zahra explained that using too much oil in the sauce was unhealthy and could cause heart problems. The producers were excited. Such nutritional advice was entirely absent from cooking shows. Even though it was only a test screening, they aired it the following day and offered Zahra work as a chef on the program three days a week. She quit her job at the UN compound but kept her job with the NGO. Working in television made Zahra feel liberated. Many Afghan families would not allow female relatives to appear on television, but her own no longer had a say over her.

Zahra hadn't spoken to her mother since leaving Herat several months earlier when one day, her sister Tahera called on her behalf. Their mother was still distressed by Zahra's deceit of the family when she fled, but she wanted to reestablish contact. The thought of Fatima's voice reignited a familiar and unwelcome anxiety in Zahra. They had never been close, and the adoration her mother showered on Parisa and Jawad hadn't changed that. It only reminded Zahra of her mother's inability to show any affection for her. Zahra's stomach ached as she called her mother.

"People talk about you a lot here. There are so many rumors," Fatima began. There was a soft timbre to her voice that Zahra didn't recognize. "But I can see that you don't suffer as much there as you used to do here. Just look after yourself," she said. Years later, Zahra's eyes would well up when remembering the phone call.

"I wish we had a different relationship, that we could speak on the phone regularly, and that she would even hug me once in a while, as she does with my sisters. But we don't," Zahra said. The phone call was as intimate as Zahra's mother would allow them to get.

9

OMARI

He woke up prepared to die. Slipping into a light blue shalwar kameez, he tied a black bandana inscribed with the shahada, the Islamic declaration of faith, around his head. On a large white sheet of cloth, he took his seat among dozens of other boys and young men. They began the morning by reading in the Quran, which they had all received a pocket-sized copy of. For eight hours a day they were taught to recite the holy book in Arabic, which Omari otherwise did not understand. The rest of the day they listened to imams preaching the glory of holy war. One cleric in particular was so enthralling that his voice, booming across the camp through crackling loudspeakers, could make the boys cry in devotion.

At fourteen, Omari was a suitable age for suicide bomber, or *fedayeen*, academy. A few boys were younger than him, some a little older. They were all easily moved. Outsiders said the young boys were manipulated at Taliban academies like the one in Miranshah, but Omari said they were just very emotional.

"Some say that if you go to Pakistan, the Taliban will brainwash you to commit suicide attacks, but that is not true. They only preach," he said. "When we got emotional, we could feel our faith grow so strong that we nearly lost our minds."

The mullahs impressed on the students that only those who fought the righteous jihad were proper Muslims. The boys should resist committing too strongly to this earthly life. Protect your families, but devote all other attention to the holy war in preparation for judgment day, they said.

"Don't study at university to make money. Make sure you have enough for your basic needs, but do not get attached to this life," Omari remembered one of the mullahs shouting over the distorting speaker. They were told that their parents would receive a generous sum of money once their mission had been completed. When they arrived, all students had their phones confiscated until the end of their training, which could last up to two years. After the training period, they would travel back to Afghanistan, where they would receive instructions. The *fedayeen* were handed detailed maps of the area of the intended target. Years later, maps would be downloaded onto smart phones with GPS trackers and 3ds Max software, which made it easier to identify exact gates or street corners. An aspiring suicide bomber had to travel slowly to his destination along circuitous routes to avoid detection by government intelligence. Before setting off, the fighter would prerecord a video message to be sent to his family after his mission was completed. He was forbidden from contacting them otherwise.

Miranshah had been a stronghold of the Haqqani network since the 1980s, when Pakistani funds and arms made it one of the region's strongest and deadliest terrorist outfits. The network also had schools on the other side of the border in Afghanistan, where the Pakistani intelligence agency ISI helped it construct a base inside a natural citadel called Zhawara. Built with financial aid from Osama bin Laden, the base in the 1980s became a hub for Arab volunteer fighters who would come to form the core of al-Qaeda. Suicide academies were a centerpiece in the violent push that made the Haqqanis responsible for some of the deadliest attacks since 2001. A Taliban spokesman, Dadullah Lang, called the suicide bombers "Mullah Omar's missiles."

The young age of the would-be suicide bombers became a hallmark of the Afghan insurgency. Despite the bloodshed they caused, Afghan suicide bombers were surprisingly ineffective compared to their peers in Iraq. An American researcher who studied patterns in Afghan suicide attacks discovered that the most common outcome by far of a suicide attack in Afghanistan was that the suicide bomber was the only person killed. In only about 20 percent of the attacks did a suicide bomber succeed in killing one or more victims. The fact that they still caused significant deaths was a testament to the number of suicide attackers under the Taliban's command. In Iraq, failures were uncommon and suicide bombers usually took a large number of fatalities with them, partly because they typically struck crowds of civilians, including women and children, to spread fear. Taliban suicide bombers, at least in the first half of the war, mostly targeted military installations and convoys. The research attributed the relative incompetence of Afghan suicide bombers to their young age, illiteracy, and even disabilities. A typical Afghan suicide bomber was twelve to thirteen years old on average, with little other schooling than an intellectually suffocating religious training from the madrassa. They often went to the madrassa without their parents' permission, as Omari had. According to the Afghan intelligence agency the National Directorate of Security, the Taliban paid the bombers between two thousand and ten thousand dollars for their mission, to be given to their families after their deaths.

Omari was fully committed to his destiny as *fedayeen*, but after about a month in the camp, a commander pulled him aside and told him he shouldn't be there.

"You're a good boy. Go home to Afghanistan and look after yourself," he said, and kissed Omari on the head. Omari was flustered. He had been a good student and was committed to the cause. It turned out his father still had contacts in the Taliban from his time working in its government. When he heard that his son had traveled to Miranshah, he was able to retrieve him. Omari returned to Sayedabad furious. His father had already fought in the jihad, and now it was meant to be his time. He expected to be punished but his father hugged him and treated him with kindness. Omari figured that his usually stern father must have been so sick with worry that, even if he was angry, he didn't want to risk his son leaving again. Once Omari had settled in, his father took his phone and broke the SIM card with all his contacts. Omari eventually acquiesced. He didn't give up on his jihad but resigned himself to fighting his war in this world.

Omari returned from Pakistan with his mind ablaze. His first trip outside Wardak had taken him several hundred miles away, abroad. Afghanistan was in the midst of historic, global turmoil, surrounded by enemies. For a young teenager with his senses and curiosity awakened, it was impossible to just sit at home and watch. Everyone Omari knew in Wardak regarded the American war in Afghanistan as based on lies. They believed the United States was there to wage war on Islam, not terrorists. The evidence was there for anyone to see. In the middle of the night on May 2, 2011, on the other side of the border, twenty-five American Navy SEALs landed in the courtyard of a two-story building in the Pakistani city of Abbottabad, stormed the house, and killed Osama bin Laden. Few Afghans were surprised that the elusive terrorism leader was based in Pakistan, but his whereabouts were so blatantly within the ISI's sphere of influence that it was insulting. Abbottabad was located eighty miles from the capital Islamabad, and bin Laden had lived under the nose of a large military academy. Even after the death of bin Laden, whom the Americans had ostensibly invaded Afghanistan to catch, the United States stayed.

"It's true that Osama bin Laden in the beginning was in Tora Bora in Afghanistan, but when the US killed him, he was in Pakistan. The US has the equipment to hit anyone at any time, and they can see from far away if someone is a terrorist. So don't tell me they have come to Afghanistan to kill terrorists. They are here to eradicate Islam," Omari said.

Omari was sixteen when he was sent into the field for the first time. The Taliban had intelligence that an American convoy was planning to cross a bridge in Sayedabad that day, and his first task was to place bombs underneath it. This was a significant responsibility for a sixteen-year-old on his first assignment. Omari was relieved that the commander gave him a motorcycle battery as a power source for the detonator rather than a cell phone battery, which was more volatile and tended to blow up in your face if you had shaky hands. He had to admit his hands were a little shaky. Three teams were dispatched to prepare the ambush. One looked out for the convoy, a second planted the explosives, and a third would detonate the bomb. Omari and his team were told to be ready for a signal from the scouts farther up the road. When they spotted four American Humvees heading their way, they signaled to Omari. He quickly buried the explosives in sand under the bridge and sprinted away. The third team watched as the convoy approached. When the last Humvee drove onto the bridge, they called the cell phone attached to the bomb, sending a signal to a circuit board that triggered the explosion. Omari was huddled in a field of tall grass. The blast sent an armored Humvee door flying over his head. He was close enough to the bridge to see several injured and dead Americans. The explosion was still ringing in his ears as some of the Americans began searching the area, shouting desperately while their comrades treated the wounded.

"I couldn't understand any of what the Americans were shouting," he said. "I was in shock, and really afraid that they were going to find me and arrest me."

Omari believed he helped kill four or five US soldiers that day. His teachers had taught him that killing seven enemies of Islam would grant him the same status in the eyes of God as that of a martyr. He was on his way.

Armed struggle was addictive. Fighting the Americans gave Omari a sense of ownership of his life. Americans controlled his country, a fact the hum of drones reminded him of every night. He had found a way to strike back. The drones made his nights restless, but when he was awake, the popping sound of bullets kicked his adrenaline into gear and suppressed his fear. Besides, war gave him something to do.

"It was a lot of fun," he admitted. Between Quran studies and war, Omari found time to read historical literature and engineering textbooks. He dreamed of becoming an engineer, and had a knack for it. His commanders noticed, and one day asked him to travel to the northern province of Jowzjan to teach at a Taliban-affiliated school. Jowzjan was populated mostly by Uzbeks and Turkmens, whose history Omari had learned in snippets in school. He remembered the story of General Dostum under whose command thousands of Taliban fighters had suffocated in shipping containers. One of his new students in Jowzjan elaborated, claiming that when the Taliban fighters in the containers had asked their guards for a drink of water, Dostum's men had given them bottles full of urine. After President Karzai implemented a law that granted government allies immunity for past crimes, Dostum supported his presidential campaign in 2009. Now, in 2012, he was part of the leadership of a northern anti-Taliban council that united prominent Tajik, Uzbek, and Hazara military commanders. Watching warlords with blood on their hands walk free hardened Omari's resolve against the government and the foreign diplomats who treated them with a deference usually reserved for dignitaries. One of the starkest examples was the Islamist former mujahideen commander Abdul Rasul Sayyaf, who in the 1980s formed a close relationship with Osama bin Laden. Sayyaf was believed to be the person who invited bin Laden to Afghanistan. His training camps and Islamic schools were accused of training terrorists, including Khalid Sheikh Mohammed, the architect behind the 9/11 attacks. The white-bearded Sayyaf was so radical that a Philippine terrorist group, which would later swear fealty to Islamic State, took its name after him: Abu Sayyaf. After 2001, Sayyaf read the tea leaves and aligned himself with the new US-backed government. It worked. Within a few years, his reputation had been whitewashed and, while not exactly a friend of the West, both the Afghan president and Western diplomats in Kabul consulted him as a respected elder. In one example of the public esteem high-ranking foreign diplomats were willing to bestow on him, the European Union in Kabul posted a photo of its ambassador, Franz-Michael Mellbin, and Sayyaf at the warlord's residence in 2015.

"I always find the views and perspectives expressed by Mr. Sayyaf stimulating and look forward to continue our relations," Mellbin said in the post.

After three months in Jowzjan, Omari returned to Wardak, eager to explore the rest of Afghanistan. First on the list was the capital. Kabul was ninety minutes' drive from Sayedabad, but provided more of a culture shock than going abroad to Pakistan. Omari's family saw Kabul as a nest of decadence, moral decay, and arrogance. Omari was curious to see for himself. On a Friday, he slipped his parents a white lie, telling them that he was going to visit an uncle who worked for a mine-clearing NGO in Kabul. He bought a seat in a shared taxi from Sayedabad going north on Highway 1, paved smooth with American and Japanese aid money, through Maidan Shar, the government-controlled capital of Wardak province. The journey continued without incident, and they soon reached Kampani, the bustling suburb where a weekly cattle market drew crowds clogging the road, through Kot-e Sangi to Shah-Do Shamshira Mosque on the banks of the filthy Kabul River, where pigeons fluttered around its two blue-tipped minarets.

Omari paid a brief visit to his uncle but spent most of his time wandering the streets transfixed. The city was sin incarnate. Drug addicts and peddlers, hustlers and women with their hijabs wrapped tauntingly loose around their hair. The country's capital embodied everything he hated about the new Afghanistan. He returned to Wardak more determined than ever to fight the Americans who had toppled the Taliban to build this cesspool.

The nation was being ravaged by an intense battle for its soul. Some people, particularly in the cities, reaped benefits of the Western intervention, which had created employment and sown seeds of social progress. The Americans and their allies wanted girls to go to school and women to become prominent politicians, presenting the emancipation of women as an unambiguously virtuous cause. The Americans would spend the entire war trying to convince Afghans skeptical of their intentions that they were not there to colonize or to wage war on Islam. They repeatedly undermined those efforts by committing grievous mistakes.

On February 22, 2012, a group American soldiers at Bagram Air Base were ordered to incinerate a pile of more than 1,600 books, some of which supposedly had been annotated with extremist content by inmates. It ought to have been a routine task. As the soldiers tossed the books onto the flames, an Afghan worker offered to help. Watching more closely, he noticed the Quran among the books and started screaming and dousing the flames with water. At least four Qurans were charred in the flames—an incendiary insult to Muslims everywhere. Some Afghan workers smuggled the burned books out of the base, igniting a riot of protesters hurling stones at coalition forces. The protests spread beyond Bagram and Kabul, despite apologies from US officials. Thirty people died during five days of protests across the country, including two American servicemen killed by an Afghan soldier who turned his gun on them. The riots added to acrimony between the United States and the Afghan people. A month earlier, a video recording had surfaced of four US Marines urinating on the bodies of three killed Taliban fighters. "Have a great day, buddy," one of the soldiers said.

It got worse. Three weeks after the accidental Quran burning, on March 11, 2012, US Army S.Sgt. Robert Bales put on night vision goggles and traditional Afghan clothing and left his outpost, Camp Belamby in Panjwai in Kandahar, in the middle of the night. Buzzing on a cocktail of alcohol, sleeping pills, and steroids, the American sniper walked to the villages of Alkozai and Najiban, where he shot and killed sixteen villagers in cold blood, including nine children and three women. It was the worst massacre committed by an American soldier since My Lai in Vietnam in 1968. Bales turned himself in and was sentenced by a US military court to life without parole. Many Afghans thought the sentence was too soft, and that justice should be

served in the country where he committed his crime. The Afghan Parliament and President Karzai demanded that Bales be tried in Afghan
court where he could face the death penalty. Many Afghans saw it as
another example of Americans trampling over Afghanistan. For years,
the United States had been arresting and torturing Afghans and shipping them off to Guantánamo without trial. But when one of their
own committed a war crime in the country, they hurried him back
home to deal with him themselves.

Another of the worst known atrocities of the war unfolded about
twenty miles from Omari's village. In 2012, a group of American
Green Berets set up base in a district called Nerkh. They hadn't been
there long before allegations started circulating that the elite forces
were kidnapping, torturing, and murdering civilians. Dead bodies
appeared, some missing limbs, others so badly brutalized that they
couldn't be identified. At the time, President Karzai was negotiating a
new security agreement for Afghanistan with the United States that
would provide the framework of the two nations' partnership after
the planned drawdown of US troops. The Nerkh scandal gave impetus to Karzai's two main demands: he wanted Afghan prisoners in US
detention transferred to Afghan control, and he demanded a stop to
American night raids. The United States at first denied any wrong-
doing in Nerkh, but under pressure from the International Committee
of the Red Cross and the UN, it agreed in 2013 to investigate the allegations. At least seventeen civilians were found to have been murdered between 2012 and 2013, but the only person punished was an
Afghan interpreter, Zikria Kandahari, who was sentenced to twenty
years for treason. Although US military commanders, according to international criminal law, could have been held accountable for the actions of their subordinates, and the UN said it was possible that what
happened in Nerkh was a war crime, the United States concluded that
there was "no credible evidence to substantiate misconduct by ISAF or
US Forces relating to the detainees or deaths in Nerkh."

Incidents piled up from the beginning of the war. American drones
bombed wedding parties and funerals. Foreign militaries collaborated

with Afghan officials involved in industrial-scale drug smuggling. In Kandahar, Western forces worked closely with a police chief who operated a private torture chamber—and went on to become the country's head of intelligence under Karzai. In 2012, a self-designated "kill team" of US Army soldiers murdered at least three Afghan civilians and took their body parts as souvenirs. That same year, the *Los Angeles Times* published photos of young American soldiers posing for the camera with severed limbs of suspected Taliban fighters and a sign saying "Zombie Hunters." In 2013, an Australian elite soldier admitted to severing the hands from the bodies of two dead suspected Taliban militants. He was acquitted of war crimes at home. In one of the grimmest incidents, in 2015, an American warplane mistakenly bombed a hospital run by Doctors Without Borders in the northern city of Kunduz. For over an hour a massive Lockheed AC-130 bomber circled in the darkness above and turned the hospital into a burning war zone. Forty-two patients and medical staff were killed, several of whom were burned alive.

In almost every instance, it took independent journalists, activists, or medical workers—Afghan as well as foreign—to uncover or document such atrocities and civilian deaths. Foreign militaries almost never divulged the truth without pressure. Treating an enemy as subhuman is a habit as old as war itself, turning other humans into faceless enemies, their mutilated bodies into trophies. Afghan government soldiers were known to strap dead Taliban fighters to the fronts of their vehicles, like figureheads at the bow of a ship, and proudly showed video footage of the scenes to foreign journalists. Taliban fighters released videos online depicting suicide missions, complete with dramatic soundscapes and cartoonish graphics that made a killing mission look like a video game. To wage war, it is necessary to maintain an us-versus-them mentality. Did Western commanders and policymakers worry that if they openly discussed the full ugly truth, public support for the fight at home would dwindle? Perhaps. Regardless, widespread impunity or lenient punishment for manifest crimes confirmed to many Afghans the hypocrisy of the West.

The American way of war was felt in Sayedabad, too. One of Omari's uncles had fought with the Taliban since the first day of the war, and the Taliban had been mentor to him. One night, a group of US soldiers abseiled from their Chinook down into the uncle's garden. In the ensuing firefight, the uncle's brother, sister, and young daughter were killed. The uncle himself was tied up, blindfolded, and flown to Bagram Air Base. He returned six months later a broken man. He had a permanent headache and his short-term memory was shattered.

"When he told stories about what he went through at Bagram, he would suddenly start crying," Omari said. "Sometimes he seemed normal but he couldn't control himself. He said the Americans had given him and other prisoners electric shock and kept them awake all night. They were constantly watched by cameras, and when they were about to fall asleep, an American would come by the cell and knock on the door with a wooden stick to keep them awake. They sprayed them with some kind of gas that made their eyes water and their noses bleed."

The uncle's treatment at Bagram fits with well-known descriptions by other inmates. Sleep deprivation and enhanced interrogation techniques were hallmarks of time spent in American detention. After he was released, Omari's uncle left the Taliban. He kept in touch with his old friends in the movement but was no longer able to fight.

"He had lost his mind," Omari said. "That's probably why the Americans released him."

10

MADS

Kabul in the mid-2010s was a place of parallel worlds. It was a city that ran on foreign money, administered by an Afghan elite who lived in secluded compounds and moved their children and families abroad. A city of spies hiding in plain sight and millionaires zipping through town, obscured by tinted car windows, where a mosque boomed anti-Western sermons a hundred yards from a gym where bodybuilders bench-pressed with 50 Cent on the sound system and Shakira muted on the common television. At the American ambassador's residence, visitors were greeted by a painting in the hallway meant to depict an everyday scene on the banks of the Kabul River less than two miles away. In the painting, the river was clear blue, not the sludgy brown of reality, and on its banks, women were fetching water in buckets, trousers rolled up to expose their legs.

In the first decade of the war, foreign aid workers, mercenaries, and journalists who came to Kabul to forge careers created a separate society buzzing on equal measures of adrenaline and booze. Aware of the absurdity of the world they lived in, they named their social scene: the Kabubble. Drag racing on motorcycles through empty streets at night, foreigners congregated to blow off steam at Prohibition-style speakeasies like the Gandamack Lodge, run by a former British soldier turned cameraman, or fancy-dress parties with themes like "Tarts and Talibs." Foreigners helped the handicraft shops on Chicken Street stay solvent and overnight turned a cohort of Afghan cleaners, cooks, and fixers into middle-class citizens. They nursed hangovers over brunch in French-style cafés or the early-morning carnage of a suicide bombing they had to document for their editors back home.

By 2014, the war had changed. The peak of the surge was over. Bin Laden had been killed in 2011, and the coalition had handed over responsibility for the country's security to the Afghan forces. Focus had shifted to training the Afghan military and police and conducting counterterrorism missions run by US Special Forces. In 2014, President Obama said most US forces would withdraw by the end of 2016, freeing them up for counterterrorism activities elsewhere. The pledge was met with skepticism among experts, and Obama would leave office in 2017 with more than eight thousand troops still in the country. But in 2014, the overwhelming sense in the country was one of transition. Tens of thousands of foreign soldiers departed as the international combat mission ended, leaving a smaller number to "train, advise, and assist" the Afghans. Aid spending decreased as belated awareness of corruption, the impact of the 2008 financial crisis, and war-weariness ate into the previous decade's lavish budgets. The number of journalists also shrank, and NGOs tightened their security protocols as life in the city became more dangerous. The excesses of expat life mostly took place inside highly secured blast walls where Western diplomats lived secluded. One summer evening at a pool party in the garden of one such residence, a muscular diplomat flaunting beefy pecs and flowery boardshorts held out a tray of yellow Jell-O shots infused with vodka to welcome newly arrived guests into the boisterous crowd.

"This is probably the only action my tongue will get tonight," he said before sealing the glass with his lips like a suction cup.

More than a decade into the war, policymakers and strategists often seemed insulated. Lessons were rarely learned, mistakes often repeated. Afghan and Western scholars and journalists produced plenty of public criticisms, but it was difficult for Kabul-based research-ers, relative outsiders in Western capitals, to influence policy. The war created its own research industry, in which Western analysts—who often had little knowledge of Afghan language, culture, and political dynamics—sought to distill complex problems into digestible nug-gets of data and analysis for policymakers back home. Some research-ers were independent, but many belonged to the military-industrial complex, funded by militaries, private contractors, and aid agencies linked to foreign ministries. The scope of their research was deter-mined by short-term contracts, reflecting the fact that most civilian and military personnel did tours of no more than a year at a time, and that no government made real plans beyond one electoral cycle. Long-time Afghan scholars complained that when they were invited by the US military to share their views, the generals tended to ignore their work and listen to small groups of insiders, and gravitate toward pre-drawn conclusions: for example, that the counterinsurgency model imported from Iraq would work in Afghanistan. When visiting embas-sies, female scholars sometimes found diplomats more interested in the mundane practicalities of life in Afghanistan—questioning them in more detail about how they dressed or got around—than in their findings from hours of interviews with tribal elders.

The American war was driven by ideology, and from some perspec-tives, it was not so different from the Taliban's holy war. Both sides were fighting for ideas. Modern American warfare has generally been waged not against states, but against ethereal dark forces and beliefs: for "freedom" against "evil," light against darkness. In the immediate aftermath of 9/11, George W. Bush had much of the world's sympa-thy when he responded to the mass murder of American civilians. He called on the world to align itself with America's ideals: "And what is at stake is not just America's freedom. This is the world's fight. This is civilization's fight. This is the fight of all who believe in progress and pluralism, tolerance and freedom." As late as 2017, influential US sena-tor Lindsey Graham, during a trip to Kabul alongside John McCain,

Elizabeth Warren, and other Senate colleagues, described the Taliban as people who "will kill women for sport in soccer stadiums." He added: "I want every American to know that we will win this thing because the Afghan people do not want to go back to the darkness. They want to pursue the light. They reject what radical Islam is selling. They just need our help."

Such simple juxtapositions help politicians explain to voters why they are sending soldiers to risk their lives overseas. But fighting an abstract enemy leads to endless wars. You can obliterate a state and topple a government, but you cannot bomb away an idea, especially if substantial portions of the local population don't share your hard-line views about your enemy.

Living sheltered lives may have been necessary for diplomats in Kabul, and many of them lamented their lack of mobility. Nevertheless, the security measures they lived under could only skew their perspective. Diplomats wrote cables that helped capitals decide that deporting refugees to Afghanistan was safe, while their own security teams banned them from even stopping their car to buy a loaf of bread. One night in 2015, the staff at one European embassy were awoken by gunfire. Frantically, they scrambled for the underground safe room, one clenching a gun, another crying in the corner. Their radios were silent. They assumed the security team was busy fighting outside. It turned out Afghanistan had won a big cricket match and the city was celebrating, as per tradition, with gunfire. The embassy security team was indeed busy, watching the game. Cricket is the biggest sport in Afghanistan and people in the city had been talking about the match for a week.

To spot a foreigner in Kabul, the best bet was to look up. From morning to evening, helicopters clattered across the sky, flying so low they made the windows below rattle. Sometimes they would shoot flares in lieu of honking horns. By the late 2010s, American and British diplomats traveled almost exclusively to and from the Kabul airport by helicopter. The road to the embassy, fewer than three miles long, was deemed too dangerous.

Outside the compound walls, it was mostly Afghan civilians who felt the waves of violence. The surge in attacks at times made the belt of checkpoints around Kabul, known as the Ring of Steel, feel like kitchen foil. Residents had gotten used to, literally, getting back on their feet following major attacks, to the sight of lifeless bodies and bloody limbs on the other side of police cordons. Outside hospitals, hundreds of crying women and men would bang their fists against the gates, desperate for news of their loved ones. There would be an awkward exchange of looks when a truck full of orange-clad street cleaners passed by. They were tasked with possibly the dirtiest job in town: to sweep away the blood and torn body parts of the same loved ones. By afternoon, the streets were clean of broken glass and mangled metal. Bakeries handed out steaming hot bread for the break of fast, and barbers polished newly replaced windows. Foreigners often marveled at the "resilience" of Afghans. It would be wrong to mistake this resilience for apathy. Life had to go on, not because Afghans didn't grieve their daughters and sons or feel traumatized by the violence around them, but because war was so pervasive, and there was no alternative in sight. It often seemed that Kabul's separate worlds were growing further apart. Sometimes, though, they met.

Mads Kundal Jensen arrived in Kabul in June 2014, six years and several tours after his first mission to Afghanistan as part of a contingent of Danish soldiers in Helmand, where he had lost several friends. Now the twenty-seven-year-old first lieutenant was in charge of a force protection team under the new NATO training mission and faced his most difficult task yet. A large delegation was due to visit Camp Qargha west of Kabul, home to the Afghan National Army Officer Academy, where foreign soldiers mentored Afghan officers. The delegation was going to look at a water-shortage problem that was complicating a $70 million American construction deal. Mads had been told seven foreign generals would be among the delegates, including two Americans, of whom one was a two-star. It struck him as unusual that such high-ranking officers would spend their time inspecting a water facility. On the other hand, he knew that in a war, the most mundane matters could have great strategic importance. Whatever the case, it was far above his pay grade to decide whether the trip was worth the risk. His job was to mitigate danger. Any movement outside the perimeter of the NATO headquarters required thorough planning, and he had been doing reconnaissance a month in advance.

The son of an engineer with the Danish shipping conglomerate Maersk, Mads had known that he wanted to be a soldier since he was a kid. His parents had taken Mads and his sister to South America, the Middle East, and East Asia, spending several months at sea and docking in far-flung places. In India, at the age of six, he saw children his own age living and working on the street. By the time he started high school, Mads had visited nearly thirty countries. Growing up in a tiny Scandinavian welfare state, he understood that he had an obligation to help those less privileged. He could have pursued a career as an aid worker but he was drawn to the physical challenge of the military. His calm demeanor and trustworthy good looks of a reliable real estate agent, with short side-parted blond hair and a controlled stubble, belied a restless soul. If he was running from anything, it was the clammy hands of boredom. Behind a quick, welcoming smile, he held strong opinions about his fellow Danes, especially those he saw as well-meaning but naive humanists.

"It's easy to sit in Denmark with your pacifist opinions and eat organic vegetables if you've never been confronted with the misery of the world outside," he said. Mads had supported Denmark's contribution to the war from the start. Europe owed the Americans for helping fight the Nazis during the Second World War, and after 9/11, it was time to repay the favor. He also believed that building schools and a new political system could transform developing countries for the better.

Camp Qargha was located on a dusty, hilly plain on the side of the highway leading west out of Kabul. The outer perimeter of the camp was visible from outside, but most of it was set back from the road. Mads had corralled a team of eleven Danes, a Croatian, and two Australian snipers. The Taliban had never attacked the camp before, and there was no intelligence suggesting they were planning to do so imminently. The delegation would fly the roughly six miles from the military headquarters in Kabul and stay in parts of the camp that were at a safe distance from the road. The most likely danger to the group would be an insider attack. Since the start of the war, about 150 foreign soldiers had been killed this way. In 2013, an Afghan soldier had injured a New Zealander and an Australian at the same academy. But more often than not, foreign officers were met with generosity and kindness, and Mads hadn't alerted anyone about the pending visit. He expected an uneventful day.

Harold Greene, a two-star major general, was unlikely to see much battle in Afghanistan. He had been sent primarily as an administrator, in early 2014, for the Combined Security Transition Command–Afghanistan, or CSTC-A, (pronounced "see-stick-uh"). He had nearly retired the year before, but decided to take on one last assignment, to serve twelve months as the deputy commander of CSTC-A, charged with distributing billions of aid dollars to the Afghan army. It was his first combat deployment and he had promised his wife, Sue, herself a retired US Army colonel, to be home by January for their thirtieth anniversary. Soldiers knew the general as easygoing, "careful not to come off as arrogant." His friends called him Harry. The academy at Qargha was the crown jewel in the international coalition's training mission of Afghan security forces. To inspire the rest of the army and police to root out corruption and improve the supply of fuel, food, and other necessities, the officers academy had to run as flawlessly as possible. Harry Greene knew that. He also knew that sometimes it took the weight of a two-star general to get things moving.

Mads and his team spent the night at Camp Qargha. On the morning of August 5, he rose early. After coffee, his men were ready at 9:00 a.m., when the delegation was supposed to touch down. When they landed on the dusty hillside at Qargha at 9:50 a.m., the delegation was already nearly an hour late. It was also larger than Mads had expected, more than eighty people. Interest in the visit had grown in the days leading up to it, but no one had told Mads the exact number of visitors.

"It was problematic, to say the least, that I couldn't get information on who and how many were coming," he said. The academy consisted of a collection of low-rise buildings connected by freshly paved roads. The visitors moved slowly until they reached the second-to-last stop, outside an underground reservoir. The group was too large to fit in the water-reservoir building, so while the generals were inside, an American advisor mounted an easel outside to give a presentation. This wasn't part of the plan. He was supposed to have given it earlier, but because two Afghan officers had gotten into a fight after being unable to fully answer a question from General Greene, the organizers had postponed the presentation. Mads hadn't planned for the group to stand just outside a row of Afghan military barracks for a briefing. Even though he hadn't told anyone about the VIP visit, the generals had been driving around the camp in a convoy of twenty-five vehicles for nearly two hours, so no one could have missed their presence. He had to think fast. He had already dispatched a group of British soldiers to sweep the area. They had left before he got there, but there was no indication of a potential threat from inside the barracks, nor had it posed a threat in the past. Mads had placed the Australian sharpshooters on the roof and now ran through a checklist of potential signs of danger in his mind. He had seen no indication of hostility. There were armed Afghans on the base, which was normal, but no one nearby. Every Afghan he had locked eyes with had smiled. After conferring with two American colonels, he decided the briefing could go ahead.

Rafiqullah wasn't meant to have been on patrol that day, but because of an unexpected absence of personnel, he was assigned to do a routine check of the perimeter of the camp with another military police officer from the garrison support unit. At twenty-two, Rafiqullah was skinny with a boyish face that had sprouted only a few whiskers on his lip and chin. Born in Paryakhel village in the eastern province of Paktia, the birthplace of the Haqqani network, Rafiqullah grew up in a family that supported Afghanistan's fledgling post-Taliban government. He was illiterate and, until he enlisted in 2012, earned money working in construction and running a shop in the village bazaar. His older brother had briefly joined the army, but Rafiqullah was the only one among five siblings to pursue a career in the security forces. He was not the most obvious candidate for the police, which made him the kind of man the police needed. The national security forces were still growing and needed to recruit more soldiers from Pashtun-majority provinces where the Taliban were vying for the loyalty of young, destitute men.

Rafiqullah set off on the patrol in a Ford Ranger with his colleague Mohammad. Halfway through their patrol, they realized they had forgotten to put fuel in the truck and had to turn around sooner than planned. They descended from a hill toward the barracks. The British soldiers and their dogs who had cleared the area were supposed to wait for the Danish protection team to arrive, but since no one had told them about the delay in the delegation's program, they had left fifteen minutes before Rafiqullah and Mohammad arrived at the barracks.

At 11:40 a.m., the generals appeared from the reservoir and along with the rest of the delegation gathered to listen to the briefing, forming a semicircle on a sun-torched patch of ground in front of the barracks where the grass had been trampled to dirt. As a sign of trust toward the Afghans, none of the delegates wore body armor. The advisor had almost finished his briefing when shots rang out. *Brrrah! Brrrah! Brrrah!*

"Why is there gunfire now? There shouldn't be gunfire now," Mads thought. The sound ricocheted off the concrete walls of the buildings around them and it took Mads five seconds to locate where it was coming from. He spun around and saw a gun barrel poking out of a half-open window fifteen feet away, in the building below one of the Australian sharpshooters. Mads aimed his machine gun at the tinted glass, not knowing who or how many shooters he was firing at. His first two rounds hit the frame but the next six went straight through the window. An American soldier helped return fire, the sound of bullets cracking over Mads's right shoulder. Then everything went quiet.

Mads felt blood roar through his body, like it had during gun battles he had been in in Helmand. His senses were sharpened, adrenaline overpowering his fear and any instinct of flight. Only this side of the barracks had windows, so he ran to the back of the building, calling his men over the radio.

"There's no time for this," he thought, and ran into the building alone. He was met by three Afghan soldiers, all carrying guns.

Mads had ordered all Afghans in the barracks disarmed, but he didn't know that these guys had arrived after the British soldiers left. For all he knew, one of them could be the shooter. Not wanting to take a bullet in the back if he continued into the building, he went to get backup. In the doorway, he ran into an American soldier who had been grazed by bullets in his arm and abdomen. One of General Greene's American bodyguards joined them and the three went back into the barracks, the Americans providing cover for Mads.

"Walk behind me. If I'm shot, take him out," he told them.

There were about a dozen armed Afghans in the dormitory. Mads paused. He had to be careful not to create panic. If one person started shooting now, it would all end in mayhem. It had been about a minute since the shooting stopped. If the attacker was still alive and hiding among the armed Afghan soldiers, he was unlikely to start shooting now. If he wasn't among them, he must be farther inside the building. Mads decided he had time to get an interpreter, but when he ran out to find one, the Afghan translator refused to go inside the building. Instead Mads asked two coalition soldiers who had arrived to join him.

"Fuck it, there's five of us," he thought, and went inside. Mads pushed open a door on the left to the latrines. The window inside was cracked by bullets. At the other end of the horseshoe-shaped bathroom, an Afghan soldier sat leaning against the wall in a pool of blood. Rafiqullah had slipped into the bathroom unnoticed, wedged his NATO-issued M16 through the opening in the window, and pulled the trigger. Mads or the American soldier must have hit him when they returned fire. He was struggling to breathe. Mads directed the soldiers to administer first aid, but when they laid him on the floor, he stopped breathing.

Outside in front of the barracks, everything was chaos. Injured people everywhere. A British soldier was hit in the groin, his femoral artery severed. Medics were applying a tourniquet above a gunshot in a woman's shin. A soldier being carried to a white Land Cruiser complained loudly about the bullet lodged in his ass. At 1:00 p.m., an hour after the shooting, the first helicopter took off with the injured. In the meantime, Mads and his team took the road back to Kabul. When they arrived at headquarters, Mads was told over the phone that sixteen people were injured, including three generals. One person had died: Harold J. Greene. The two-star general had been hit in the pelvis, head, and neck, and died almost instantly. He was the highest-ranking American general killed in a war zone since Vietnam.

"Fucking hell, I am going to get fired," Mads thought as the casualty toll registered. He had apparently said it out loud because one of the other Danes looked at him.

"Yeah, maybe," he said.

In the inquiry that followed, the American and Afghan militaries found that Rafiqullah had managed to let off twenty-five bullets in three-round bursts, pulling the trigger eight or nine times in six seconds. Because the group had been standing in such close proximity, some bullets penetrated several people. They learned that Rafiqullah likely had no links to the Taliban or any terrorist groups, according to his superiors, colleagues, and military intelligence. "There were no signs or indications of anti-U.S. or ISAF forces sentiments," a five-hundred-page US military report about the attack stated. "However, our investigation indicated he may have had some bias against Coalition Forces." Afghan intelligence found nothing on his phone apart from religious songs and some pornography—neither uncharacteristic for an Afghan man in his early twenties. The intelligence chief at the base, Col. Mohammad Sapo, said he regularly planted spies among the recruits at the academy to identify potential Taliban infiltrators, and Rafiqullah hadn't stood out. Three months before the shooting, he had passed a polygraph test.

"He wanted to work for the government, to serve Afghanistan," his teenage brother, Sefidullah, said. Rafiqullah didn't have a lot of friends back in Paktia, and didn't make many on the base, but his acquaintances said he largely kept to himself and was friendly. Rafiqullah occasionally complained that he didn't get enough leave to go home and see his family, especially during religious holidays, but those were the circumstances for everyone at the academy. One of his dormmates at the academy had noticed that he declined an energy bar from a foreign soldier, an unusual spurn of a friendly gesture; the dormmate presumed he'd rejected the gift as a way to rebuff the foreign soldier but didn't make much of it until after the shooting. That was the only outward sign of hostility toward foreigners anyone could think of.

Sefidullah never got the sense that Rafiqullah had grievances against anyone at the military academy.

"He would call me from time to time. He was happy there," he said. The brothers were close, and Sefidullah was certain that Rafiqullah did not have ties to the Taliban. Everyone in his family supported the presence of the United States.

"We all think the Americans came to rebuild Afghanistan. We still think that. I don't know why he would shoot the general."

The absence of a clear motive for the shooting made it difficult to recommend steps to prevent similar incidents in the future. "This investigation finds no negligence on the part of any leader, or event planner," the report concluded. It left the US military in an uncomfortable conundrum. Treating Afghans as equal partners came with inherent risks, but increasing security, such as wearing body armor and limiting the contact between Afghan soldiers and foreigners, disempowered the people meant to take over the responsibility for security in the country. It wasn't unusual for a perpetrator of any insider attacks to not have Taliban links, which made it difficult to anticipate threats. A 2012 report from the Pentagon's inspector general criticized the US Army for conducting full counterintelligence screenings on only 15 percent of the more than four thousand Afghan interpreters hired during the troop surge from 2009 to 2010; one interpreter ended up killing two American special forces soldiers. But what could those screenings have found? When asked about Rafiqullah, Zikrullah Saleh, his company commander, said, "I never saw anything bad in him."

The results of the inquiry brought little satisfaction to General Greene's bereaved family, who were looking for answers. Greene's son, Matthew, a first lieutenant, said his family felt "completely betrayed by the Army's investigation." The Afghan army, too, felt left in the dark.

"The US never shared their investigation with us in order for us to prevent incidents like this," the top commander at the training academy, Maj. Gen. Jalandar Shah Behnam, said. The reluctance of the US to share intelligence increased the likelihood that similar incidents could happen again, he added.

Mads was not fired. Instead, he was awarded a Bronze Star Medal for Valor for quickly identifying the target, returning fire, and reorganizing his security detail. Rafiqullah's brothers heard about his death on the radio, but kept it secret from their elderly, ill parents. Three months later, their father heard the news from men in their village.

"Why didn't you tell me this before?" he cried to his son, but agreed not to tell his wife. She only found out when Rafiqullah's body was finally brought to the village with help from the International Committee of the Red Cross.

"She was beating herself in the face and crying," Sefidullah recalled. The family held a funeral for Rafiqullah in Khost, a nearby city.

"The elders were talking about him," Sefidullah remembered. "Some said they wished they could have stopped him. Some said he was a martyr. Some just said he died."

11

ALEX

Kabul was a cacophony of sounds. The center was enveloped in a wall of white noise characteristic of South Asian cities—the rumble of traffic, hollering of street hawkers, rattling of old taxis, bleating of children. From early spring the tinny melody of "Happy Birthday" would pierce through the noise and travel down alleyways. It was either that or "My Heart Will Go On," the other default tune programmed into the speakers on ice cream carts, tormenting the mental health of the sunburned vendor pushing the trolley for fifteen hours a day.

"It's like a dick in the brain," one of them said succinctly.

There were regular gunshots, most often from policemen trying to get drivers to pull over, or the more serious clap of mortars and explosions that made everyone pause. Sometimes, the blasts continued for hours. Once, a one-man insurgency kept the Afghan security forces busy from midnight until dawn as he ran around Wazir Akbar Khan Hill near the diplomatic quarter letting off rounds from his AK-47 and a rocket-propelled grenade launcher, hiding from a helicopter's searchlight. Foreign reporters having drinks in their garden a few hundred yards away dubbed him the Talib John McClane. After five hours he met his martyrdom having caused no casualties.

On Fridays, the city fell quiet as people slept in and went to the mosque before meeting family and friends for freshly grilled kebabs. The sound of ice cream being churned by hand filled the early evening. On one such Friday, in a rooftop restaurant in the city center, a waiter escorted the last visiting family to the exit and locked the door. He pulled a sound system in from the storage room, turned on a garland of string lights on the wall, and sent a bass-filled Tajik pop beat pumping from the crackling speaker, drowning out any attempt at conversation among the dozen or so young men still at the restaurant. A young man took to the floor, wearing fresh mascara and rings with fake gemstones the size of his knuckles. Hands over his head, he writhed his hips and smiled seductively at his friends, who snapped their fingers on beat. Juli usually danced for tips at a karaoke bar in town where older men paid younger dancing boys to perform. This night was different. Juli and his friends were here for their own pleasure. As the volume from the first song faded, the night sounds from the city below stepped in, led by the unmistakable tremble of the call to prayer. It was considered blasphemous to play music when the muezzin sang. The guys glanced at each other. A look of hesitation stole over their faces. Then they burst out laughing. Juli grabbed the aux cable, connected his phone, and scrolled to a pumping dubstep remix of Michael Jackson's "Beat It," prompting his friends to crowd the floor break-dancing. They all filmed each other. A waiter opened the door to the rooftop and the phones turned like periscopes toward the birthday cake collapsing under the weight of whipped cream. If anyone asked what they were doing here, they would say it was Alex's birthday. Might as well play the part. Alex was handsome, with high cheekbones and sharply groomed eyebrows. He cut a large chunk off the cake and handed it on a plate to Jalal, a short stocky guy with a warm smile strung out between two deep dimples. He poked his finger in the cake and wiped a trail of whipped cream on Alex's cheek, which he then licked clean. The next man in line did the same, but ignored the cheek and slipped his finger into Alex's mouth, then followed it with his tongue. The mood was electric, perhaps partly due to the risk they were running.

The rooftop was concealed from view yet more public than most of the men had ever been with each other.

It was Alex who invited them all here tonight. At twenty-eight, he was the oldest of the group. Because of social stigma and the fact that homosexual acts were illegal, though practiced, there was little community among gay men in Kabul, and Alex wanted to establish the first gay bar in the Afghan capital. This restaurant, where the waiters were also gay, was a perfect site, but he needed money and commitment from his friends. There were no regular nightclubs in Kabul, full stop, and in theory, opening a secret gay club would be easier than opening a club where women would come. The presence of women would be impossible to explain if the place was raided, but if they were only men, the cops wouldn't necessarily suspect anything. Yet, the dangers were immense. If law enforcement or neighbors were to find out that an establishment allowed homosexual activity and decided to mete out vigilante punishment, nobody would come to their rescue, particularly not the cops. Afghan parents exerted strict control, too. Your mother nagged you to get married. Your father spied on you to see if you hung out with girls before getting married. If they only knew. The whole group agreed it was a great idea and asked Alex to let them know when he was ready to open.

Alex hadn't always been a leader, or a social dissident. As a teenager, he never felt at ease. At twelve, when he still went by his birth name, Naqib, his parents had taken him and his four older brothers to Peshawar to escape the Taliban regime. He stood out among the darker-skinned Pakistanis with his delicate facial features. His long eyelashes were the envy of the girls. As a young teenager Naqib worked as a makeup artist in a women's beauty salon. Pakistani men were vain, and if you kept your thoughts to yourself, you were mostly left alone. Life in Afghanistan was more precarious. One of Naqib's friends, whose family returned to Afghanistan before his own did, was accosted by a group of men after a wedding. When he refused their advances, they drove him to the mountains of Paghman near

Kabul, where they raped him before killing him and disposing of his body.

After Naqib's parents took him and his brothers back to Afghanistan, he found work for a construction company at Bagram Air Base, where he got to know an American aid worker in his late twenties, nine years his senior. They fell in love. Naqib had known his desires were different from most other guys he knew, but he had no words to describe how. He learned to dance by watching beautiful Indian Bollywood actresses, but had always been tickled more by Brendan Fraser, the strapping lead in *The Mummy Returns*. The American contractor gave him a vocabulary and an entry to a new emotional life. After the American returned to his own country, Naqib took his name: Alex.

As he got older, Alex naturally made more gay friends. Most of them were plagued by shame and fear of God. Alex had no such religious qualms. He believed in God, and as a way of explaining the intolerance among his fellow Muslims, he said: "Islam is complete. It is Muslims who are not complete. We cannot control our own sexuality. It is in God's hands."

Being gay in a conservative Islamic society was a test from God. Alex had no hope that Afghanistan would ever become a safe place for him, but if he could endure, God would reward him in the end. And endure, he did. One evening when he was in his twenties, Alex was invited to a party in Kart-e Naw, an impoverished neighborhood in east Kabul. A friend had arranged transportation, and when the car arrived, the driver had brought a friend, both of them scruffy-looking and impolite. Hesitating for a moment, Alex got in the back seat with his friend, who assured him everything was fine. The mood in the car was uneasy. Suddenly, the car slowed down and the friend jumped out, leaving Alex alone. The car sped through the streets and Alex rolled down his window to call for help, but the passing motorcyclists ignored him. At a speed bump, the driver had to slow down. Alex kicked the door open and ran to a group of elderly men, shouting that he was being kidnapped. The men formed a protective ring around him, and he escaped unharmed. Weeks later, he was in danger again. Male dancers were often hired to dance at weddings, and after one he had been hired for wrapped up, a group of men offered him a ride home. Once in the car, they said they had another party to attend on the way. They took him to a large abandoned house on the highway toward Jalalabad, where they offered him drugs and alcohol. He pretended to get drunk. As they became increasingly intoxicated, some of the men left the room to make phone calls. Alex didn't know who was on the other end, which made him nervous. When they were all in the room, he asked to use the toilet. Outside, he didn't waste time looking for his shoes, then opened the gate and ran as fast as he could down the dark alleyway until he emerged into streetlights. In the taxi home, he saw that the soles of his feet were ripped and bloody.

Sex between men was not uncommon in Afghanistan, though romantic relationships were taboo. The practice of *bacha bazi* (meaning "boy play") had long roots in Afghanistan and referred to a custom of young, prepubescent "dancing" boys who performed for older men as part of the entertainment in social settings—because having female dancers would violate cultural norms for segregating the sexes. The custom would frequently involve sexual abuse of the boys who, dependent on the money to support their families, were kept as virtual child sex slaves. The Taliban banned the practice when they came to power in 1996, but after the collapse of their regime, *bacha bazi* again became common in certain areas of Afghanistan, especially among warlords and former commanders from the anti-Soviet insurgency who were now allied with the Western coalition. Powerful men preyed on poor families, whose boys were kidnapped, trafficked, and raped. Sexual abuse was so rampant among army commanders and warlords that some American and European military commanders told their soldiers not to intervene in order to maintain good relations with the security forces they relied on to fight the war. The prevalence of *bacha bazi*, which most Afghans found deeply repulsive, added to stigma around homosexuality because it was the best-known type of sexual relations between two males, when in fact, *bacha bazi* was an act of coercive sex as dominance, used by men in power who were often untouchable. It was seen as morally reprehensible, but it also fit into a prevailing image of predatory masculinity that these men had built reputations on.

The emancipation and protection of the rights of women was fundamental to Western aid programs, but the ideological impetus behind that fight did not extend to Afghanistan's gay and queer communities. Afghanistan's LGBTQ community got very little assistance from foreign donors. In private, Western diplomats said Afghanistan had bigger problems to deal with, and that even raising the issue of LGBTQ rights with the Afghan government could backfire. Many Afghans already viewed the West as morally depraved, and attaching the struggle for gay rights to a Western foreign policy agenda would only undermine, the argument went. Some countries went further. In 2017, the British government announced that rejected asylum seekers who were gay could be deported to Afghanistan. While acknowledging that homosexuality was illegal and "wholly taboo" in Afghanistan, the British Home Office said that "a practising gay man who, on return to Kabul, would not attract or seek to cause public outrage, would not face a real risk of persecution."

On June 12, 2016, around two a.m., a gunman ran amok at a gay nightclub in Orlando, Florida, called Pulse. Stalking partygoers and taking hostages in the bathroom, he killed forty-nine people. The shooter, Omar Mateen, was a twenty-nine-year-old American citizen of Afghan origin. During the carnage, he demanded that the United States stop bombing Syria and Iraq, and pledged allegiance to Islamic State. Evidence later suggested that Mateen likely did not pick Pulse because it was a gay club, and that targeting the LGBTQ community wasn't his motive. Yet, the attack deeply affected Alex. Whether or not Mateen was gay himself and closeted, as media reports in the days

following the attack suggested, Alex thought he saw in him the stigma
of growing up homosexual in an Afghan family.

"His family had discovered that he was gay, and to cover up what
he thought was a shameful act, he went and killed other gays," he the-
orized. Meanwhile, people around Alex praised the shooter.

"They were congratulating Mateen, and some said, 'The son of a
lion will always be a lion, regardless of where they are born,'" Alex said.

He eventually abandoned his plans of opening a gay nightclub. The
waiters at the restaurant got cold feet, his friends lost their nerve, and
he couldn't find investors. Gay life in Kabul was a series of complex logistical maneuvers. Still living at home, Alex had most of his financial
needs taken care of by his family and spent whatever money he made
dancing on himself.

"First of all, it's hard to have sex anywhere," he said. Conveniently,
his room at home was two floors above his parents, and with his
brothers all married and moved out, he could have guys over without
anyone suspecting they were more than friends. Away from home,
they would meet up in certain places on designated days. On Wednes-
days, they met at a specific shopping center; on Fridays, at an agreed-
upon park. They were largely self-taught in the ways of romance and
sex. Movie sellers in Kabul could burn you a CD or a USB with anything you wanted, if only you knew what to ask for.

"When you go to a movie shop, they ask what you want. When you
tell them 'Playboy movies,' they will understand what you're looking
for," Alex said. "I watched so many gay movies."

The invention of social media also made life easier for gay men.
Dating apps like Grindr or Scruff were mostly used by foreigners, but
there were ways to signal your preferences in a more public square
like Facebook. Attaching the word "over" or "under" in Persian to your
profile name indicated your sexual preference. Alex was facing mount-
ing family pressure. Now in his late twenties, the marital clock had
been ticking for years, and he was expected to find a suitable wife. His
parents were understanding when he told them he wasn't ready to pro-
pose to a woman, but it strained their patience when he even turned

down offers from women who approached him. Once, he rejected a girl's hand with the excuse that she was like a sister to him. Another girl, a nursing student who was part of his circle of friends, found his address and came to his house.

"I lost my mind when I first saw you," she said. Alex tried to be as respectful as possible.

"I'm not the person you expect me to be," he said.

"How?"

"I don't have feelings for the opposite sex."

"That's impossible," he remembered her replying. "Don't ruin your possibility of having a life with me." She refused to leave. It was improper to have a girl foist herself on you like this. Alex asked his sister to come up with an excuse, so she told the girl that her parents would come ask for her hand in marriage in a proper way. When they didn't, the girl started calling Alex every day, asking where his family was, until he broke his SIM card and asked his mother to tell the girl that he had gone on a trip to Pakistan. At last, she lost interest. He was sure his family didn't suspect that he was gay but just accepted that he for whatever reason wasn't ready for marriage.

"They don't understand why I keep avoiding marriage, because some of these girls are really beautiful, I have to admit," he said with a laugh.

As he grew into himself, Alex wanted to be the kind of teacher to others that the American had been to him. He was in several serious relationships with men who were much more unsure about their sexual orientation, often because of fear.

"I teach the ones I know who are gay but aren't aware of it. I help them realize who they are, what kind of feelings they have, and why they haven't been able to express themselves," he said.

He got "engaged" to a couple of them, meaning they exchanged rings and vowed to be monogamous. For a while, he was in a couple with a man named Arash who needed daily reassurances that they weren't sinning. For months, Arash stayed a virgin, even though he would follow Alex into his bedroom at home.

"People can love whoever they want to. But my religion doesn't accept gays. It's haram," Arash said. Alex looked at him forbearingly.

"He isn't very experienced," he explained, as if all Arash needed to do was give in to his desires. "He has only smelled the kebab, he has yet to taste it."

Inevitably, their relationship had to end. Arash's father was the founder of one of Afghanistan's largest companies, and the family's reputation was staked on his son's marriage. Eighteen months into their relationship, Arash's family married him off to an Afghan girl from a good, affluent family. Alex later heard they had moved to Europe.

Alex suffered a string of breakups that left cracks in his armor. One breakup in particular was tough. They were madly in love, but when his boyfriend's family discovered their relationship because he was careless, they swiftly arranged a marriage for him. Soon after, they migrated to France. Grief-stricken, Alex punished himself and slashed his arms with a knife.

"I wasn't really aware of what I was doing. It looks superficial now but the cuts were deep," he said, pointing to a red spider's web on his arms. He had a cut on his forehead from banging his head against the wall. A doctor prescribed antidepressants, which helped him sleep.

Yet things were slowly changing. By the late 2010s, even as the country was getting more dangerous, it was as if the air in the city was becoming slightly easier to breathe. The violence of the war was getting closer to Kabul, but nearly two decades after the Taliban had been toppled, more liberal attitudes were consolidating in the cities. It became a little easier for Alex to find like-minded people. He was gaining local fame as a dancer through social media videos and word of mouth. He taught private dance lessons out of a rented house in the neighborhood of Karte 3 and was often invited to dance at parties where people treated him respectfully. Some of the invites came from government officials. President Ashraf Ghani, who took office in 2014, was educated abroad and had spent many years in the US. He never voiced public support for the LGBTQ community—regardless of his personal views it would have been political suicide to do so—but his administration was friendlier than the previous one. High-ranking officials held gay parties and told Alex he shouldn't worry, since the president was quietly supportive. Alex hooked up with some of them, who would send cars to pick him up and take him to VIP rooms at upscale restaurants or hotels. They assured him that he would be safe, even as the Taliban advanced in the provinces and many of his friends started fleeing the country. The government would never fall, they said. Still, he worried about the Taliban toppling the government, in which case he would never be able to leave his house.

"How will I be able to live like I used to do? It would be like playing with fire."

PART III
THE UNDOING

12

HINTERLANDS

If Kabul was undergoing a small cultural revolution, in the countryside, things were moving at a much slower pace. Engineering modernization from the center of the country had always been difficult, and introducing liberal ideas on the back of an armed invasion didn't make it easier. Policies conceived in Kabul, whether by Western nations or the national government, were frequently out of touch with realities in the provinces. The disconnect between decision-makers and the marginalized, mostly rural population was a major reason why the Kabul government struggled to gain a decisive foothold in the provinces where it mattered the most: the Taliban's southern and eastern strongholds. Another reason was that rural communities didn't enjoy the same levels of development during the war, so they had less of a stake in the political project promoted in Kabul and Western capitals. The failure to build strong loyalties to the central government doomed the Western-led military campaign, even if foreign soldiers outnumbered the Taliban by about four to one during the surge that lasted from late 2009 through the fall of 2012. Nowhere was this more evident than in the embattled southern province of Helmand, for more than a decade the target of the country's most concentrated foreign military intervention.

By the spring of 2015, a few months after the international combat mission had officially wrapped up, driving through Helmand, one could sense an invisible front line moving. Foreign forces mostly operated out of larger bases now, training and assisting Afghan forces, or conducted clandestine counterterrorism missions under the auspices of the CIA. On the streets of Lashkar Gah, Helmand's administrative capital, footprints of the intervention were visible but fading. Fifteen years after the ouster of the Taliban, the ninety-mile stretch of highway from Kandahar to Lashkar Gah, intended to be the logistical spine of Afghanistan's economic revival, was so risky that anyone who could afford it flew.

A traveler flying into the southern province could look out of the window and see the Helmand River as it meandered through the jagged mountains of the north and flowed into the southern irrigated farmlands. In spring, the bright green fields stretched across the tan-colored plains, providing cover for the fighting insurgents. The clay walls that always surrounded private houses and farms looked like tiny rectangles on an ancient map. As the plane descended, the buildings took shape and passengers could make out children playing inside the walled-off compounds. The plane touched down at Bost Airport, built in 1957 and since 2001 renovated to the tune of $52 million, a cost shared by USAID and the UK's Department for International Development. In 2015, the airport handled only one civilian plane per day. There was no control tower, no luggage carousel. A porter transported the luggage in a motorized cart to the arrivals area, where he handed the bags to passengers over a barbed-wire fence. Outside the airport, a ten-year-old boy sold snacks out of a shipping container. The boy had one thing for sale: energy drinks. But seven types of them: Speed, Sting, Golden Power, Party, Ginseng, Carabao, and Best VIP. He noted his sales in a notebook using a nearly dried-out Red Cross pen. On the roof of the airport building, a young man watched the scorching heat flicker in the distance. He claimed to work for the Afghan intelligence service and bemoaned the departure of foreign troops.

"I prefer American girls," he told foreign visitors with a pensive

American drawl, leaving the impression that he had never met one. "They have the tightest pussies."

The English vernacular among young men who worked for foreign troops was peppered with similar macho, Anglo-Saxon jargon.

"I'm gonna go pump my guns," Abdul Rauf, a local journalist and former interpreter for the British, said when heading to the gym. He picked up more lurid slang, too. Once, at a dusty outpost in the war-torn district of Sangin, he had approached an English soldier crouched in the corner of the camp with his back turned.

"Are you okay?" Rauf asked.

"Mate, I'm wanking," the soldier snapped back. "Fuck off."

The paved streets of Lashkar Gah were busy with traffic. On the edge of a roundabout, a group of children dressed in pastel-colored shalwar kameezes stood straddling bicycles, handlebars adorned with glitter tape, waiting for a pause in the stream of cars. Spotting a hole, they dove headfirst into traffic like pelicans. Few places on earth had received as much foreign aid as Helmand. A perpetual stronghold of the Taliban, the province was the nexus of ill-planned international attempts to win Afghan hearts and minds through a combination of expensive economic incentives and military coercion. Other parts of the country that were also desperate for aid but did not have a significant Taliban presence got very little. Now, burqa-clad women crowded the pavement in front of the governor's office asking for handouts. Outside the city, schools and government buildings stood decrepit and mostly empty. In Gereshk, a large administrative building belonging to the education ministry looked like an entire civil war had unfolded inside. Every single window had been blown out. All the walls were riddled with holes. Charred pieces of paper were scattered across the floors. Opposite the destroyed building, the police headquarters had deteriorated nearly as much, without a shootout. The grimy hallways stank of urine and paint peeled off the walls. The police chief, whose office was sequestered behind massive steel doors, was mostly absent, according to the lonely cleaner who walked the hallways pushing a mop like a bartender after closing hours.

One didn't have to drive far outside Lashkar Gah before the lines of loyalty started shifting. A few miles beyond the city limits, traffic petered out and one was almost alone among fields of opium poppies. The drug industry turned the cogs of the Taliban war machine and fed the corruption that was eroding the government's legitimacy. Nowhere did poppies grow as proud and uninhibited as in Helmand, several feet tall, their bulbous heads nodding in the wind. It was April and almost harvest.

Down the road, with Afghan pop music blaring out the windows, a white Toyota Corolla approached the small town of Babaji at punishing speed. Riding shotgun was Mohammad Abdali, baby-faced counter-narcotics police chief of Helmand, assigned the Sisyphean task of choking the world's largest source of heroin in the most violent part of Afghanistan. His escort, a Toyota Hilux, carried four armed men in the back and struggled to keep up. At twenty-five, Abdali had risen fast. Part of a new Western-trained military class, his five-o'clock shadow that half obscured his chin dimple, and Oakley shades under a tuft of gelled curls, made him look the part. The poppy fields of Helmand were not where he wanted to be, but his father, an elder of an influential Pashtun family, had a short audience with President Karzai when Abdali was sixteen, and took his son. Abdali wanted to go abroad to study, his father told the president, who replied that the nation needed its young men to rebuild it. Abdali stayed and enrolled in the police academy, which wasn't a completely alien idea to him. As a child he had watched Bollywood movies about honest, hardworking policemen. After the 2001 invasion, Afghan and foreign police officers patrolled the streets of his home city of Kandahar, bringing a sense of peace by catching thieves and deterring criminals. But after graduation, he immediately found out that police life was not what he'd expected. Rather than creating safety, he knew he was actively stoking unrest.

In Babaji, seven miles north of Lashkar Gah, the spring sun was pleasant, and blooming poppy fields stretched all the way to the mud villages on the edge of the highway. Babaji used to be one of the most

dangerous Taliban strongholds in all of Helmand. In 2009, hundreds
of British troops were airlifted into the area as part of what the British
defense ministry described as one of the largest air operations of modern times, Operation Panther's Claw. They managed to secure the area,
but the insurgents could still intimidate residents into boycotting that
year's elections. Only 150 of Babaji's estimated 80,000 residents came
out to vote. Now, Babaji was safer, even as the situation in much of
Helmand was worsening.

"Before, we couldn't even go here with twenty Humvees," Abdali
said as the cars pulled onto a dirt road where a group of villagers had
gathered around a field of about four acres. The white and pink poppies reached to the men's elbows, their bulbs the size of golf balls.
The farmer would normally have begun his harvest around now. He
would have gone out in the afternoon, cupped his hand around the
bulbs, and lanced them with a sharp knife, making a fine diagonal
cut in the poppy head. Overnight, sticky resin would have oozed from
the bulb and thickened like caramel. In the morning, farmers would
have scraped the sticky sap with a large blade into cans around their
neck, before repeating the task three or four times until the bulbs
were empty. The opium would then be sold in markets in areas of Helmand under Taliban control, from where it would be sent to Pakistan
or driven to one of the four hundred to five hundred clandestine labs
in the southern Afghan wilderness. Smugglers transported the drugs
south, through the lawless Balochistan province, to Iran or Pakistan
and then on to Europe, the Persian Gulf, or Africa. Similar processes
took place in northern Afghanistan, from where much of the opium
was shipped through Tajikistan to Russia.

If the harvest was good, a field that size could yield 150 pounds
of opium, at a price of about $50 a pound. That could be made into
about 15 pounds of heroin, which drug dealers would sell for $60 to
$150 a gram, depending on the destination and purity. On European
street markets, this field's harvest could have yielded roughly between
$400,000 and $1 million. Abdali's men got out of the truck with the
swagger of cavalry. The eyes of the villagers crouched in the shade

vacillated between mistrust and loathing. In the field, six tractors raced in circles, turning the crops into mulch. The drivers, faces obscured by sunglasses and scarves, raised their fists in greeting. They were Abdali's men: local workers hired on a meager salary to carry out orders from Kabul and fight America's war on Afghan drugs. Choosing which field would get crushed was arbitrary, often determined by a farmer's ability, or lack thereof, to pay off local law enforcement.

Abdali knew the resentment his work prompted in locals was damaging to the government, but he was following orders from the provincial governor. The Western coalition had long since given up on poppy eradication. In 2002 and 2003, a British poppy eradication program offered farmers $1,750 in compensation for each hectare of poppies destroyed, less than half of what they could have generated from harvesting and selling their crops. Eradication was often conducted in locations that received little development assistance, so farmers were left without alternative livelihoods. After recognizing its failure, the $34 million program was scrapped. In 2005, US members of Congress became concerned about Afghanistan's opium cultivation and its destabilizing impact and called for action.

The US embassy in Kabul issued the first US counter-narcotics strategy for Afghanistan, emphasizing crop eradication. The campaign never destroyed enough poppy crops to meaningfully dent the drug business. When eradication was at its highest in 2007, when roughly nineteen thousand hectares were destroyed, Afghan opium production was also at an all-time high. But the policy provided a boon for private companies. Until 2009, the security contractor DynCorp operated an eradication force funded by the State Department, eliminating poppy cultivation at nearly $74,000 per destroyed hectare. By comparison, when the Afghan government in 2015 embarked on a new national drug plan that again included eradication, the US government paid the provincial governor $250 per destroyed hectare. The plan emphasized that eradication should be accompanied by improvements in law enforcement, security, governance, and economic development, all of which suffered as the United States gradually disengaged from

Afghanistan. Successful or not, it was Abdali's job to make sure the eradication teams were safe. He wasn't blind to the futility of his work.

"Every year, farmers grow one hundred seven thousand hectares of opium in Helmand. Last year we eradicated eight hundred. This year, our goal is a thousand. What difference does it make?" he said. "The people are very poor and feel compelled to do these things," he said. "As long as we aren't able to control our border and prevent the drugs from being smuggled out, it doesn't do any good. It's nothing but a political signal."

Everyone seemed to think poppy eradication was a joke, except the farmers whose fields suffered.

"What can I do?" said Abdul Hadi, a farmer who had just watched Abdali's men destroy his crops. "I have children. Now I don't have a choice but to get them to beg, or maybe steal."

Abdali feared he was doing the Taliban's recruitment work for them. Because of the security situation in Helmand, his orders were to only eradicate poppy cultivation in government-controlled areas. Anything else was too dangerous. That put the farmers in a dilemma: support the Taliban and risk being arrested or killed by government forces, or support the government and risk losing their livelihood.

"We are turning the population against us. We should not be eradicating poppy in areas where people support us. We should do it in Taliban areas," Abdali said. A week later, one of his men would be killed by an IED in a field while on duty.

When the US-led coalition attacked Afghanistan in 2001, opium cultivation had nearly ceased after Taliban leader Mullah Omar, seeking international recognition for his government, had banned it as anti-Islamic the year before. Outlawing Afghanistan's most valuable crop was economic suicide for the Afghan state. Production immediately fell from nearly 90,000 hectares to about 8,000. The drop brought economic ruin, particularly to rural areas where tea shops, fuel stations, and other local businesses depended on the drug trafficking route for survival. Thousands of farmers and traders earned a stable income from the cultivation. The war allowed poppy cultivation to spring back to life. In 2017, poppy cultivation spread across a record-large area of 328,000 hectares, and not only in the south. Helmand alone, an area slightly smaller than the state of West Virginia, produced more narcotics than Colombia, Mexico, and Myanmar combined. The United States boosted the drug industry by partnering with dubious strongmen, corrupt governors, and law enforcement officials who had their hands deep in the business. One of them, Sher Mohammad Akhundzada, was an ally of President Karzai who was appointed governor of Helmand and whose late uncle had been one of the country's most powerful drug lords. In 2005, British soldiers seized nine tons of heroin and opium at his house. Akhundzada claimed he had confiscated the drugs from smugglers and was going to turn it over, but no one believed that. His arrest did nothing to stem the drug trade. Narcotics flowed freely across the border to Pakistan, which was impossible for Afghan government forces to seal. Foreign forces never tried.

The vast majority of the drugs that left Afghanistan, either as raw opium or as heroin produced in mobile labs, was transported through the desert of Nimruz province on the southwestern edge of Afghanistan, bordering Iran and Pakistan. Nimruz was a postapocalyptic wasteland straight out of *Mad Max*. Sandstorms kicked up without warning, swallowing the horizon in a thick beige mist. In storms, visibility was limited to fifteen feet ahead. Curtains of sand slid down car windows. Pickups raced across the plains, whipping up tails of dust, carrying policemen armed with AK-47 assault rifles and rocket launchers poking out from the truck like quills on a hedgehog. Behind them, a group of motorcyclists, their hair stiff with grit and their eyes hidden by goggles.

Nimruz was Afghanistan's rawest and most untamed province. At the same time, it was a microcosm of what went wrong in the Afghan war. The province's lawlessness was a testament to the Western-backed government's failure to assert authority and curtail rogue strongmen. As Afghanistan's drug-smuggling hub, it provided a financial artery for the Taliban, as well as a gateway for the growing number of Afghans fleeing economic destitution and violence.

The provincial capital Zaranj was home to about 160,000 permanent residents, its contours shaped by streams of passers-through
and torrents of money flowing from drug barons, arms dealers, and
human smugglers. Residents in hushed voices warned each other of
kidnappings. In the scorching daytime heat of summer, Zaranj was
comatose. In a roundabout, a young boy break-danced for change, but
nobody paid attention to him. The city came to life late in the evening when buses from Kabul and Herat arrived, throwing open their
doors to hundreds of bleary-eyed men spilling into decrepit, neon-
lit hotels carrying belongings in plastic bags or knockoff US military
backpacks. Most of the buses were German, relics of a bygone era.
There was some poetic justice in that they now helped migrants go
back toward Germany. Inside the hotels, clusters of migrants waited
often up to a week for a smuggler to call and tell them to get ready for
departure. Huddled around a few floor fans that pushed around stale
air, many of the men looked undernourished from drug habits picked
up on previous trips to Iran. Afghanistan produced more than 90 percent of the world's illicit opium, the majority of which was smuggled
through Nimruz. The industry left a trail of addiction from Helmand
to Nimruz and back to Kabul. After sunset, addicts congregated in
corners of the city to smoke opium, heroin, and crystal meth, all of
which could be purchased for less than a dollar a hit.

Nimruz had been one of Afghanistan's unruliest areas for centuries, partly because governments paid it little heed. In 2017, Kabul's
political representatives in the province were keeping up that tradition,
even as they lived in the center of Zaranj. For Haris Stanikzai, Nimruz
was not, as it was for migrants, a gateway to freedom. It was prison.
In his early twenties, the son of the provincial governor was officially
in Nimruz as an advisor to his father, who was often absent. The Stan-
ikzais were from Logar, near Kabul, and came here when Haris's father,
Mohammad Samiullah, was appointed governor in 2015. They were
outsiders, and due to the risk of kidnapping, Haris's father banned him
from leaving the secured compound alone. Haris's only friends in Nimruz were his bodyguards. With stubble and striking green eyes, Haris

exuded self-confidence, and the smell of an entire duty-free perfume shop. He was twitchy and struggled to keep himself busy. Young and rich, trapped in a much too grown-up world. A playboy in a desert without a woman in sight.

"Afghanistan is only good for senior citizens," he said. "They are totally respected in the house. They sit around doing nothing. Every family is a dictatorship."

It was a starry night, and he was sitting on the grass in the garden of the compound, picking at a plate of freshly barbecued lamb, which he washed down with a glass of whiskey mixed with lime-colored energy drink. He signaled to a bodyguard, who retreated into the darkness and reappeared a quarter of an hour later with another bottle of Jack Daniel's in a black plastic bag. Supplies flowed freely in this smugglers' den.

Haris's upbringing was relatively liberal for an Afghan family. His father forbade him from joining the army and said if Haris wanted to serve his country, he should study law. In school, Haris learned that Islam was superior to other religions, but a trip to India taught him that even people who worshipped differently were decent folks.

"Everyone believed in God so what's the problem?" he said. Afghanistan's greatest enemies were fundamentalism and closed mindsets.

"Islam is a good religion. It's a religion of peace. But it is in bad hands. If Europe was Muslim, the world would be a peaceful place. There, people are educated," he surmised.

Banned from leaving the grounds, he would give his rare visitors a tour of what he called his "zoo"—a large garden in the governor's compound.

"Look at those two beautiful goats!" he exclaimed and gesticulated at a small enclosure where two springboks were languishing in boredom. The price tag for flying the antelopes from Kabul was $6,000 a head, he said. He built the zoo to have company and something to do, and it was home also to various birds, including peacocks and parrots, but most of the animals had died in the heat that summer.

Haris's life was worlds apart from those of the impoverished migrants flocking to Nimruz, and he was disparaging of their reasons for leaving.

"No one cares about their country. Everyone thinks about their own benefit," he said, whiskey singing in his throat. "They are happy to go to Iran to do manual labor, to clean toilets, to be treated in a very bad way. But they won't stay in their own country to serve in the police and the army."

Haris did, however, share their lack of hope, and he was himself a prospective migrant. He had been engaged for seven years to a cousin who lived in Germany. He was madly in love, although they had only met a few times. After dinner, lounging on pillows with flowery perfume emanating from his crisp shalwar kameez, Haris puffed on a hookah and practiced a sincere but badly out-of-tune rendition of "My Heart Will Go On" to later sing for his fiancée over the phone.

When the governor left town, which he did often, Haris would rev the engine of his government-issued Land Cruiser and tear through the streets of Zaranj. One morning, giddy with excitement and for all intents and purposes the acting governor, he drove deep into the desert and fired his machine gun blindly into the sun while screaming to the heavens.

"I was feeling totally free," he reminisced, grinning.

If Nimruz was the port from which migrants set off into unknown terrain, Lashkar Gah was the shore that the bloodbath of the war lapped against. Helmand's provincial capital was home to the only hospital for war wounded in Helmand, run by the Italian NGO Emergency. Located near the banks of the river in a low-rise building, the hospital was an oasis of calm. Inside the concrete compound walls, patients rested on shaded benches in the neatly groomed garden, hobbling on crutches among pink and white roses. Staffed by dozens of Afghan medics, the hospital was run by a motley crew of southern Europeans in their thirties who looked like survivors of the anarchist left. One female nurse dyed her hair blue; another had a bull's ring pierced through her septum. The head nurse wore long sleeves so the tattoos covering every inch of his arms didn't offend his conservative Muslim patients. A few years earlier, an amateur tattoo artist visited the organization's headquarters in Kabul and inked ten of the staff members on the shoulder with the initials "RNR KBL"—rock 'n' roll Kabul. They were unwaveringly professional. They saved mine-blast victims from bleeding out with surgical precision, and gingerly nursed children who had lost limbs, tickling their necks until they giggled and teaching them to walk on crutches. Powered by batteries of espresso, they barely sat down until evening, when they would gather at a long table at their compound around bowls of pasta, like an extended Italian family.

"I take my coffee bitter like the present and black like the future," the organization's country director Luca Radaelli said.

During a round through the hospital, an Afghan nurse concluded, "Bullets are good." What he meant was: if you are admitted here with injuries from gunfire, you are lucky. Homemade mines pulverized limbs, not infrequently those of women and children. As the nurse entered the operating room, a police officer on the operating table closed his eyes as the anesthetics rinsed through him, arms stretched out as if crucified. A medic lifted the two metal pegs skewering what remained of his right leg to allow nurses to wash the bloody stump of skin and pink flesh. The bone had been snapped off so it exposed the marrow. Before an IED ripped off his leg, he made $150 a month. He was single, and when he woke up, his family would have to support him for the rest of his life.

Yet the most unsettling sights at the hospital were perhaps the subtler ones. Resting in a ward, twenty-four-year-old Habibullah, who was missing both legs after stepping on an IED, flashed a wide grin and a thumbs-up, but rambled incoherently and repeated that he was three years old. A couple of beds over, ten-year-old Abdullah was recovering from surgery after being hit by a mortar on his way to school. On the floor was a single sandal. He would not be needing a second one.

Emergency treated everyone, regardless of affiliation in the war, and enjoyed the protection of both the government and the Taliban.

Occasionally Taliban and government soldiers recuperating in the same wards got into shouting matches. Food fights broke out in the cafeteria between warring parties armed with bread and beans. The local community supported the hospital as well. After a particularly gruesome suicide attack in central Lashkar Gah, more than fifty civilians gathered outside the hospital offering to donate blood. Puzzled medical staff, who hadn't yet sent out a call for donations, asked how they knew they were needed.

"Facebook," they replied with one voice.

Emergency's entire Afghan operation, including three surgical centers, a maternity center, a series of medical outposts, and salaries, cost around $11.5 million per year, roughly the equivalent price tag of keeping six US soldiers in the country.

The Taliban were getting closer to Lashkar Gah. To the west of the city, it was largely up to about one hundred members of the Afghan Local Police in a village called Sayedabad (not to be confused with Omari's home district of the same name) to hold them off. If the militants took Sayedabad, little more than the open highway separated them from Lashkar Gah. Some of the men were hunkering down in a civilian house. A teenage police officer, Nowrooz Ali, had tied a piece of white cloth around his rifle, which he grinningly presented at any given opportunity. A Taliban flag. A few days earlier, he and three other policemen had snuck into the insurgent-occupied neighboring village in the dead of night and stolen it. It was a small victory in a war that was uncomfortably close.

"We never thought we were going to fight on the front line," another of the men said. As part of the local police, the men had received only twenty days of training by the British, primarily in searching houses, target practice, and a bit of first aid. They were never meant to man a front line. Local police units were not authorized to conduct offensive operations. They could only sit and wait and defend. Cannon fodder.

"It's very difficult to see from here who is a Talib," Habibullah, another policeman, said. "They wear big scarves that cover their weapons, and if I open fire without being sure, I might kill a civilian." It was the Taliban who determined when to fight. A month earlier, some of their colleagues had been caught out when the Taliban fired rockets against their base a few hundred yards away. When the police fled, insurgents who were hiding in the grass mowed them down one by one. Twelve were killed. The rest only survived by jumping off the roof of the base and fleeing.

Around dusk, a firefight broke out on the other side of the village. On a rooftop, a group of government soldiers discussed the direction of the incoming mortar fire. They fired back blindly. In between explosions, cicadas sang and dogs barked. The soldiers, soothing their impatience with cigarettes and buckets of green tea, were waiting for the Taliban to storm. They never did. Instead the radio crackled.

"It's the Taliban," a soldier said to his comrades.

The warring sides often killed time by tuning into each other's radio frequencies and shit-talking, like teenagers on a basketball court. An insurgent on the other end called the soldiers infidels.

"Surrender and fuck off," the voice said.

"You are the dogs of Pervez Musharraf," one of the soldiers shouted back. Using the former Pakistani president's name as a slur made him cackle.

Later that night, the dull thud of airstrikes could be heard in the distance, coming from Marjah. It was the sound of counterterrorism gone wrong. In 2010, Marjah had been the scene of the largest operation of the entire war, Operation Moshtarak. In 2017, the insurgents controlled 80 percent of Marjah. The thump of airstrikes was America trying to prevent them from taking the rest.

Local police units tended to get overrun, unless they got support from special forces, who were often summoned at the last minute. In 2017, these well-trained elite troops, numbering some thirty thousand and constantly dispatched around the country, made up 7 percent of the total number of security forces, but accounted for 70–80 percent of the fighting. In Chah-e Anjir, a hamlet north of Lashkar Gah, a unit of forty-four special forces had taken position in a civilian *qala*, a collection of houses surrounded by clay walls, supporting a group of fifty regular army soldiers. The Taliban were a couple of houses away. A young soldier wearing a Rambo-style bandana in the tricolors of the Afghan flag manned the gate. The commander of the unit, 1st Lt. Rohid Paykar, sat in the shade, leaning against a window frame, smoking a cigarette. Handsome and lean, with days-old stubble and dirt on his biceps, the twenty-five-year-old had just finished the first bout of fighting of the day. They had been there for a week, fighting about two hundred insurgents. It was a fairly straightforward task for Paykar and his well-trained men with sophisticated equipment. But soon, they would be dispatched to another front line, leaving the government soldiers on their own. The Taliban lived here and were going nowhere.

"The army soldiers don't have night vision. At night, when it's dark, they can't stand outside the base for even one minute," Paykar said. "If I wasn't here, the army and the police would flee immediately. I guarantee it."

Minutes later, the crackle of gunfire rang out over the base. Paykar directed his men to take position in three different corners of the *qala*. One soldier tossed hand grenades from the shade of a small grove, another climbed a rickety ladder to tilt the barrel of his M4 carbine over the edge of the wall. They were calm and experienced. The regular army soldiers swiftly pulled back to a narrow passage between two houses, from where they fired frantically into the air. It was a Hail Mary shootout, and their bullets were depleting fast. One of the soldiers screamed. A bullet had grazed his neck and ripped the skin. As he was patched up, a flash of madness in his eyes showed just how close a call it had been.

After the firefight, the soldiers concluded they had killed three Taliban fighters. How they reached that number wasn't clear, and the difficulty of assessing casualties illustrated how the government in Kabul was able to issue figures unchallenged, often downplaying its own losses and exaggerating those of the enemy. The units on the front line were severely understaffed. Officially, there were supposed to be twenty-five thousand government soldiers in Helmand. In reality, 40 percent of them didn't exist, according to confidential government documents. Ghost soldiers haunted the official statistics. Army officers boosted rank numbers to get more funding, or hid the actual number of casualties to downplay military failures, which meant their dead were never replaced. It was a betrayal of young men on the front, which cost lives.

"Our commanders said we were four hundred policemen at our base. In reality there was only a hundred and twenty of us," said a young policeman, Omar Shah, who had lost both his legs when insurgents snuck up on his vehicle, placed a bomb, and remotely detonated it. He said his commanders' exaggeration to Kabul of their troop numbers was the reason their base was overrun.

Helmand's civic space belonged almost entirely to men. Outside Lashkar Gah, even schoolgirls were rarely seen walking the streets. In town, women shopped in a specially designated bazaar. At the weekly livestock and farmers' market on the banks of the river, only men manned the stalls selling pyramids of watermelons or hot green tea. Bleating goats and sheep arrived at dawn. In the afternoon young men washed trucks for three dollars in the river. Fathers took their sons for a swim. On the opposite bank, the men might notice the outline of a few young women washing clothes in the river, but they were too far away to make out their faces.

And then there was Narges Rokhshani. A member of the provincial council, she was one of Helmand's most prominent women and human rights defenders. Raised in Iran, her parents returned to their homeland, Helmand, in 2004, imbued with more liberal ideas about women's role in society. Rokhshani began working as a teacher at a girls' school, and two years later, at the age of twenty, founded a girls' high school called Bibi Fatima Zahra. She didn't wear a burqa, but dressed in colorful long dresses and scarves.

"Women can do the same jobs as men. If a man can work, then so can a woman. Women make up half of the population, so we should have the right to work as well," she said. "Since we arrived here, I have done my best to change the social life of Helmand. But people here have different ideas than they do in Iran. They're different."

Years earlier, Rokhshani's car had been struck by an IED as she traveled between Lashkar Gah and Gereshk. She survived because her driver, aware of the risks of the journey, drove so fast that the bullet-proof vehicle didn't take the full impact of the explosion. Gruff-voiced men routinely called her with threats. Unknown gunmen shot at her family members in the street. She took note of the dangers inherent in her work rather drily.

"Of course, if you stick your neck out, you make enemies," she said. "The situation in Afghanistan is not favorable to women who want to work. The constitution and Islam give women the right to work, but it's a right that exists only on paper."

If the advancement of women's rights had moved at a glacial pace in places such as Helmand, they were already sliding backward. Rokhshani was grateful for foreign aid money, but by 2017, more than 150 schools had already closed due to threats and absence of funding. Those that had remained open offered such poor education that it almost didn't matter, she said.

Rokhshani's career was only possible because she had been willing to make radical choices. She had refused to get married, even into her early thirties when she by Afghan standards was considered a spinster. Few men would allow their wife to work, particularly in such a prominent position. For women in Helmand, political office seemed incompatible with marriage, so she avoided it. Her parents, a day laborer and a homemaker, supported her choice.

The terrorists never got to Narges Rokhshani. She finally married in 2018. A year later, she was about to give birth when something went terribly wrong. She died in May 2019, at Lashkar Gah's understaffed and underfinanced public hospital.

13

ZAHRA

When she was young, Zahra sought solace in other people's stories, but it had never occurred to her that anyone might find consolation in hers. In 2009, a friend told her there was a man she should meet. Hjalmar Jorge Joffre-Eichhorn was a German Bolivian activist and director who had recently cofounded an NGO with the goal of bringing reconciliation to Afghanistan through theater. He was interviewing candidates for a workshop he was organizing. Zahra's family had seen the US intervention as a hostile occupation, and she had never had a conversation with a Westerner before. She spoke no English, but agreed to meet Joffre-Eichhorn for tea in a leafy garden in central Kabul. Fast-talking and bald, with a chin strap of beard, the director explained through a translator how he and some colleagues for the past two years had been working underground in Kabul, collecting stories of war victims and replaying them through theater. His NGO, the Afghanistan Human Rights and Democracy Organization, or AHRDO, had just started doing things out in the open, and was organizing a workshop two weeks later. Joffre-Eichhorn found Zahra withdrawn at first, but charismatic. He asked if she'd like to join them. Zahra hesitated. She had never seen theater and wasn't convinced it was for her.

The director's presentation seemed alien to her. But when he called her
a couple of days later, he had made her curious enough that she agreed.

They met again in early October in the same garden, now furnished with a large open-sided tent. Dozens of men and women had
arrived to participate. The workshop was led by a Colombian actor. The
first couple of days had little to do with theater in a traditional sense.
The organizers had the participants play a game, such as tag, then
asked them how the game might be symbolic of concrete experiences
in their life. Some participants said it reminded them of fleeing Kabul
during the civil war. Zahra found it all rather silly. After two days,
Zahra approached Joffre-Eichhorn.

"These games, running around, screaming and yelling. Yes, we talk
about issues," she said. "But what is this?"

Joffre-Eichhorn had seen Zahra reluctantly engage but not fully
commit to sharing much about herself. He conceded that it was "a bit
of a strange method." He told her that if she wanted to leave, there
would be no hard feelings, but that it usually took a few days for the
method to click. He was right. After two more seven-hour days of ex-
ercises, he watched Zahra open up, telling other participants small
snippets of her life, laughing and crying. She carried an unspoken
darkness with her, but he also saw how charismatic she could be when
she let her guard down. She laughed often and humored him when he
attempted to tell jokes in halting Persian. Joffre-Eichhorn recognized
in her an ability to cope with tragedy with humor and a buoyancy that
inspired others.

Joffre-Eichhorn's method derived from a type of participatory
theater called "Theatre of the Oppressed," a movement started by the
Brazilian artist Augusto Boal during that country's military dictatorship in the 1970s. Inspired by Bertolt Brecht, Boal viewed theater as
a tool of social and political change, using nonprofessional actors.
Performances followed a protagonist going through hardship, and
featured a facilitator, a so-called joker, who would interrupt the play
and ask the audience to help the main character deal with a difficult
situation. The idea was to forge a collaboration between actors and

audience to find alternative storylines, and in turn inspire them, in
collaboration, to affect change in their actual communities. Dubbing
his method "rehearsal for revolution," Boal had clear political intentions. In Afghanistan, Joffre-Eichhorn focused on victims of war and
domestic abuse. The organization's work wasn't explicitly political,
but by challenging the male-dominated status quo, it indirectly challenged people in power. During the workshop, Joffre-Eichhorn noticed
a man who didn't seem to fit in. Sporting a thick mustache, he moved
around awkwardly and claimed, unlike the other participants, to be
an experienced actor. He drew attention from everyone and Joffre-
Eichhorn confronted him and asked if he was spying for the government. In the next tea break, he excused himself and didn't return.

At eight thirty in the morning of October 9, 2009, a passenger car
crept out of Kabul's rush hour and up to the perimeter of the Indian
embassy, three blocks from where the theater workshop was taking
place. Zahra had just made it inside the garden when the vehicle detonated a load of explosives in the middle of a road busy with traders
and pedestrians, sending small missiles of glass whizzing over the
garden wall. Seventeen people were killed outside, but inside the garden, miraculously, only a few people were slightly injured. The garden
fell silent. Some of the workshop participants cried inaudibly. The Colombian actor broke the silence, asking if anyone in the group had
anything to say. The conversations that followed broke the spell, and
the workshop continued, though some of the participants did not return the following day. The war was moving closer to Kabul, bombings
hitting the city with frequent intervals, and public gatherings were
fraught with danger.

Among the participants who never returned was the woman
meant to play the lead in the next performance. Joffre-Eichhorn asked
Zahra to step in. In her first public performance, in front of an audience of women at the offices of a German association, she played a
newly married bride who had been beaten by her husband, perform-
ing a monologue, sitting on a pile of firewood. She received a standing
ovation. Joffre-Eichhorn offered her three hundred dollars a month

to join the troupe permanently, more than she had ever made. She immediately quit her other jobs.

"Imagine! To get that kind of salary you usually needed a university degree and to be able to speak English. I had only finished twelfth grade, and I spoke no English," Zahra said. "They told me, 'It doesn't matter. You have other skills.' That was completely new for me."

Zahra was able to provide Parisa and Jawad with schoolbooks, clothing, and healthier food. After two years with the NGO, when the children were old enough to spend the night at a friend's house, Zahra began traveling around the country with other members of the organization to collect stories for plays. Because she didn't need permission from a male relative to travel, she could be relied on to go to Nangarhar, Kandahar, Mazar-e Sharif, and Bamiyan. She received directions from Joffre-Eichhorn on how to collect stories that would be acted back to audiences as a way of working through trauma. Sometimes, they performed at gatherings of women who were asked to use the plays as inspiration to pressure local politicians to pass legislation that better protected their rights. Zahra found a new interest in law, poring for hours over reports and legal documents as part of her own investigation into why so many women suffered domestic violence. It was a therapeutic form of self-study, and a crash course in women's rights.

"I learned to ask 'Why?'" she said. "It helped me a lot." The trips outside Kabul gave her perspective on her own situation.

"I met a woman in Nangarhar who hadn't left her home since she got married, except to go to her father's house. Even then, she was only allowed to go there after dark so nobody would see her. By comparison, I was very fortunate," she said. "I saw so many new provinces for the first time. That was more valuable to me than a university degree."

She met women who had never met a non-Pashtun woman, and had to speak through a translator.

"The women asked me how I had the courage to travel there. I said, 'Girls, it's not like you're zombies, you are not going to hurt me,'" Zahra laughed. She heard stories of war, and met parents who had been forced to watch as the Taliban tied up their son and stabbed him to death. "It took a month before I could get their story out of my mind. It kept returning in my nightmares."

As a teenager, Zahra had steeled herself against abuse by taking control of her emotions. The stories of fellow Afghans left her raw and exposed. Her smile was easy, but she also found herself constantly pushed to tears. She initially thought there might be something wrong with her but came to see her tears as a sign of health, that she hadn't become numb.

"I think that if you're not distressed by everything that's happening in Afghanistan, you have a problem," she said.

Over six years, Zahra helped put on nearly fifty performances in five provinces, reaching nearly five thousand women. Joffre-Eichhorn said the role seemed like second nature for her. He saw her facilitate a session at a girls' high school in Kabul for about two hundred students clamoring to be part of the workshop. Zahra was calm, thought quickly, and directed the girls as if she were conducting an orchestra.

As she took on more responsibility, Zahra's salary rose to seven hundred dollars a month, about four times that of a young soldier on the front line. She was now part of a growing, Western-funded middle class whose presumed loyalty to the new political order was meant to bolster the country against a Taliban resurgence. She moved out of her small apartment and took a three-month lease for a house in Qala-e Fatullah, a more affluent, central neighborhood. Her new landlord, an elderly truck driver, lived with his family in the adjacent building in the same compound. Living alone as a divorced mother was still widely seen as shameful, so Zahra told him that her husband worked in Iran and occasionally returned to Afghanistan to visit her and the children. The landlord spent a lot of time on the road and Zahra rarely saw him. After a month, he started spending more time around the house. Zahra felt his gaze when she entered and exited the compound. One evening, he invited her for dinner with his family. During the meal, every time she caught his eye, she saw him staring at her in a way that made her shudder. Weeks later, the landlord invited her over again. This time she turned him down. She suspected he might have caught on to the fact that there was no husband. Or perhaps he didn't care.

One evening around midnight, she was about to go to sleep on the floor between Parisa and Jawad when she heard a knock on the window. The room was lit by candlelight, from ten p.m. when the electricity cut off. A man's silhouette loomed outside the window. She recognized the landlord's long beard, then his voice, addressing Zahra according to the polite custom.

"The mother of Jawad, open the door," he said. "I can't stand it any longer, I must have you. Just for ten minutes," he pleaded and continued to knock on the door. The hinges, already loose, wouldn't sustain much force.

"For God's sake, open the door," he shouted.

Zahra wanted to call for help, but suspected the landlord's wife would then blame her for enticing the husband. She pulled the blanket tight around her face, pretending to be asleep. The landlord was loud and the neighbors would no doubt gossip about this in the morning. She heard him return four times to hammer on the door before he finally gave up. In the morning, Zahra called a girlfriend and told her Jawad had gotten into a fight with the landlord's children so they needed a new place to stay. She didn't tell her friend the whole truth, to avoid drama. The girlfriend asked her to hold on. Ten minutes later, she called and said she had found space for Zahra at a shelter for widows. Although Zahra wasn't a widow, they were willing to house her for a month. The next time the landlord's wife left the compound to buy groceries, Zahra went to him and said she was moving out. She handed him a month's rent plus ten dollars for the electricity bill. The family could fit all their belongings in a taxi, and less than an hour later, they arrived at the shelter. She settled in with seven other women who all worked outside the shelter to support three or four children each. Space was tight. They all shared one kitchen, but also a kinship. While she was there, she found a room in Dasht-e Barchi, her old neighborhood, in a flat owned by a woman living alone, whose husband worked in Iran. Once her month at the shelter had come to an end, no one asked her for payment.

In 2011, Joffre-Eichhorn came to Zahra with his biggest plan yet. Along with the NGO's cofounder, an Afghan activist named Hadi Marifat, he had written an hour-long script based on ten war victims' stories. He wanted to perform the play in different parts of Afghanistan, and he wanted Zahra to play the lead. Her role was to sit toward the back of the stage in front of a wood-fired oven while other actors enacted their stories. Holding a stack of photographs depicting people killed in the war, she would count, slow and steady—"One, two, three"—while feeding one photograph after another into the oven in a rhythmic death chant. Zahra agreed, and based her performance on a homeless woman she had seen walking the streets of Kabul, out of her mind with grief, looking for her sons who had died in the war. At the end of the play, the three protagonists killed each other over ethnic disputes. Zahra, wearing a green dress and a bloodred scarf, got on her feet. As she approached the front of the stage, it became clear that she was pregnant. Wailing with grief over her dead compatriots, she walked around as if roaming the streets of Kabul like the homeless mother, saying that she was going to kill herself and her unborn child, who didn't deserve to be born into such a cruel world. In the final moments of the play, she had a change of heart, leaving the audience with a sliver of hope. They performed the play a dozen times. Every time, some members of the audience cried.

"It was haunting," Joffre-Eichhorn said. Later that year, AHRDO secured visas for the performers to take the play, called *Infinite Incompleteness*, to the United States. In November 2011, they performed in Washington, DC, and in New York at the Helen Mills Theater. Zahra got standing ovations.

"Sometimes people deserve to be stars," Joffre-Eichhorn said. "And she was a fucking star."

Spring came, and in the countryside grasses and herbs were flowering. After a relatively quiet winter, the blooming vegetation allowed the insurgency to regroup and fight. President Obama had pledged that this would be the final chapter of America's war in Afghanistan, but in 2012, the war looked endless. As foreign soldiers were packing up ahead of a planned end to the international combat mission in 2014, boarding Chinooks out of embattled provinces back to Kabul, they could see violence rising in their trail. The Taliban advance was already devouring many of the hard-won gains foreign and Afghan soldiers had fought and died for. In Kabul, emboldened insurgents openly threatened organizations they saw as serving a Western agenda, including AHRDO. Adela Mohseni, Zahra's activist friend, encouraged her to travel to India to seek asylum. From there she might be able to resettle in Europe or the United States. Zahra, wanting to keep Parisa and Jawad safe, took the advice. Joffre-Eichhorn helped her raise money for plane tickets and the first few months' rent in India, and they flew to New Delhi. With her life story and the threats against the NGO, she received asylum in less than two months. Adjusting to Indian culture was easy but life in Delhi was unpleasant, with no end in sight. The UN's refugee agency told her that resettlement to Europe would take between three to five years, during which she would not be allowed to work in India. Sitting idle, she felt the depression of her past creeping up on her. In Kabul she had been able to distract her thoughts with meaningful work, but here she didn't know the language and had no friends. If India, a neighboring country, was this tough, she couldn't imagine how difficult life in Europe would be. After a few months, she returned to Afghanistan. The next summer she was invited to accompany Joffre-Eichhorn and Marifat to Utrecht in the Netherlands for a conference. It was her first visit to Europe, and she arrived on the first sunny day after a period of gray weather. She watched the Dutch flooding the streets, faces turned toward the sky.

"It was as if they had never seen sunshine before," she laughed. She met actors from across the world, including Palestinians and Israelis doing theater together. Some of them encouraged her to stay in the Netherlands and apply for asylum. Afghanistan was only getting more dangerous. But Zahra had made up her mind. She had spent the first two decades of her life outside Afghanistan, and that was enough.

"Afghanistan is my mother. She is wounded, but she took me under her wing," she said.

Besides, Parisa and Jawad were back in Kabul, and she couldn't leave them behind or have them travel overland to Europe on their own. In Afghanistan, at least they could go to school. She no longer feared the wrath of Hussein or his family. She had built a network of friends she dared to rely on and confide in. After she returned to Kabul, she started reading again for the first time since her marriage had extinguished her childhood thirst for literature. Wandering Kabul's dusty streets, she sought out secondhand bookshops to find her old passions Victor Hugo and Benazir Bhutto. She picked up memoirs and poetry. One day, her brain brimming with other people's stories, she sat down to write her own.

14

SAIF

In the back seat, Saif blinked the sleep from his eyes and opened them to see
the martyr with eyes the size of car wheels staring down at him.
He had been asleep since they crossed the border but woke up when the
car entered Karbala. Portraits of Abulfazl Abbas stretched across entire facades of buildings. For all his ten years of life, Saif had heard
stories of Abbas and Hussein, descendants of the holy Prophet Mohammad, who were slaughtered mercilessly with their families in the
desert of Karbala 1,300 years ago. Now, he was only a few miles from
the mosque where the family was buried. Saif felt his senses sharpen.
It was 2003, and Saif's parents were returning to Afghanistan after
twenty-five years in Iran, using the opportunity to detour to the sites
in Iraq that for Shia Muslims, like his family, are among the holiest
in the world.

In Karbala, two mosques on opposite sides of a square commemorate Imam Hussein, grandson of the Prophet Mohammad, and his half
brother Abbas. Among throngs of pilgrims lumped together in an an-
archic act of worship, the air was punchy with the sweet scent of rose
water. A rhythmic sobbing escaped from the doors of the mosques.
The pilgrims cried for Imam Hussein, considered by Shias to be part

of the rightful lineage from the Prophet Mohammad. To Shias, Hussein is a symbol of resistance against tyranny and injustice. In AD 680, Hussein was traveling with a band of followers and family members through the desert toward Damascus to usurp the formal ruler of the Muslim world, Caliph Yazid, a risky endeavor he undertook after people in the town of Kufa, south of Baghdad, assured him that they would join him. But when the caliph's soldiers intercepted the group in the desert, the people of Kufa did not come to the rescue. For a week, the soldiers surrounded Hussein and his family, cutting off their access to water. They killed first Hussein's half brother Abbas, when he rode on horseback to collect water, then attacked Hussein's family, including the women and children. By sunrise Hussein was dead, his head mounted on a pike to be carried to Damascus and paraded in front of the caliph.

The story has for centuries drawn Shiite pilgrims to Karbala, where Hussein perished. Inside one of the mosques, pilgrims shuffled in an impenetrable mass around a mausoleum. Saif surrendered to the crowd and allowed himself to be swept along by the gently swaying stream of men, who slowly carried him toward the silver cage in the middle of the room where Hussein's earthly remains are believed to be buried. Mosque servants sprayed the room with rose water and Saif, overwhelmed, started to cry. He felt his father's strong hands on his shoulder, and the presence of his four brothers somewhere in the crowd. When they finally reached the mausoleum, they placed their hands and a kiss on its silver bars. Together, father and sons, they cried for Hussein.

After two weeks in Karbala, Saif's family packed up and continued toward Kabul. Saif's parents were both from the mountain town of Bamiyan and neither of them had ever been to the capital. But times were changing and the Western military coalition had brought money, and something even rarer: a sliver of hope of a brighter future. Saif sat on the roof of the bus, among brothers and luggage. They rested in hotels without electricity, sleeping on the floor. After four days, the family reached Kabul. They settled among fellow Hazaras in Dasht-e Barchi. Kabul was an assault on the senses after the spiritual cleansing of Karbala. Any trace of the soothing smell of rose water was erased; the harsh reek of burnt plastic and feces from open sewers ambushed Saif's nostrils. Yet somehow Afghanistan felt like home, and the family had arrived.

With money they had saved in Iran, they bought a small plot of land and built their own home. They faced discrimination. Iranians had called Saif and his brothers "Afe," a colloquial slur for Afghans that was used to connote anything poor and dirty. In Afghanistan, people called the boys "Zawarat," a demeaning term for those who had spent the tough years under the Taliban in the safety of exile. Generally, though, Saif's family found religious freedom. After 2001, President Hamid Karzai held up ethnic diversity as a strength for the nation and called on Afghans in the diaspora to return home to rebuild their country. And they did. Having grown up working in the brick kilns of Tehran, the brothers were used to manual labor and toiled every day to keep poverty at bay. Saif and his brother Safa worked as painters, balancing fearlessly on rickety scaffolding as they splashed various shades of pastel across walls, and climbing shaky ladders to decorate intricately carved ceilings.

When Saif was fifteen, his mother passed away from illness. Two of Saif's three brothers had married and left the house, and he had no sisters. Immediately after his mother died, with no one to do the grocery shopping, to cook and clean, to do the laundry and put out fresh clothes for the men, the home began to unravel. After eight months, his father shook him awake one morning.

"Come with me. You're getting married today," he said.

At sixteen, Saif had dreamed of finding love and marrying a woman of his own choice. Before the end of the day, he had met his future wife—a cousin named Asal. They married two days later. She stood next to her mother among a small group of family members. Had Saif's mother been alive, she would have been there as well, to lead her son into married life and adulthood. Instead, he stood there, bereft of any female family members, and felt crushingly alone and robbed of his future. He fought back tears.

"The only words my wife and I exchanged that day were 'Hello' and 'How are you?' I was so young and knew nothing about life," he said.

In 2011, when he turned eighteen, Saif joined the army. The Taliban were growing stronger, and President Obama's troop surge was underway. Saif wanted to serve his nation. The government was encouraging men from the Hazara minority to join the armed forces, and after a short training period with the army's 133rd Battalion, he was dispatched to Nuristan, a remote mountain province bordering Pakistan. The unit he joined was exhausted and struggled to contain the Taliban fighters in the area. Their M4 carbines, hand-me-downs the Soviets had left in the 1980s, were worn out and jammed constantly. The local Taliban knew the area far better than the soldiers who came from various other parts of the country. From their hideouts in the mountains, the insurgents ambushed government soldiers who were too busy staying alive to ever gain any terrain. Saif's unit developed a network of informants among shepherds and children, who warned them about Taliban positions. On a September day in 2011, they were on patrol on the edge of a forest below the mountains. By a bridge, a group of boys caught their attention. They pointed toward two men underneath another bridge, whom they said were drug addicts. Saif and the soldiers could tell the men weren't smoking. Four soldiers from the group split up and, instead of crossing the bridge as planned, snuck up on the men.

"Don't move," Saif shouted. The two men reached for their guns, but one of the soldiers kicked their weapons away. The men had been digging mines into the sand. The soldiers crossed the bridge several times a day, and if the boys hadn't warned them, someone would likely have been killed or badly injured. Weeks earlier, Saif's unit had caught a Taliban commander but had seen him released after a few days. The only reason for his release, as far as Saif could tell, was bribery.

"Money can melt even a rock," Saif said. "The enemy has infiltrated everything, from the president down to lowest-level soldier. Corruption is like a wound that never heals. Sometimes it bleeds here, the next minute it bleeds there." He was not going to let these insurgents get away.

After a kicking, the soldiers blindfolded the Taliban fighters and tied their hands behind their backs, then led them into the mountains. When they were out of earshot from any village or army checkpoint, Saif shouted at the insurgents: "When we join the army, we put our hand on the Quran and swear to never betray our country, that we'll defend our soil with honesty and dignity!"

"Are you Hazara?" one of the Taliban fighters responded. They recognized his accent.

"Yes, I am Hazara, and this is my country to fight for as well," Saif replied angrily, knowing that many Taliban resented Shias like him. "When the Russians came, did the Hazaras not wage jihad against them? Did we not fight them even with our shovels?"

The other Taliban interrupted him and accused soldiers of being lackeys for foreign powers.

"Us?" Saif thought. "You are the ones being paid by Pakistan to kill your fellow Afghans." He tightened his grip around his rifle. He had attached a knife to the mouth of the gun, like a bayonet, and pointed it at one of the young insurgents. A month earlier, the Taliban had stormed an army checkpoint and killed thirteen soldiers, some of whom were said to have been found with their decapitated heads placed on their chests. Now these two Taliban had the nerve to claim that Saif wasn't a true Muslim. He took a step toward the fighter who had first mocked him for being Hazara. He jabbed the knife as hard as he could into the fighter's stomach. The Talib jerked, and as he doubled over, Saif stabbed him four more times. The other soldiers followed and started beating the other Talib with the butts of their guns until both men lay lifeless on the ground. They carried the bodies up into the hills.

"We threw them in the mountains for the dogs to eat," Saif said.

Back at the base, one of the soldiers in the group, perhaps burdened by guilt, told a commander about the incident. When they located the bodies in the mountains, Saif and three fellow soldiers were arrested. Saif was strung up to the ceiling with a rope. One of his interrogators grabbed a stick.

"So, you hazaragi want to kill some Taliban?" he said as he thrashed Saif's calves and arms. Saif and his three friends, who were also being interrogated, claimed they had killed the Taliban fighters in self-defense. Had they wanted to execute them, they said, they would have simply shot them. The army interrogators didn't buy it. They kept the soldiers on the base for two weeks, and afterward sent them to Pol-e Charkhi, a large prison on the outskirts of Kabul. After languishing for two months awaiting trial, Saif was sentenced to six years in prison for murder. He was furious. When he signed up for the army, he swore to risk his life in the fight against the Taliban. But when he rid the world of two of the miscreants, he was punished.

"Tell me, if you were a soldier fighting for your country, facing an enemy who decapitated your friends, and you knew your corrupt government would set the enemy free if it had the chance, what would you do if you caught one of them?" Saif said.

In the Afghan legal system, a case had to pass through three different courts before it was finalized. Six months after his initial judgment, Saif had to face trial in the second court. He had heard of a high-ranking general who was also Hazara, who had been appointed to a prominent position in Kabul. Through relatives, Saif knew the general's bodyguard, a man named Black Mohammad, who agreed to ask the general for a favor. In the second court, Saif was acquitted. He never returned to Nuristan. His faith in the new government had vaporized. The new Western-backed government, the Taliban, they were all traitors. After Saif returned home, he folded up his uniform, kissed it, and placed it in the bottom of his cupboard. He promised himself to always serve his country but never this government.

After the army, Saif would go back to Iran regularly to work at construction sites, scraping together enough money to support Asal and his father. In 2014, he heard stories about the martyrs. Afghan migrant workers in Tehran spoke of a group of twenty-five of their countrymen who had gone to Syria to fight against Islamic State, or ISIS. Twenty-one had been killed in the fight. After a popular uprising in Syria had morphed into a civil war three years earlier, ISIS had used the opportunity to conquer large swaths of territory across that country and Iraq, killing and torturing civilians. The group adhered to an extremist version of Sunni Islam and targeted Shias as much as Christians, pillaging and vandalizing holy Shia sites. They threatened the rule of Bashar al-Assad, a long-term strategic ally of Iran, which intervened to prop up his rule. Assad's grip on power in Damascus allowed Tehran a beachhead in the Arab world near the border with its archenemy Israel. The war drew in regional and global actors and pitted state-sponsored militias, terrorist groups, and secular separatists against each other. Defectors from the Syrian army formed Islamist factions supported by Gulf states. Extremist jihadist groups allied with al-Qaeda also took advantage of the chaos. In the northeast, the United States supported Kurdish groups opposed to both Assad and ISIS.

From the beginning, Assad found support from Iran—and, from 2015, Russia—and Tehran's web of Arab Shia militias. The most powerful was Hezbollah, a Lebanese paramilitary group formed in 1982. Hezbollah had since become Lebanon's most powerful political party and an Iranian insurance policy against an Israeli attack: if Israel bombed Iran, Hezbollah missiles could strike Tel Aviv. Iran now replicated the model in Syria, recruiting fighters from countries in the region to fight for Assad's regime in groups formed, funded, and trained by Iran's Islamic Revolutionary Guard Corps. Iran cast itself as a champion of the world's Muslims, Shias in particular, and used ISIS's attacks on holy shrines and mosques, in combination with cash payments, as a way to draw fighters to Syria. Afghans formed the biggest of the militias, the Fatemiyoun Brigade, estimated to number from several thousand, according to some Western analysts, to twenty thousand, according to Iranian media.

Saif didn't care for geopolitics or Bashar al-Assad, but Islamic State's vandalization of religious antiquities made him angry. The extremists threatened sites such as the Sayyidah Zaynab Mosque in Damascus, believed by Shias to house the grave of a granddaughter of the Prophet Mohammad. Saif had never shaken the humiliation he felt in the Afghan army. Not long ago, his brother Safa had been killed in Helmand fighting for the Afghan army, after stepping on a mine while carrying injured comrades. Saif lined up outside the Ministry of Martyrs and Disabled Affairs to receive state compensation. Day after day, he queued for hours, while he saw relatives of Pashtun soldiers walk past him and promptly receive financial compensation. Even pleading for a modest benefit after his brother had made the ultimate sacrifice, Saif believed he faced discrimination.

Iran might treat him like a second-class citizen, but it respected and protected his religion. He had first come into contact with Iran's Revolutionary Guard when he was nine years old. Outside the local mosque in the Tehran neighborhood where his family lived, a group of youth volunteers invited him to Quran lessons. The volunteers were the first Iranians Saif met who treated Afghan and Iranian children equally. They were the Basij, a paramilitary group under the Revolutionary Guard, known mostly in the West for harassing young women for wearing clothes they deemed immodest and beating up protesters in the streets of Tehran. The Basij also arranged religious ceremonies, made propaganda, and organized community activities. In the Basij school Saif attended, the teachers didn't beat you—unlike his other teachers—as long as you tried. Saif found their religious morals incorruptible.

"If you offered them a house full of gold for eating even the smallest piece of opium, they wouldn't do it," he said.

The Basij didn't accept Afghans as members, but Saif stayed in touch with some of the volunteers while in Afghanistan. He supported them in spirit when they beat pro-democracy protesters, such as members of the 2009 Green Movement, because he believed the Iranian regime's claims that the uprising was sponsored by Western powers. To Saif, the Basij represented the true path. The Basij had provided teenage suicide warriors to fight Iraq in the 1980s, and now they were at war again.

In July 2015, Saif stood at a central bus station in Tehran, carrying a small backpack. The summer heat beat down on him. At twenty-two, Saif had the dark, leathery complexion of the Afghan working class, testament to hundreds of hours of outdoor labor. Had it not been for his faint wisp of a mustache, he could have been mistaken for a man in his thirties. He had packed light. He had told Asal and his family that he was going to Sweden to look for work, but he had different plans. Going to Europe felt cowardly. He had no children and nothing to show for his twenty-two years on earth. The load of his backpack seemed light, like his life, weighed and found wanting. He turned around, turned off his phone, and walked toward the Revolutionary Guard's recruitment office.

The Revolutionary Guard accepted his request to join the Fatemiyoun, few questions asked, and sent him to a training camp in Qarchak, south of Tehran. During four weeks of training, his target practice with a Kalashnikov was so good that his officers agreed to let him handle the larger M249 machine gun and rocket launchers. Having completed his training, before he left Tehran he visited Jamkaran, a village where legend said the Twelfth Imam, a Messiah-like figure who went into occultation and will reappear at the end of days, had shown himself centuries earlier. By the mosque, visitors threw notes of paper expressing their deepest wishes into a well. Saif wished for a safe return from Syria. He strived for martyrdom, but knew that he was needed in this life, too.

He was flown on a government-owned passenger plane to Damascus. When he arrived, he called Asal and his father and told them where he was. It was important to Saif to get their blessing before he started fighting. Asal approved, partly persuaded by the five hundred dollars he would be making per month.

Saif's first week in Damascus passed peacefully. The Syrian capital was calm, and he visited the blue-tiled Sayyidah Zaynab Mosque, which he had dreamed about seeing for years. When the time came to go to war, his commanders, much to his surprise, did not task him with guarding the shrine, but sent him to Aleppo in the north, where

Islamic State and various offshoots of al-Qaeda were stronger, but where there were fewer Shiite holy sites. This was not what Saif had hoped for, but he committed to being a good soldier.

Saif viewed his place in the world as an extension of the seventh-century massacre of Imam Hussein and his family in the desert of Karbala. They were slaughtered as martyrs, and Saif drew moral guidance from that battle like Christians did from the crucifixion of Jesus, or Palestinians did from the Nakba. It was his Holocaust, his 9/11, a tragedy never to be repeated. He had traveled to Syria to defend the holy shrine, but what good were the holy sites if all Shias were exterminated? So Saif went to Aleppo, and he fought in the villages, and he found direction and weight in his life. The phlegmatic, skinny day laborer turned into a warrior.

In between deployments, Saif traveled back to Kabul. He found it hard to establish a life while waiting to go back to war. God had yet to gift Asal and him a child, and the first couple of years of their relationship had been tainted by Saif's anger against his father for marrying him off against his will. With age, their marriage improved. They traveled to Bamiyan to see the caves where the famous Buddhas used to be before the Taliban blew them up in 2001. They pedaled a swan-shaped boat across the piercingly blue mountain lake of Band-e Amir before feasting on freshly barbecued kebabs. It was their happiest time together. But Syria was where he found meaning, a high that would linger for months after he returned. He sprayed the house with rose water bought in a gift shop in Damascus to make the memories last longer. Every Friday in Kabul he posted photos from the day's prayer at the mosque to Facebook and received cutting comments in return from Afghan militia fighters in Syria.

"Hey, you son of Shias, are you sitting at home watching football and eating melon, while we're out here crying blood and defending the shrine of Bibi Zaynab," one post read.

On battle deployments, his skin grew furrowed and he took on an authoritative confidence. While his younger brothers had their hair cut into modern pompadours, he wore his in a stiff, highly

unfashionable side sweep that seemed to preserve months of bat-
tlefront grease. Over meat skewers at the local kebab restaurant, he
treated anyone who would listen to long, fabulizing tales from the
front lines.

"I swear, we once saw the dead bodies of one thousand children
under the age of six, just like Imam Hussein's sons," he reminisced one
afternoon. Once, he said, his unit had chased after an enemy squad
when they suddenly saw a vision in the sky: a white horse carrying a
warrior, sword in hand and his face glowing like the sun. Factual accu-
racy was not his concern. He was trying to get symbolic points across,
and did so with the élan of a preacher as he showed his battle scars to a
dozen middle-aged men sipping green tea. He had been injured three
times. One bullet was still lodged in his thigh. He carried another as a
necklace. He assumed a similar evangelist role in Syria, where he had
risen quickly in the ranks to squad commander. When they wound
down for the night, he would use his phone to play for his men songs
by the Iranian religious singer Mahmoud Karimi, whose chanting
verses aired constantly on Iranian state radio.

"Boys!" he implored them. "We have been chosen to be here tonight, so cry your hearts out." He wrote his own poems that he recited
under the glow of the stars:

We will hold our heads low
Solve the impossibilities of the world
When they look back on history and see you
In the warmth of Bibi Zaynab
We are the nightmare that Daesh [Islamic State] see in their sleep
Like Alawi I will die
Like Murtazai I will die
For Zaynab's grave, I am the chosen one

Even the thought of Islamic State made Saif's blood boil. Many
of them, he imagined, were young men who had grown up in Europe, where they had spent their youth chasing women and drinking

alcohol. Now they were bored and had gone to Syria to fight innocent civilians. They deserved to die.

"My aim was to defend innocent Shias in Syria. Islamic State show no mercy. They kill children, old people, everybody," he said.

On a January day six months after he first arrived in Syria, Saif sat crouched behind a hill outside the Syrian village of Duwayr al-Zeytoun. His unit of forty-five men had done well, until now. They had moved steadily forward, advancing about four hundred yards since the morning. Not bad for an area that for a long time had been under the control of Islamic State. Now they were in trouble. Dressed in fatigues and helmet, Saif wore black kohl around his eyes and black finger-thick commando lines drawn across his cheeks. He had the name of Bibi Zaynab—the Prophet's granddaughter whose shrine he had come to defend—scribbled on his forehead. On his breast pocket, Saif had attached an embroidered patch depicting Abdul Ali Mazari, a legendary Hazara leader who fought the Soviet occupation in the 1980s and was later tortured and killed by the Taliban. His men called him Kaleh Kharab, meaning Broken Head, or more colloquially, the Crazy One. He would need to live up to that name now. The enemy had arrived out of nowhere. As the Fatemiyoun had advanced through the area, it had seemed nearly deserted, with the exception of a few Islamic State fighters who took potshots at them. As the afternoon waned, the Afghan militia fighters corralled to plan a night operation against the village. All of a sudden, enemy fighters surged toward them from all sides. It turned out they had dug tunnels underground, and now, as daylight had dimmed, they crawled out of the earth like roaches.

"They had an entire city underground," Saif said. There were too many of them. Saif's unit was surrounded. They had to retreat. Saif ran, zigzagging, bullets snapping at his feet, and dove behind a mound some fifty yards away. He received a call on the radio. His friend Sardar was left behind. They had to go back. Saif took three men with him. Every ten meters they had to take cover, but the shooting didn't let up. The man next to him, who was armed with a rocket launcher, took a bullet in the chest and was killed on the spot. Saif asked the two remaining guys, an Iranian and an Afghan, to stay behind and provide cover while he ran toward Sardar. He set off, and immediately a grenade exploded about thirty yards away and sent dust and rocks flying, leaving his face scratched. He turned around and saw two Islamic State fighters, bearded and wearing bandanas. They hadn't noticed him.

"For Bibi Zaynab!" he remembered screaming, firing his Kalashnikov blindly. The two fighters fell to the ground. Saif picked himself up. It felt like an eternity before he reached Sardar. His friend was alive, and together they ran toward their unit in a hail of bullets. One struck Saif in the leg, but he limped back, with Sardar several yards ahead of him. Behind a mound of sand, he reached into his backpack for the last of his homemade bombs and tossed them in the direction of the enemy. Under cover of the explosions, he ran to his unit, where an Iranian doctor patched him up and sedated him with painkillers. While the sun set, bleeding its orange light over the plains, the adrenaline seeped out of Saif and left him drained. The sound of Islamic State's artillery fire faded as the temperature dropped. The entire unit was about 250 men, armed with M249s, .50-caliber machine guns, and rocket launchers. They couldn't move.

"They were all around us, like the rind on a melon," Saif recounted. They held their ground for forty-eight hours until reinforcements arrived and helped them break the siege.

He returned home to Kabul with battle scars to show. For months at a time, he lived a chest-thumping warrior's life, followed by periods of being a stay-at-home husband. His family and close friends knew what he did in Syria, but he had to hide his activities from government intelligence agents who were wary of young Afghan men returning from a foreign war who could potentially be radicalized against their own state. Even his closest knew only what he told them—stories of valor, stripped of doubt or regret. Yet, his internal life was fraying. He had watched friends die. He had held a young man in his arms, his brain tissue visible through a crack in his skull, as he took his dying breath. Afghan men rarely discussed feelings that might arise from such experiences. Many people carried trauma but had no words for it. At home he kept himself together. He didn't fight with Asal or contradict his father. When he went to his mother's grave alone, he mourned loudly, sobbing, allowing the gates to the darker corners of his mind to open. He paced around the graveyard aimlessly, sometimes staying until four in the morning, while his mind played a movie on repeat: of friends dying, their eyes wild with fear; of Islamic State fighters surrounding them, chasing them; of the pop of his AK-47 and the silence as enemy bodies absorbed the bullets with the sound of sucking teeth. The projectiles disappeared into soft flesh as easily as the bayonet with which he had stabbed the Taliban fighter to death. Saif banged a rock against his forehead. Whether he was trying to chase the memories away or simply just feel something, he didn't know.

Saif always made sure to be home in Kabul on July 24. That was the day his mother had passed away, and his father would invite relatives to the house to read the Quran. If they read continuously from dawn, taking turns, they could get through the book before sundown. During the day, the guests were offered fruit, bread, and tea. That was all the family could afford. In the evening, everyone went to the mother's grave. After Safa was killed in Helmand, he was buried next to her.

On his mother's anniversary in 2016, over sixty relatives had gathered in their home. Around three in the afternoon, they were well under way in the Quran reading and preparing to head to the grave when they heard a massive explosion. A couple of miles away, thousands of Hazara citizens had gathered in a demonstration against what they saw as government discrimination, and a suicide bomber had walked into the crowd and detonated a backpack of explosives. Nearly a hundred people lost their lives, all civilians, making it one of the deadliest attacks of the entire war. The bombing was a watershed moment for a different reason, too. It was the first attack inside Kabul claimed by Islamic State. A new enemy had arrived in Afghanistan, and it had Hazaras in its sights. In the coming months, more Islamic State attacks would target Afghanistan Shiite communities. The new development put Saif in an uncomfortable dilemma. The enemy he had fought against for years in a foreign country had now reared its head close to home. He no longer had to cross borders to defend Shiites against the extremists; he could drive three hours to Nangarhar province, where Islamic State's regional affiliate, Islamic State Khorasan Province (also known as ISIS-K or ISKP), had based itself in the mountains. He decided he would rather fight for the Iranians than for the Afghan government. Iran had never betrayed him.

"I served my own army well, but I suffered so much while I was in the military that I quit. Our country is in the hands of traitors," he said. "I trust Iran. It is a religious country, and it acts with determination. Iran is the only independent Shiite government in the world."

He continued to go back to Syria to help free villages from the grip of the extremists. The Iranian-commanded militias were gaining momentum, helping to turn the war decisively in Assad's favor. Near Aleppo, Saif led his platoon into the village of Tal Jabin, recently cleared in a major operation. They found a settlement littered with dead bodies, killed by Islamic State before the extremists had retreated. They continued toward Hardatnin and Ratyan, spending six days freeing the two villages, before reaching their goal: the villages of Nubl and Zahra, which had been under siege for four years. The towns had changed hands several times, from the Syrian government to its enemies in the Free Syrian Army and most recently Jabhat al-Nusra, a brutal al-Qaeda offshoot. Now, the Fatemiyoun stormed the villages alongside Syrian government forces, assisted by a barrage of airstrikes conducted by Russian warplanes that had joined the fray to defend Assad. More than five hundred airstrikes and barrel bombs hit the two towns during the two-day offensive. When it was over, Saif would recount back in Kabul, he strolled into the liberated streets, where he and his fighters were welcomed by cries of gratitude.

15

OMARI

To get to Kabul from the southern provinces, a traveler would pass through parts of the city where the international presence wasn't immediately obvious. The Kampani suburb was a pandemonium of rattling, ancient buses vying for space with goats and sheep herded by stick-wielding, bearded men on their way to the weekly livestock market. Driving toward the city center, one would pass the zoo housing two lions, a brown bear, and an aging pig gifted by the Chinese government, and the amusement park with the ominously creaking carousels. In the roundabout by the Abdul Rahman Khan Mosque, hordes of child *espandis* waved tins of coals so pungent smoke wafted through the windows of cars, to ward off evil spirits. Street stalls sold sunglasses, sheepskin hats, and SIM cards. Hawkers pushed carts full of fruit candied in layers of dust. Behind the luxury Serena Hotel, two police officers plucked the body of a dead dog from a sewer, carried it wet and pathetic across the street, and dumped it in the river. Historic buildings in the heart of the city, such as the presidential palace, had been hidden from the view of the Afghan public for nearly two decades. The biggest Western embassies and the NATO military headquarters were all located near the palace, connected by a small network of roads behind blast walls and barricades restricting access for regular citizens to an entire quarter of the city.

For those stuck in traffic, ubiquitous decals on car windows imparted words of wisdom or swagger in broken English: "Fighter Car. If You Follow Me Will Be Die," warned an old Toyota Corolla. Another counseled: "Live Well, Love Mach, Laug Often," accompanied by a Che Guevara stencil inside an Apple logo. A third offered consolation: "Don't Cry Girls, I Will Be Back." In a sign of the hard times, one simply said: "If I make, I make it. If not, I'm going to Germany."

By 2016, even as the country was becoming increasingly dangerous, and the liberal order was under growing threat from antimodern insurgents, Kabul's cosmopolitan side was growing stronger. You could start your day with an omelet and espresso in the grapevine-shaded garden of a French-inspired bistro. Outside the café, Chicken Street's rug and handicraft shops that had attracted travelers for decades—hippies, Russians, Americans—collected dust. Few customers were around anymore. Continuing down Flower Street to Peace Street, coffee shops furnished with Scandinavian-style wooden interiors brewed cappuccinos. In a fashionable bakery, Stanley, a Black Zimbabwean pastry chef, made birthday cakes to order with custom photographs printed on them. Indian, Pakistani, and Uzbek restaurants rubbed shoulders with upscale supermarkets where street kids politely held the car door for you and shouted, "What's up!" if you looked foreign. Around the corner, the opulent Shahr-e Now wedding hall was built to look like an Arab desert palace.

Shirpur, known as a "posh" neighborhood due to its wealthy residents, was home to warlords and politicians who had illegitimately seized land and built gaudy villas surrounded by blast walls and guards. One house was built to resemble the US Capitol (but was nicknamed the White House), its big white dome illuminated at night. In another, the Uzbek warlord Dostum sheltered behind blast walls and dozens of guards in a mansion filled with aquariums and tropical plants. The neighborhood was also home to an excellent Chinese restaurant serving tongue-numbing Sichuan cuisine to contractors drinking black-market whiskey and Carlsberg lager for ten dollars a can while belting their hearts out at a karaoke screen. Despite the rich residents, the roads remained potholed and streets unlit. Walking toward the glow of streetlights would lead you to the Wazir Akbar Khan square, surrounded by Western embassies, travel agencies, and a freshly opened café selling American-style frozen yogurt. In Parliament, about one-fourth of the elected lawmakers were women. At the city's universities, students immersed themselves in secular law studies and pursued master's degrees in women's and gender studies, alongside more traditional Islamic jurisprudence and theology. It was an uneasy coexistence, but Afghans, for the most part, coexisted.

Omari had seen all this on his few trips to the capital. He did not like the coexistence. He resented how the Afghan government had opened the country to foreigners who poisoned the minds of young Afghans. So when Haji Muhib one day approached him with a new task, he was skeptical. His mentor asked him to apply for university. The Taliban were infiltrating the city in preparation for future military operations, and universities were a good place to suss out the mood of the young and mobilize anger against the government. Besides, Muhib said, the Taliban needed its young fighters to be well educated so they could help run the country once they were back in government, inshallah. Omari was keen to leave the battlefield without giving up the jihad, and his parents, too, would be thrilled to see him get a degree. He agreed, and prepared to live in the capital he despised.

He enrolled in Pashto Literature at Kabul University. On his first day, he was met by inquisitive looks. His classmates stared at his beard, which, at twenty-two, he kept long and bushy like the Prophet's, reaching about two inches below his chin. His hair was jet-black, and he wore glasses with thin frames that he thought exuded a scholarly look. His teacher pulled him aside and frowned at his traditional tunic cut in village style with a thick, brown patu wrapped around his shoulders.

"You look like a terrorist. You look like al-Qaeda," he said.

Most other students wore jeans and button-downs, which to Omari was Western fashion. To get the teacher off his back, he bought a pair of jeans, but only wore them to that particular class. Omari felt on edge at university. About 40 percent of students at Kabul University were women. Barely any of them wore the burqa, just headscarves. He didn't know where to look.

"I just sit in a corner by myself, and don't look at them. I try to close my eyes to them. It upsets me a lot to see a girl hanging out with a boy who is not her *mahram*. Why do they need to have relations? I don't get it. So, I just sit in the corner. Sometimes I even leave the classroom," he said. He paraphrased an Islamic teaching: "Lock me in a room full of gold, and I won't steal anything. But lock me in a room with a woman, and I don't know if I can control myself." He took to wearing a wedding ring at university, "just so women don't expect anything from me." He almost dropped out several times but Haji Muhib pressured him to bottle up his anger and keep going.

"We need learned people in the movement," his Haqqani mentor said. With an education, Omari would also be able to earn more money for the Taliban. Omari reminded himself that university was part of God's lifelong test, as were the temptations he encountered there. He passed his exams, sometimes with a squeak, and when he occasionally stole a glance at the girls around him, he reasoned that all humans are flawed.

"Our sins are measured up against our good deeds. God doesn't expect Muslims not to make mistakes. If we weren't able to make mistakes, what would be the point of creating us?" he said. Gradually, Omari settled in and found his people. He could tell another Taliban supporter from his behavior and the cliques he moved in. He didn't have to ask, and he didn't tell anyone about his own loyalties. He shared a dormitory room, but the other guys never revealed their life stories. He was right to sense that he wasn't alone. Islamist groups, including but not limited to the Taliban, were solidifying their presence at Afghan universities, particularly Hizb ut-Tahrir, a group that considered democracy un-Islamic and sought to establish a caliphate encompassing the entire Muslim world; it had a large following among university students. The trend bucked the idea that all Islamists were country boys. Young people in the cities were usually the most politicized, and included both proponents of secular education and activists advocating against what they saw as Western values. About one-fourth of university students in the larger cities, Kabul, Jalalabad, and Kandahar, favored a political system more rooted in Islam than the current one, polls showed. Kabul did not represent all of Afghanistan, but it was where change began, and a new national identity was most visibly being forged. Universities had become ideological battlegrounds. At Kabul University, the country's largest academic institution and one of its most reputable, the faculty of law and political science was populated mostly by secular students and professors, including many old Communists. It was located across from the faculty of Islamic law, and students from the two regularly squared off against each other. Omari knew which side he was on.

"Democracy is incompatible with Islam. Democracy is irrational. It's the rule of the people, which means that people rule according to their desires and wishes. In a democracy, you can do whatever you want. But you can't do that under Islam, which is the rule of God," he said. His scholarly appearance was matched by a calm temper. He rarely raised his voice and would merely shake his head and smile when he disagreed with something. Although the Afghan constitution stipulated that no national law could contravene Sharia, that wasn't enough, he said. This was a common Taliban talking point, but the movement didn't clarify what part of the existing constitution they wanted to change. Omari said he wanted the whole package from the Taliban's 1990s rule back in force, including corporal punishment for theft and the death penalty for adultery. Such punishments, and the absence of corruption, were the reason Afghanistan had been peaceful under the Taliban, he said.

"In the current situation, it doesn't make any sense to put a criminal in jail. If they get twenty years, they will pay their way out of prison after one year anyway."

As for foreigners, Omari distinguished between soldiers and civilians. Journalists were welcome in the country, as long as their work was "honest." Aid workers, too, but they should not design development projects to buy the loyalty of Afghans, but only work to the benefit of the country.

Yet, Omari was curious about Christianity, especially the resurrection of Christ and the Holy Trinity. Jesus is an important prophet in the Quran, where he is called Isa, but Muslims don't believe that he is the son of God.

"Astaghfirullah," Omari exclaimed to ask forgiveness from God, and shook his head when he confirmed that Jesus was part of the Holy Trinity, along with the Father and the Holy Spirit. He took that to mean that God wasn't one, but three, a heretic idea as it contravened Islam's central tenet that there is only one God. He kept friends who weren't Taliban, who had grown up in his home district of Sayedabad. One of them would occasionally test him teasingly, to see how Omari ranked different sins: "What's worse, sex, murder, or alcohol?"

Omari didn't even have to think about it.

"Alcohol." He illustrated with a hypothetical example. A woman tells a man he can choose between sleeping with her, killing her, or drinking wine. He chooses the wine, thinking it is the most harmless of the three. As soon as he has drunk it, he loses control, sleeps with the woman, then kills her. To Omari, the lesson of the story was clear. Intoxication leads to total loss of control and morality. Regardless of your sins, however, fighting a holy war could rectify everything. "No matter how often you pray, one day of jihad counts more than all of your prayers," he said.

As he grew older and learned more about the Taliban's operations, he wrestled internally with some of their practices. The insurgency earned millions of dollars from the drug trade, which it condemned as anti-Islamic, and it received support from Pakistan while criticizing the Afghan government for being a puppet of a foreign power.

"Drugs are illegal, but the Taliban don't have a choice. They only sell drugs to non-Muslims," he claimed. "The Taliban only sell opium, which can also be used for medicine. If others choose to make heroin out of it, that's their problem." He gently sidestepped the fact that, according to US intelligence, the Taliban operated between four and five hundred heroin labs in the desert in Helmand.

He said about Pakistan, "They only give us money and weapons to fight the foreigners, they don't control us. Our fight is for Afghanistan."

Omari had earned enough trust among his Taliban commanders to be rewarded with more sensitive tasks. He had made up his own coded language and taught it to other fighters so they could communicate safely over WhatsApp during missions. On a day off from university, he was asked to accompany half a dozen young men from the provinces around town, using his knowledge of the capital to point out landmarks and government facilities. Only halfway through the trip did the driver tell him that the men on the back of the truck were suicide bombers acquainting themselves with the city they would later plan to attack. He traveled to Nangarhar posing as a maintenance worker to access a government army base and map it. As he walked around taking note of fuel tanks and other targets, he raised suspicion and was kicked off the base. The soldiers didn't find anything on him and let him go. In early 2017, he was ordered to Sheberghan to plan an attack on Abdul Rashid Dostum, the feared Uzbek strongman. Dostum had long been a target of the Taliban, and Omari helped plan three attack scenarios: hit his convoy with a roadside bomb, send a suicide bomber to infiltrate his compound, or strike his helicopter with a rocket. He was still in the early stages of planning when Dostum left the country following allegations that he had ordered his bodyguards to kidnap a political rival and rape him with the barrel of a rifle.

When spring came, announcing the start of a new fighting season, he spent the week studying, then traveled back to Wardak on Fridays to fight. A weekend warrior.

"My parents and my brothers don't know that I fight. They believe that when I am not at home, I am at university," he said.

In the provinces, casualty figures were higher than ever, and almost all were Afghan. Muslim soldiers and Muslim insurgents killing each other.

"It is acceptable to fight Muslims if they are spies for the enemy," Omari said. However, a nagging doubt had crawled up on him. What's a young holy warrior to do when the foreign enemy has left the country but the war continues? When you never see the real enemy, but only see him circling the sky with drones or hear the whoosh of his powerful bombs dropped from above? Omari's friends and commanders in the Taliban believed it was a religious duty to kill Afghan soldiers as puppets of America. Omari, who most of all dreamed of an Afghanistan free of foreign interference, and who had maintained a friendship with the neighbor's son despite Rahimullah's contracting work for the Americans, felt increasingly uncomfortable.

The arrival of Islamic State's regional affiliate had given the war an even more ruthless edge. In March 2017, a group of Islamic State militants stormed a military hospital in Kabul, killing fifty government soldiers and doctors who were treating them. Omari was disturbed.

"Those doctors were important to Afghanistan's future," he said. The Taliban also stepped up violence in a way that grated. In April 2017, Taliban fighters stormed a military base in Mazar-e Sharif, killing and injuring more than 150 soldiers while they were praying or eating lunch.

"There were no foreign soldiers there, and the Afghan soldiers who were there were not fighting with the Taliban when they were attacked. It was just a base. As an Afghan, I hated to see it," he said.

The emergence of Islamic State complicated the war. It distracted the US-led coalition from its original mission of fighting the Taliban, and put further pressure on the government in Kabul. The extremists had an explicit goal of establishing a caliphate and using it as a base to plan attacks on the West, so the coalition could not afford to ignore it. ISKP, as the group's Afghan affiliate came to be known, numbered no more than a couple of thousand fighters, if that, but their brazen attacks on civilian Afghans rattled the country and forced the army to stretch further beyond its capacity. Ghani's administration appeared to have no idea how to stem the violence, apart from relying on foreign soldiers, whose presence was not going to last forever. Patience in Western capitals with the Afghan war was running out. Further complicating the conflict was the Taliban's deepening entanglement with drug gangs as a source of revenue, which blurred the lines between insurgency and organized crime.

By 2017, the government controlled or influenced slightly more than half of Afghanistan's roughly four hundred districts. The Taliban controlled and influenced 11 percent. The remaining one-third was "contested," according to US military data. Those numbers masked the fact that in the provinces, the war had settled into an intractable stalemate that was growing bloodier by the year. The Taliban continuously stormed army and police bases and briefly held areas, and even district centers—towns that housed the government's administrative representatives—before often being pushed back. Front lines seesawed through villages and outskirts of towns, causing a growing number of casualties on all sides. The deadly grind took a worse toll on the government, for the Taliban appeared to have no problem recruiting fighters to replace their dead. Meanwhile, the army and police ranks were ground down, and the government's international backers were itching to pull their soldiers home and leave the long war behind. The United States had an official aim to increase the strength of the Afghan security forces to about 350,000, but the real number of forces, if known, was classified by both Washington and the Afghan government. A *New York Times* report in 2017 estimated that government recruitment was down by 50 percent. The US congressional watchdog for Afghanistan, the Special Inspector General for Afghanistan Reconstruction, estimated that by 2017, the Afghan national army on average lost one-third of its soldiers to attrition every year, and the police one-fifth of its officers. The Taliban's incessant attacks on government positions also gave them material advantages. While their control of large bases was often temporary, the raids allowed the insurgents to capture government equipment, including heavy weapons and vehicles such as Humvees and Ranger pickups paid for by the United States. Insurgents would dress in government army uniforms, pack the vehicles with explosives, and ram them into other government bases, causing massive casualties. Sometimes they wiped out entire units.

At the same time, the Taliban took a cue from Islamic State and resorted to ever-deadlier attacks, targeting civilians seemingly without remorse in a way that had previously been rare. In May 2017, a massive car bomb exploded in Kabul's diplomatic quarter and killed more than 150 civilians in one of the bloodiest attacks of the entire war. Nobody claimed responsibility, but the Afghan intelligence agency, the National Directorate of Security, said it had traced the bomb-laden car back to Haqqani members in Wardak, Omari's home province. Such attacks seemed to do more to dent the population's faith in the government than deplete support for the Taliban. Most civilians looked to the government, not the insurgents, for safety, and were gradually losing faith in Kabul's ability to protect them. Omari, however, was disturbed by the attack in the diplomatic quarter. He hoped the Haqqanis weren't behind it, but suspected they were.

"They only killed Muslims. There were no foreign soldiers present. The true jihad has rules that must be followed," he said. He had come to believe that excessive force was not always the right way. "We have to guide bad Muslims. They are on the wrong path," he said.

He did not feel the same sympathy for students. In 2016, when a group of terrorists stormed the American University in Kabul, chasing students around the hallways with machine guns and hand grenades, killing sixteen of them, Omari had not a shred of doubt: the students deserved to die. The university was the most prestigious place of higher learning in the country, and privately funded, but its name signified values that were in direct opposition to everything the Taliban stood for.

"Those who try to change the mentality in society are even more

dangerous than soldiers because their work is less obvious," Omari
said. Education was the biggest threat to the Taliban's ability to recruit supporters. He was tiring, physically and mentally, of the armed
struggle.

"If my commanders ask me to fight, I will," he said. But he preferred
not to. When at the front line, he preferred to keep a lookout from
a hill above the highway while his comrades ambushed government
soldiers, so he didn't have to shoot at anyone.

Ramadan in 2017 began on a sunny Friday in late May. Omari woke
up in his father's house. He had slept badly, plagued by a nightmare in
which a drone had struck the village. When he woke up startled, he felt
something was wrong and asked his father what had happened.

"Nothing."

"What happened?" Omari repeated.

"Nothing."

Unconvinced, Omari lumbered outside and called a friend, who
told him a drone had just bombed an area nearby but that no one knew
exactly where. An hour later the friend rang back. The strike had hit a
village, he said, and Haji Muhib, Omari's mentor of almost ten years,
had been killed. Omari nearly keeled over. Dizzy, he reached for a water bottle before he remembered he was fasting. Haji Muhib had been
traveling in a car alongside another Haqqani commander who was visiting Sayedabad from Miranshah, where Omari had attended suicide
academy a decade earlier, when they were hit by a drone strike. His
friend picked him up and they drove to Haji Muhib's village. The place
was tense with anger and sorrow. On a strategic level, the stalemate
in the war served the Taliban more than the government. The Taliban
had time on their hands. But on a personal level, the war was exacting
its toll among the insurgents, too. Haji Muhib had seemed invincible.
With him gone, Omari thought, his own luck could be about to run
out, too. If he was arrested in Wardak, the authorities didn't even have
to prove in court that he was a member of the Taliban. They could just
kill him. Kabul was safer. It was easier to disappear among people, and
the police in the capital were preoccupied with other things.

"Sometimes I feel that life is better in the village. Sometimes I want to move to Kabul to start a new life," he said. He wanted to move his parents and thirteen siblings to Kabul and try to live a civilian life.

"If they send foreign soldiers back here, there's no doubt that I will fight them," he said. "But if the foreign soldiers don't return, I will live a simple life."

16

PARASTO

On a sunny spring day in 2015, a twenty-seven-year-old female student of Islamic law went to the Shah-Do Shamshira Mosque in central Kabul. The square in front of the blue-domed yellow mosque was, as always, busy with peddlers and men feeding flocks of pigeons by the bank of the Kabul River. Outside the shrine, Farkhunda Malikzada approached a group of mullahs and chastised them for selling good-luck amulets to visitors, which the mullahs claimed would help prayers come true. Farkhunda suffered from mental illness that her parents had long sought to get her treatment for, and she showed little restraint as she berated the mullahs until an attendant at the shrine interfered. Loudly enough for bystanders to hear, he falsely accused her of a far more serious crime: burning the Quran. In minutes, the crowd surrounding Farkhunda grew into a mob of hundreds. The men cornered Farkhunda, pelted her with rocks, and stomped on her body. When a small group of police officers saw the commotion, they tried to intervene, firing warning shots in the air. They managed to pull Farkhunda up onto a corrugated metal roof. Then, as a video recording from the scene showed, the men below struck her with poles and planks of wood until she slipped back into the crowd. Clutching her hair, her face covered in red bruises and blood, she looked terrified as she appeared to have just realized that she had dropped her hijab. When she was dead, the men tied her body to a car and drove her to a nearby bank of the Kabul River, where they burned her corpse.

In death, Farkhunda became a martyr for Afghanistan's women's rights cause. Weeks later, a group of activists gathered outside the mosque to reenact her killing. A memorial with her photo on the side and a fist on top was erected in her memory.

Parasto, who was about to graduate from high school and was immersing herself in books and documentaries to try to understand the inner lives of the heroes and villains of history, thought there had to be a deeper explanation to Farkhunda's murder than pure evil. The investigation into her murder showed that several policemen had stood at a distance and watched the spectacle. What crime had she committed to deserve such a fate? What was the evidence against her, beyond the word of a random man? Farkhunda's killers were driven by a stronger force than just their individual wills, Parasto thought. Farkhunda was killed by violent mass ignorance.

"The men were illiterate. Who taught them these things? Who made them monsters? The family did. The culture, the illiterate society did," she said. The men killed Farkhunda out of a twisted perception that they were protecting Islam.

"When things go wrong, it is not because the Quran is incomplete. It is our understanding of it that is incomplete."

Farkhunda's fate was an extreme and tragic conclusion to a pattern Parasto had recognized in Afghan society. No matter how ambitious or talented a woman might be, if she stepped outside certain lines, men would take her down. To be successful, Afghan women needed men to lift them up, or at least get out of the way. For years, Parasto wanted to study at a Turkish military academy to be a military pilot, a dream her father supported once she turned eighteen. Abdulhakim pleaded Parasto's case with her mother. But Sofia was hard set

against her daughter becoming a soldier. She worried about Parasto's
safety in the presence of male soldiers, and she knew that a career in
the military could taint a girl's reputation in society. Over dinner, Sofia and Abdulhakim argued openly in front of Parasto about whether
to let her join the military. Eventually her mother enlisted Parasto's
uncle to help persuade her not to go.

"Look at me, girl," the uncle said when he pulled her aside one day.
"If you go to Turkey for this, nobody is going to want to marry you
when you come back home. I know you are a good girl, and you won't be
distracted. But why would you want people to accuse you of something
you didn't do?" He was referring to sex in the typical, circumspect
way people usually did in Afghanistan, especially around unmarried
women.

"Even in five years, or ten years, when a husband comes to ask for
your hand, his family will ask you if you slept with a boy when you
were in Turkey."

The discussions went on for two whole years until Abdulhakim
relented.

"If you had been a boy," he told Parasto—again—"you would have
made a great commander."

Parasto's older sister Gul became the first person in the family to attend university, and Parasto followed the year after, in 2016, enroll-
ing in political science at Kardan University. She carried herself with
a confidence that belied her young age. Often dressed elegantly in all
black, she added a couple of inches to her height by wearing pumps,
which she kicked off in informal settings, pulling her feet up in a lo-
tus position in her armchair. When appropriate, she swept her black
headscarf behind her ears to reveal a pair of pearl earrings. Whenever
she was told no, she asked why. When she asked the dean why they
had no school newspaper and he replied that they didn't have students
who wanted to make one, she retorted, "I'm going to make it happen."

He asked her to find fifteen girls willing to work for the paper, and to send him examples of her work.

At the time, Parasto was enthralled by a movie making waves in Afghanistan and beyond. *A Letter to the President* by the female director Roya Sadat followed Soraya, a female police detective and mother of two in a toxic marriage. The lead was played by Leena Alam, who had played Farkhunda in the activists' play on the banks of the Kabul River, where she had doused herself in a liquid meant to look like gasoline. In a crucial scene in the movie, the detective responds to her husband's violence by slapping him, a delicious smack across the face that made cinema audiences in Kabul gasp and break out in applause. In a final scene, Soraya accidentally kills her husband in self-defense by pushing him through a glass window. She ends up on death row, from where she writes the president, asking for her life to be spared.

For the dean, Parasto wrote her own "Letter to the President," asking why Afghans were treated as subhumans in the world. Among her questions to the Afghan president: "Why am I only allowed to travel to six countries when Afghanistan has embassies in more than 20 countries?" This was in Parasto's eyes a symbol of Afghanistan's pitiful global status. For a second piece, Parasto wrote a profile of a local businessman. She found five girls keen to work for the paper, fewer than the dean had asked for, but he was nevertheless impressed enough to let her set up an editorial office for the new publication. As it turned out, Parasto had little time for the school newspaper. The businessman was so pleased with the profile, which ran in the paper's first issue, that he introduced Parasto to the deputy head of President Ghani's administrative office, a man named Khan Wali Khan Basharmal, who had just returned from India where he had received training in a method of education surveying developed by an Indian organization called the Annual Status of Education Report Centre. Basharmal was planning to implement the ASER model in Afghanistan, and invited Parasto to volunteer at his office. She threw herself into the work and impressed Basharmal with her willingness to learn and her

English. Shortly after, he offered her a salaried position as a project manager. Parasto was the first woman in her family to have a job. It was an extraordinary opportunity—for a woman in her early twenties from a modest background to work with the government.

The government launched a pilot project in the neighborhood of Paghman Charaye Siah, where they surveyed 1,500 schoolchildren. Parasto then traveled to India, where she spent ten days with the ASER team surveying Indian kids. She learned Afghan tenth graders were about as educated as Indian fifth graders. The trip was an epiphany. The way to combat the violence, intolerance, and misogyny in Afghan society was not, as with the police officer in *A Letter to the President*, to slap it across the face, but to undermine it through education. Parasto saw how women were left to fend for themselves. There were not enough women in high positions to lift each other up.

"In Afghanistan, you always need a man to help you get from one stage to the next," she said. Prominent women talked about female empowerment through solidarity. Parasto rarely witnessed that in reality.

"Other women would never support me," she said. She understood why. All of them had fought hard for their position of influence and guarded their privilege ferociously. Women who spoke English and had connections with foreign embassies got invited to international conferences and included on the short lists of women's rights activists that got passed down from one Western political officer to the next. The ecosystem of women who had the ears of diplomats and journalists was small and insular. Even if women were willing to share their influence, they were too scattered throughout the system, too disorganized, to pierce the thick skin of the patriarchal order that stymied their advancement.

In families, women also needed men to cede space. By 2020, Parasto had graduated with a bachelor's degree in political science, and the president's office and the Ministry of Education were discussing how to update the national curricula. Parasto was asked if she would be willing to travel to the rural province of Uruzgan to survey the level of education. As an unmarried woman, she needed the permission of her male guardian to travel. Uruzgan was one of the most dangerous and conservative places in the country. The government controlled only spots of the province, and outside the capital, Tarin Kot, the Taliban operated openly. Officials in government had told Parasto that their forces only controlled 3 percent of the province. Her mother didn't like the idea but deferred to her father's judgment.

"It's just a two-day trip, it's not a big deal," Parasto pleaded with her father. The plan was to fly into Tarin Kot, then drive to the nearby district of Deh Rawood. She knew no other young woman whose family would allow her to travel outside Kabul without a *mahram*. And they needed a woman to visit girls' schools and talk to female teachers. To her own surprise, Abdulhakim agreed. Parasto traveled to Uruzgan wearing a burqa, purchased for the occasion. She was uncomfortable, enveloped in synthetic fabric, but it allowed her to do the job. In Tarin Kot, she stayed at a guesthouse that belonged to a local NGO. She got up every morning before dawn to visit schools in the districts. Life in Uruzgan, less than three hundred miles from Kabul, was how Parasto imagined life in the sixteenth century, she said. Children walked several hours to school at four a.m. In the afternoon, many of them worked. Women died during pregnancy because of lack of healthcare, and didn't know about contraception.

Parasto's work with ASER got the attention of other officials in the Ghani administration, which had taken power back in 2014. She suspected they were intrigued by her because there were so few young Pashtun women in government, but she also performed well. Basharmal recommended her for a job in the administrative office of the president, evaluating educational programs. In 2020, she applied for a job monitoring assistance at the anti-corruption secretariat, and got it. The assignment put Parasto in the vicinity of Ghani's inner circle, and at the heart of one of the fiercest political battles at the time. Ghani had failed to live up to his electoral promise to clean up nepotism and corruption, both of which benefited mostly men. The son of a female parliament member, a young man named Zubair, the self-styled "Eagle of Takhar," regularly drove around the streets of Kabul in his mother's car, letting off rounds from his Kalashnikov through the sunroof. The antics prompted President Ghani to stand up in Parliament and demand that Zubair's mother, Habiba Danish, get her boy under control. The Eagle of Takhar was eventually arrested but released after a couple of days, reappearing shortly after in an Instagram video from Dubai.

"Who is Ashraf Ghani?" he declared. "I don't know him."

Such antics were only the most visible symptoms of a disease that was eating the Afghan state from within. Since the beginning of the war, the United States had been fully aware of the endemic corruption among powerful anti-Taliban power brokers but chose to rely on them as allies in the new Afghanistan. According to a 2005 cable from the US embassy, "Garden-variety corruption—the use of public office for private gain and the greasing of palms to secure delivery of government services—has been a hallmark of daily life here for many centuries. The highly informal and relationship-based nature of Afghan society, including a strong element of nepotism, has reinforced this." The United States could not dodge responsibility. To gain control of the country, it had relied on shady strongmen who built their power on financial patronage. American money nurtured corruption, which soon grew far beyond "garden-variety" theft of Afghan citizens' money.

In one shocking incident in 2011, American military officers working as mentors at Afghanistan's main military hospital discovered that corrupt doctors and nurses were demanding bribes from patients for food and basic needs, leaving injured soldiers to die of simple infections. Some even starved to death. One of the worst scandals had occurred back in 2010, when the country's largest private bank, Kabul Bank, was revealed to have been operating as a massive pyramid scheme. Deposits from ordinary Afghan citizens worth hundreds of millions of dollars had been fraudulently lent to fictitious companies. Some of the money was invested in a real estate bubble in Dubai that had since burst, some was sunk into questionable projects and political donations in Afghanistan. The scandal was particularly problematic, as the bank was the main conduit for payment of Afghan security forces. It had also been a main financier of then president Karzai's election campaign. The two main benefactors of the fraudulent loans were the president's elder brother, Mahmoud Karzai, and Haseen Fahim, the brother of the vice president. At least $982 million disappeared. According to an Afghan corruption watchdog, the Independent Joint Anticorruption Monitoring and Evaluation Committee, Karzai later paid back $13 million of the $22 million he owed, though he claimed to have paid back all his loans with interest.

That same year, Afghan investigators raided the offices of a money transfer firm called New Ansari Money Exchange. The company had been moving as much as $2.78 billion out of Afghanistan on behalf of drug traffickers, insurgents, and government officials between 2007 and 2010. During the investigation, a wiretap had caught a close aide to President Karzai, a man named Mohammad Zia Salehi, soliciting a bribe in return for obstructing the investigation. After US officials presented other palace aides with the wiretap, Salehi was arrested. Hours later, Karzai ordered him released. All charges were dropped.

The Salehi case illustrated a troubling pattern of Afghan government officials evading prosecution, even when evidence of their involvement in corruption was blindingly clear. It left many to ponder whether if this was the new order, perhaps the old one was preferable after all.

Washington and Kabul were now both in transition. In 2017, Donald Trump entered the White House promising to end America's war in Afghanistan (a pledge he would abandon almost immediately after taking office, instead ordering more troops). In Kabul, President Ghani, who styled himself a modern intellectual technocrat, also pledged an overhaul of his country's political agenda, saying he would do away with impunity for corruption "root, stock and branch." After returning to Afghanistan from a job at the World Bank in 2001, Ghani had served as finance minister under Karzai and authored a slim book called *Fixing Failed States*. The book, and Ghani's academic air, had been seen as an encouraging sign that here was finally someone with reformist ambitions who knew what he was talking about. Parasto, attracted to Ghani's veneer of professionalism, had high hopes. But so far, little had improved. Three years into his presidency, Ghani's self-labeling as a fixer of failed states had become a punch line at dinner parties, an intellectual albatross around his neck. His critics were eager to point out that the scholar-president was failing more than he was fixing. A consummate micromanager, notorious for a foul temper, a high self-regard, and very thin skin, Ghani had surrounded himself with a close-knit circle of loyalists. Former aides said the president always thought he was the smartest man in the room and as such wanted to be his own chief of staff, defense minister, and finance minister. Cabinet members were afraid to contradict Ghani because he would bite their heads off. Former acting US envoy to Afghanistan and Pakistan Laurel Miller said Ghani made "more enemies than friends" this way.

Parasto saw the deficiencies of the president and the system but knew that she had no choice but to make her job work. She was privy to government reports showing the Taliban gaining ground, and it frightened her. Taliban commanders had suggested that if they took power, they would be more lenient toward women than in the past, but Parasto didn't believe they had changed. A friend from Kandahar told her that if Mullah Haibatullah, the Taliban leader, knew the extent to which Afghan women in Kabul were working, he would want them all killed. She became convinced that backing the current government was the only choice.

17

ZAHRA

In the summer of 2016, the hallways of Kabul's universities were abuzz with chatter about something that rarely created a buzz: a new book. Written by an unknown female author, the book contained unusually vivid portrayals of female life, depicting domestic violence, marital rape, and even graphic descriptions of women's periods—completely unheard of in Afghanistan.

> I hated marriage, the wedding night, the idea of a husband and a wife and all the things that would end up in pain. Hatred clung to me like a tight dress. In the evening, when we were led to the bedroom without exchanging a word between us, I found Sultan by my side. Suddenly I felt sharp pain pierce my body. Afterwards I couldn't remember a thing. When I opened my eyes, I saw I was in a hospital bed.

Some had heard the author wasn't even living in the safety of exile. She was here in Kabul. Young people loved the book. In its first few weeks it sold nearly a thousand copies, a bestseller by Afghan standards.

Zahra had quit acting and become a full-time activist and writer. Part memoir, part fiction, her book *Light of Ashes* combined her own life with stories of women she had interviewed for the theater project. Writing the book helped her reconcile with her past. She had ditched her family name, Hosseini, and taken a new one, Yagana, meaning "unique." She had told her parents about the book but hadn't heard from them since its publication. Her sisters had read it and told Zahra they were proud of her. She had used her savings to rent a bigger house. In the courtyard was parked a little red Daewoo Matiz that she drove on weekends to take Parisa and Jawad for picnics. She never saw another female driver in the streets, and often faced verbal abuse when she got behind the wheel, but the traffic police were friendly and stood up for her.

Among her readers were many young men. Where women identified with her book, men found revelations about women's lives previously unavailable to them. Some of them reached out to her for advice. They were often men who had lost their own mothers and were looking for a maternal guide. For her birthday that year she received nine cakes from young men. Some of them visited her for Eid. Dozens more connected with her on Facebook and would recognize her at cultural events in the city. Zahra was both baffled and flattered by the attention, none of which seemed to be romantic. Teaching young men to see the world from a woman's perspective was a way to drive change in society, as Theatre of the Oppressed had taught her to do. When some of the men asked permission to call her "Mother," she obliged.

It had been years since she last heard from her ex-husband, Hussein. In 2016, Parisa's phone rang one day from an undisclosed number. Parisa at first didn't recognize the voice on the line and admonished the man for calling a young woman from a secret number. When he cursed at her, she recognized her father's voice. He must have gotten her number from his parents, whom Zahra insisted they visit regularly to keep them in her children's lives.

"You haven't called me for so many years, and this is how you talk to me?" Parisa said, and burst into tears.

After the call, Zahra had to reassure her frightened children that
Hussein couldn't hurt her or them. He was still in Iran, she reminded
them, and even if he were to return to Afghanistan, he had no money
to travel to Kabul.

Jawad, who had just become a teenager, the first feathery hairs appearing on his upper lip, was uncomfortable around the many young
men only a few years older than him doting on his mother. Having
spent much of his childhood with his grandmother, he was more conservative than Zahra and Parisa. His mother's rebellious nature put
him in an awkward position as the male representative of the household. Parisa, at seventeen, occupied space around her like an adult
and, like her mother, often behaved in ways the community considered inappropriate. She would ride Jawad's bicycle up and down the
quiet alleyway outside the house, prompting the local boys to bully
Jawad mercilessly for not being able to put his sister in her place.

Jawad spent less and less time at home. He sought guidance in
the Quran and from the imams at the local mosque. During the holy
month of Muharram, when Shia Muslims commemorate the martyrdom of Imam Hussein, he went to the mosque every day and volunteered to organize street processions. Zahra saw his predilections as a
phase, a teenage identity crisis.

"It's fine that he has some rules to live by until he is old enough
to decide how religious he is," she said. But she kept an eye on him.
Kabul's Shia community was fidgety with anger and unrest after a
new wave of terrorist attacks had targeted their community, even in
their mosques. Some of the imams running mosques in Dasht-e Barchi, where they lived, were known radicals. Other local leaders were
calling on the community to be ready to mobilize and arm themselves.
Most of the Hazaras who organized did so peacefully. A new political force had emerged called Junbesh-e Roshnaye, the Enlightenment
Movement. The name's double meaning signaled an aspiration to educate Afghans about what the activists saw as persistent discrimination of Hazaras, as well as the more literal aim of bringing electricity
to Bamiyan, the underdeveloped province in the highlands dominated

by Hazaras. The government had long planned to build an electric power transmission link to bring electricity from Central Asia, but had decided to circumvent Bamiyan, contrary to the original plan. The rerouting amplified a sense among Hazaras that they were neglected and discriminated against by the central government. Politicians and activists had seized on the moment to rally Hazaras in the street.

On July 24, 2016, at six a.m., thousands of Hazara activists and other citizens gathered in several meeting points in western Kabul to march toward the presidential palace, the Arg. It was one of the largest mass protests in decades. Characteristically for the Hazara community, hundreds of women participated. Zahra had brought Parisa and Jawad to the protest, and gathered with other activists outside a mosque. She didn't usually get involved in politics, but discrimination of Hazaras was personal. As the procession moved from the mosque, the women took position in the back, carrying colorful umbrellas to shield themselves from the sun and lending a photogenic touch to the rally. One banner read: "Don't extinguish us," a plea that would prove gruesomely prophetic.

The government of Ashraf Ghani, who had cast himself as a leader ready to finally listen to the Afghan people, had blocked protesters from reaching the palace by placing shipping containers on the roads leading downtown. Instead, the rally convened at the Deh Mazang square, a roundabout just outside the city center, where activists and lawmakers spoke to the crowd. Early in the afternoon, Zahra's legs started aching and she decided to go home. She led Parisa and Jawad out of the crowd and hailed a cab. They had barely entered the front door at home when a massive explosion sent them scampering for cover. The blast could be heard across the city, and left a plume of smoke rising from the square. A teenager had walked into the crowd by the square, sidled up to a man selling ice cream from a bicycle cart, and detonated the explosives in his backpack. The bomb tore bodies apart and scattered bloodied limbs across the square. The pressure wave shattered windows several hundred yards away. An exact death toll was never made public, but nearly one hundred people were believed to have been killed. During the same protest, Saif, the young militia fighter home between deployments in Syria, was at his mother's memorial. Both he and Zahra missed the blast by chance.

Three months later, on October 11, 2016, hundreds of Shia faithful were gathered at the Karte Sakhi shrine at the foot of TV Hill to mark the beginning of the Ashura mourning holiday when three armed men stormed the complex, firing machine guns and lobbing hand grenades indiscriminately into the crowd. They killed eighteen people, including four women and two children. Among the dead was a young man named Abbas, one of Zahra's young admirers. They used to text almost every day, and that same morning Abbas had asked to come over later and borrow a book. She could not muster the strength to go to his funeral. It had been years since she had lost people close to her, and she worried that her misfortune had returned. The Hazara community was under attack. Like the demonstration bombing, the attack on the mosque was claimed by a fast-rising local affiliate of Islamic State, which was spreading fear among Kabul's Shias, demonstrating a willingness to kill civilians, including at holy sites, which even the Taliban had never shown. A new enemy had come to Afghanistan.

The day after the attack on the shrine, a procession of about fifty vehicles raced recklessly through the streets, forcing all other traffic to make way. Three men occupied the passenger seat of one car, limbs splaying out of the open door. A man had strapped himself to the roof of another, waving a large flag depicting a child wearing a green headband, the color of Imam Hussein, whose death the faithful had mourned when they were massacred. "Ya Hussein!" black-clad men shouted in religious fervor. The scene had the marks of a sectarian conflict in the making, although the men said that's what they were determined to prevent. They said they were intent on mourning their fellow faithful who had been killed the day before the same way they emulated the suffering of their imam: by self-flagellating with fists, chains, and knives.

The Karte Sakhi shrine sits in the middle of a sprawling cemetery at the bottom of Kabul's TV Hill, named after the antennas poking out of its sepia-colored peak. Headstones crowd the ground outside the shrine like scattered timber from a wreckage on a beach. On weekends, the area doubled as a fairground, with Ferris wheels and balloon sellers. When the Ashura procession pulled up outside the mosque, hundreds of men spilled into the courtyard and stripped down. They brought out chains with five-inch blades and started whipping their bare torsos. Boys, some looking as young as ten, with thin arms and backs betraying no trace of muscle, swung the chains up high then brought them down, cutting their skin open with every strike.

Many Shias find the ritual archaic and repulsive. But for those who partake, from Iran and Afghanistan to Pakistan and India, self-flagellation is a pure form of worship. For many years, the Ashura rituals were kept underground, but the new religious freedoms of the post-2001 era had brought them out in the open. This year in Kabul, the Ashura ceremony was also a way for the mourners to protect their religious identity and to defy the threat posed by the Islamic State.

"In the past, we have been accustomed to political and tribal war," Sayed Yusuf Hosseini, the head cleric at the Karte Sakhi shrine, said. "But we did not experience religious war." The thirty-five-year-old cleric was dressed in a crisp white tunic and black vest, carried a pleasant smell of rose water, and wore a ring with a big yellow stone.

"The enemy is trying to bring religious divisions," he said, managing a confident demeanor despite being visibly shaken. "But it will be impossible for them."

A month later, a suicide bomber sent by Islamic State killed more than thirty worshipers in another Shia mosque in Kabul. By the end of 2016, a year after the Islamic State first appeared in eastern Afghanistan, it had killed at least 125 Shias in the capital alone.

Two days later, on a Friday, Zahra took Parisa and Jawad for a simple picnic on a hillside overlooking Shahrak Haji Nabi, a neighborhood in west Kabul. She tried to take them here every Friday before the weather turned cold. Snacking on dried apricots and sunflower seeds, she topped up her green tea from a thermos and looked down at the city that had changed so much since she moved there nearly a decade earlier. An uncharacteristic gloom settled over her face.

"Only last year, I was so optimistic. I still have hope but I really don't know what's going to happen. I just try to convince myself that it's not going to get worse than it is now," she said.

It had been years since she had lost her faith in the God she was raised to believe in. The hardship she had gone through made God as described in scripture even harder to accept. Did the promise of eternal peace in the afterlife have to come at the price of interminable pain now? She still found solace in prayer, as she had as a child. She prayed to a God of her own mind, one who didn't impose rigid doctrines of a past era or punish you for trying to change what was obviously unjust.

"When I'm alone, I sit for a long time, offer prayers and cry. Then I feel calm and talk to my God. This is how I get some peace of mind," she said. She gazed to her left toward another hillside, this one dotted with twenty green flags, one for each of the protesters killed in the Deh Mazang bombing, who were buried there.

"I don't usually care about politics, but many of these attacks target Hazaras," she said. "I have seen Pashtuns on social media celebrate the attacks. And I have seen fake Facebook accounts trying to manipulate Hazaras and create divisions among people. But Shias still go to mosque. They will continue to protest. People will not sit down and remain silent. It may become difficult to control. The young generation is very emotional and pained."

Parisa was only fifteen years younger than her mother, but her childhood was a world apart from what Zahra's had been. Against all odds, Zahra had managed to provide her children with opportunities that neither she nor her parents had. But inherent in their lives was a new danger that she had never faced. Kabul was engulfed by violence that did not discriminate between children and adults. Walking back down the hillside, Zahra passed a group of young boys flying kites. On a gravel road, taking advantage of the remoteness and quiet of this suburb on a sleepy Friday, a lone woman was practicing her driving, stopping and starting in bursts as she maneuvered her Toyota Corolla slowly around the bend.

Despite the bloodshed, to the untrained eye, everyday life in Kabul went on seemingly undisturbed. Throngs of schoolgirls in white headscarves continued to flood the city's sidewalks in the afternoon after the end of classes. The man who made a skimpy living writing love letters in beautiful calligraphy for young, illiterate paramours still turned up on his rickety wooden chair outside the swanky supermarket. The butchers still got up before dawn to skin animals and attach them to hooks in the doorways of their shops. Young Afghan women still dressed and acted in ways in public they knew extremists did not approve of. But the Islamic State attacks palpably changed the mood. At no point in the past twenty years had Afghanistan's Shias been as targeted as they were now. The Taliban viewed Shias as apostates, suppressed them when they were in power, but did not systematically persecute them after they were toppled, perhaps because they hoped one day to rule Afghanistan and believed they needed broad legitimacy to do so. Islamic State had no such concerns. Their goal was to destroy the Afghan nation state and make it part of a transnational caliphate. The Afghan government at the time estimated that 90 percent of Islamic State fighters in Afghanistan were foreigners, with a mostly Pakistani leadership. Islamic State also drew the attention of the United States. In April 2017, true to style, President Trump chose the most blustering-sounding weapon on the shelf to deal with the new threat in Afghanistan. Formally known as a GBU-43/B Massive Ordnance Air Blast, the weapon better known as the Mother of All Bombs was released from an American C-130 Hercules cargo plane over the Islamic State headquarters in the mountains of Nangarhar. It was the largest nonnuclear bomb ever dropped. The US military never publicized casualty figures from the blast, which did not significantly set back Islamic State's capabilities in the country, but MOAB became a marker that things were escalating.

Afghans prepared for the worst. Queues outside passport offices snaked around the block. Conversations among friends became tinged with anxiety. Nobody wanted a sectarian war, and many community leaders were trying to quell tensions. On social media and in coffee shops, young non-Hazaras expressed solidarity with their Shia compatriots, swearing that extremists would not be allowed to tear the nation apart. But there were also signs that the atmosphere was getting increasingly bitter. The recent wave of sectarian attacks carried an unmistakable echo of the past and boded ill for the future. Government officials said they had distributed up to five hundred machine guns to Shia mosques across the city, a stunning admission that it wasn't able to protect the city's Hazaras, that they were largely on their own.

The Islamic State attacks kept coming. In January 2017, alleged Islamic State militants killed thirteen coal miners in the northern province of Baghlan. Zahra watched restlessly. Her book had gained her a modest public profile and a sizeable following on social media. She found herself in a role of community leader that she hadn't sought. She decided to use it. One of the miners who survived, Hanif, had been injured and badly needed treatment. Zahra posted his story on Facebook, asking for money for his medical bills. The post went viral. Afghans from across the country came together to fund Hanif's treatment.

"Everybody, regardless of their ethnicity, jumped in to help," she said. An eight-year-old boy who had saved 1,300 afghanis, about twenty dollars, through the year to buy a cell phone donated his money. Zahra raised enough for Hanif to go to India for treatment, but he died before doctors could operate.

Hanif's death gave Zahra purpose. She had found a way to help, even if doing so meant confronting the darkest sides of the Afghan experience. She had cofounded an NGO, Green Home, aimed at economically empowering marginalized groups by providing courses in computer literacy and English and other skills. On the side, she kept fundraising. In August 2018, a teenager walked into the Mawoud Academy tuition center and detonated a backpack of explosives at the end of algebra class. The lecture hall was packed and the explosion killed

more than forty students. Most of the students had moved to Kabul
from the provinces to pursue higher education, a ladder out of poverty
for their families. In the past, an attack of this magnitude would have
paralyzed Zahra. Now she got to work. For three weeks, she spent her
waking hours shuttling between hospitals and homes, helping victims.
She spent most of her time helping a seventeen-year-old girl called
Shukria who had been paralyzed in her lower body and still had shrapnel in her waist. Doctors told Zahra that the girl wouldn't recover. Re-
moving the shrapnel was too risky. Facebook had become the closest
Afghanistan had to a public square, and this time Zahra raised more
than $60,000, a significant chunk of which was paid by four wealthy
Afghan brothers in Dubai. The money was sufficient to send Shukria
to the renowned Medanta Hospital in India, where doctors removed
the shrapnel. One month after the surgery, the girl regained feeling
in her legs.

While Shukria was in India, Zahra tended to other victims of the
bombing. She had just helped the last injured student of the Mawoud
Academy home after being discharged when Islamic State terrorists
attacked a wrestling club in the same neighborhood. Zahra rushed
back to the hospital where she had spent much of the past month, just
in time to help with the new victims.

"I was in the hospital when I saw the wounded wrestlers being
brought in. I lifted them with my own hands," she said. "I saw victims
whose heads, hands, or legs had been blown off. The dead and injured
were all mixed up. I saw that they mistook an injured person for dead,
putting him among the corpses. His brother told them that the man
was moving, but they insisted that he was dead. Then he pulled him
out and we saw that he really was alive."

The bodies of the young men, athletic and strong, stripped to their
underwear, piled up as Zahra worked the phones, calling other hospitals to see if they had space for patients. When she returned home
and bent over the sink to wash the blood off her hands, a sharp pain
shot through her body, forcing her to lie down for the rest of the evening. That night, the face of one of the wrestlers she had watched die

in the hospital visited her. In her dream he died once again, and lay down next to her on the bed, his head on her pillow, his face a mask of blood as it almost touched hers. She startled awake and saw her hand on the pillow where the dying man's face had been. She couldn't feel the right side of her body. In the morning, she called a psychotherapist, who recommended that she stop working with war victims, at least temporarily. They stayed in touch, and Zahra allowed herself time and space to talk. Between sessions, she would suffer fits where she found it hard to breathe and her heart was racing. But she slowed down, got on medication, and got better.

A few weeks later, Zahra called her mother while walking down the street. They didn't speak often but stayed in touch, and Zahra had news she wanted to share: she was on her way to register as a candidate for the October 2018 parliamentary elections. National politics was a comparatively welcome avenue for women. According to the Afghan constitution passed after 2001, at least sixty-eight seats, or 27 percent, of the Wolesi Jirga, the lower house of the national assembly, were reserved for women. She didn't know how her conservative mother would react, but Fatima shrieked with joy when she heard.

"You'll achieve more this way, I am so proud of you," she said on the phone. "I hope you get what's good for you."

Inspired by her charity work, Zahra ran on raising the voices of people she said had been forgotten, particularly women and children, and to funnel more resources to literacy and job creation for disenfranchised citizens. Parisa helped out, doing media interviews on her mother's behalf and canvassing in the street. In the end, Zahra got 1,385 personal votes, but didn't win. Of the two seats up for election in her neighborhood, one went to a sitting parliamentarian, and the other went to another female candidate who accused Zahra of pocketing money she had raised for war victims. She didn't produce any evidence, and Zahra countered that she only facilitated the online fundraising campaigns and reported all the spending to donors, providing documents, videos, and other proof.

"But people couldn't see that from the outside," she said. She thought the allegations had doomed her campaign. "I was heartbroken. I felt judged."

After the election, she was unemployed for a year and had to borrow money for rent, Parisa's tuition, and to service her debt. After a short stint as a public relations officer at the Ministry of Mines, she was hired by the Liaison Office, or TLO, an Afghan NGO focused on good governance and on including rural communities in peace processes.

The two deaths came months apart. Her father had high blood pressure and his cholesterol numbers were off the charts. The stroke that hit him in the spring met with little resistance. Her father's death had little impact on Zahra, perhaps evidence of how emotionally absent he had been for her. She was more surprised by how rattled she was when Hussein passed away. No one seemed to know how he died. Since he had gotten out of prison in Iran, Hussein had lived secluded in a remote little Iranian town. Some in the family said he had suffered an overdose, others said he slept through a gas leakage in the house.

"Although we'd separated for years and I had no feelings toward him, the news broke my heart," she said. "I told myself I didn't love him. I didn't expect it to hit me that hard." Maybe it was the thought of her children losing their father that saddened her.

"We lived together for ten years, and for the first six of them, I loved him," she said.

Jawad had been five years old when Zahra and Hussein separated, but Parisa remembered him well. Zahra suspected that her daughter blamed her somewhat for the divorce that deprived her of having a father. One late night soon after his death, Zahra felt Parisa come into the room and hug her from behind. She knew then that her daughter grieved. And that she forgave. She also supported her mother if she wanted to find another husband.

"I don't have a problem with her marrying someone. It's she who doesn't want to marry," Parisa said. Zahra claimed she didn't have the emotional space for a romantic relationship. But she did hope to re-marry one day.

"I don't want to marry a younger man. Perhaps when I'm older, I'll find a divorced man to spend my life with," she said. She did not want to settle for being a second wife, the only role many families would accept for a divorced woman.

A male friend had once told Zahra, "No one will marry you if you're old."

"Then I will marry an old man," she laughed.

Parisa was herself entering a marriageable age. When she had turned thirteen, Zahra told her that it was only natural to feel attracted to boys, so there was no need for alarm when it happened. It was also okay to talk to boys, she said, but be watchful. Only fifteen years apart, they were each other's confidantes. When Parisa was twenty-two, the first suitor came and asked Zahra for her daughter's hand. Zahra hadn't expected to feel so resistant. The boy was educated, respectful, and from an affluent family.

"But it was unthinkable for me to give her hand away in marriage," she said. She didn't have to make a decision because Parisa rejected the boy herself. There was a Persian saying, which the family had always applied to Zahra: "A thorn will forever remain sharp." Parisa was her mother's daughter, only feistier. She was the most liberal of all her cousins, and of her friends. She was into fashion, and made it a point of pride not to care about others' opinions. She wore cargo pants, dyed her hair white, and shaved the sides of her head.

"I look way too strange for my classmates," Parisa admitted. The girls started calling her *byadar*, "brother," pinched her cheeks, and said she looked cute. She knew that behind her back, those same girls would accuse her of not being a good girl. She had more male than female friends at university, which kept other girls at bay.

"Gender doesn't matter to me," Parisa said.

"She used to be harassed for her style, and she would punch those who catcalled her," Zahra said.

Parisa smiled. "It's been a year since I last fought anyone," she said.

There was one thing Zahra shielded her children from. She had always asked them not to read her book. She didn't want them to read their mother's own account of the violence and trauma she had endured. She still got occasional backlash for writing it. One of her own nephews in Herat had threatened to kill her in a Facebook message. Jawad saw the message and replied to his cousin: "If you ever write to my mother again, comment on her posts or threaten her, I'm here and you can deal with me."

Some readers were triggered by her indirect criticism of Islam. The book made the case that there was no justice for women in Afghanistan, and by extension, in Islam. As the Taliban seemed poised to return to at least some measure of power, Zahra began to worry. Rogue Taliban members wouldn't even have to read the book to hurt her for it. Merely knowing that the book existed could be enough. Among the messages she received was a warning from a woman educated in an Islamic seminary who had in fact read her book: "If I ever come across you, I'll spit on you."

18

PARASTO

In February 2018, President Ghani had made an unprecedented offer to the Taliban, inviting them to participate in peace talks with his government without preconditions. The offer was remarkable because it officially recognized the Taliban as a legitimate political stakeholder in Afghanistan. It was the result of months of talks among various political groups, figures, and civil society members. The president also offered to have Taliban officials removed from the UN sanctions list. From her desk at the anti-corruption secretariat, Parasto dreaded what might come of this.

After months of silence, the Taliban rejected the offer. The militants maintained that they would not speak directly to the Kabul government, which it considered illegitimate, until after reaching a deal with the United States. But even as Ghani's initiative collapsed, a new one was underway, for the Trump administration was eager to pursue a deal—with or without Ghani's government at their side.

In late July, high-level American diplomats agreed to meet with the Taliban directly in Doha, Qatar, without the Afghan government, reversing nearly twenty years of foreign policy. And in September, President Trump appointed Zalmay Khalilzad, a slick, affable, Afghan-born veteran diplomat, as his special envoy to negotiate directly with the Taliban.

Khalilzad, or Zal as he was known to scores of colleagues and journalists, was a former ambassador to Afghanistan who early in the war as President Bush's envoy had been one of the main architects of the overthrow of the Taliban and of the country's new constitution. Previous US efforts to engage the Taliban had not gone well. The first serious attempts had begun in 2010 but floundered, partly due to disagreements between the military, whose counterinsurgency campaign was intensifying under the command of Gen. Stanley McChrystal, and Obama's Afghanistan envoy Richard Holbrooke, who considered the push for military victory doomed to fail. Karzai was skeptical of Holbrooke's outreach, and the insurgents refused to deal with Karzai. Holbrooke's case suffered in 2010 when, in an almost comical case of intelligence failure, NATO and Afghan officials met at least three times to negotiate for peace with a man they thought was the Taliban's second-in-command, but who turned out to be an imposter, likely a shopkeeper.

Another attempt failed in 2013 when American officials had convinced Qatar to allow the Taliban to open a political office in Doha, as a sweetener. Karzai reluctantly agreed, on the condition that the office was not elevated to anything resembling statehood. When Al Jazeera broadcast the grand opening of the office live in June, the camera panned to the black-and-white former flag of the Taliban's Islamic emirate on the building, and a massive sign behind the speaker's podium that read: Islamic Emirate of Afghanistan. Karzai immediately withdrew from the peace process.

Khalilzad was now trying to do better. As a former ambassador to Iraq, he had played a key role in the disaster unfolding there, too. He was also an old acquaintance of President Ghani. The two had studied together in the 1970s at the American University in Beirut, an intellectual hub of the Middle East. They both went on to pursue degrees in the United States—Khalilzad at the University of Chicago, Ghani at Columbia University in New York—with the aspirations of playing roles in their country's future. Their personalities and politics were radically different, and their working relationship during the peace process was often contentious. Khalilzad favored American-style capitalism and was a compromise-seeker, whose detractors said he could not be trusted. Ghani was socialist-leaning, insular, and so confident in his own ideas that many found him arrogant. In one of their first meetings after becoming the US envoy, Khalilzad claimed to Ghani that he had yet to meet with the Taliban, even though he had already sat down with them. In another meeting, Ghani treated Khalilzad to a PowerPoint presentation laying out his vision for peace, which involved his government and the United States sitting on one side of the table, across from the Taliban on the other. Khalilzad, who knew the Taliban would refuse to meet with the Kabul government, found the proposal completely unrealistic. Khalilzad saw Ghani as an obstacle to peace, and to the American withdrawal. Ghani was obstinate. He knew that any peace deal would require him to leave office, as the Taliban would never accept his authority—and he wasn't the only one in Kabul who suspected that Khalilzad might be gunning for his job.

Khalilzad's leverage was undercut early on, when President Trump announced in late 2018 that he would unconditionally withdraw seven thousand troops—half of the American contingency in Afghanistan. When the United States and the Taliban opened formal negotiations in Qatar the following month, on January 22, 2019, Khalilzad faced Taliban officials who knew that his boss in Washington was in a hurry. His counterpart was Sher Mohammad Abbas Stanikzai, a veteran Taliban diplomat. The negotiations centered around a four-part accord that Khalilzad had conceived of. In return for a full American withdrawal from Afghanistan, the Taliban would guarantee that al-Qaeda and other terrorist groups would not threaten the United States from Afghan soil, commit to entering into peace negotiations with the Afghan government, and engage in a cease-fire. Taliban negotiators would not commit to a cease-fire, insisting they would only consider it as part of later talks with the Afghan government. Khalilzad, worried that too hard-line a stance at this early stage would collapse the process, kicked the question down the road.

The negotiations went on for months. Throughout the process, Ghani was skeptical and felt sidelined. The United States was not negotiating a peace deal with the Taliban, but a withdrawal arrangement. The Americans had brought the war to Afghanistan draped in ornate language about democracy, nation-building, and human rights. Now, in order to exit the war, they prioritized outreach to the Taliban over the autonomy of the Afghan government, which had been democratically elected—albeit in elections plagued by fraud—according to a constitution the United States had helped write.

They reached an accord in February 2020, when Khalilzad and the leader of the Taliban delegation, Mullah Abdul Ghani Baradar, inked the deal. It committed the Afghan government to releasing thousands of Taliban prisoners as a precondition to launching Afghan peace talks with the militants.

Like many others who feared a Taliban return, Parasto was distraught. When the two negotiators shook hands, they were standing outside Afghanistan's borders, making commitments on behalf of the Afghan government without including it in the process. She felt betrayed.

The Americans hadn't shared the full text of the deal with Ghani before signing it. Ghani had seen a draft, but his notes and comments had largely been ignored. The final deal contained no agreement on a cease-fire or reduction in violence, even though it had been a central US demand at the outset of the talks. The deal also contained a secret annex and a series of verbal agreements that could be seen as double-crossing the Afghan government, including a guarantee that the United States would not help its Afghan partners conduct offensive operations against the Taliban, but only help them defend if they came under attack. The Taliban in return promised not to attack Americans in their bases or on their way out of the country. Meanwhile, reports filtering through Parasto's office showed how the Taliban slowly but steadily gobbled up territory in the provinces.

The peace accord also included a deadline for the US exit: May 2021. Over the coming months, the United States tried to persuade

Ghani to honor his part of the bargain—which they had negotiated on his behalf. The main sticking point was the prisoner release. The Taliban submitted a list of five thousand prisoners they wanted set free in order to begin talks with the Afghan government. Ghani's advisors were worried about freeing hard-core criminals, killers, and drug smugglers, and in May released just under a thousand Taliban prisoners they assessed to be of low risk. The Taliban insisted they would only enter into negotiations once all five thousand had been freed. The insurgents were in a position to play hardball. They knew the Americans were eager for the intra-Afghan negotiations to begin so they could leave by May the following year. They had momentum on the battlefield. The peace process had not meaningfully addressed the issue of Pakistan, which continued to supply insurgents with support and safe havens. As long as Taliban fighters were able to slip across the border, they stood a much better chance of being able to defeat the Afghan government.

The Trump administration pushed Ghani to relent but he stood firm. He saw himself as the rightfully elected leader of a constitutional democracy. "The U.S. doesn't owe us anything," he told Khalilzad. "If you want to leave, then leave—no hard feelings."

Some people around Ghani, and perhaps the president himself, still did not fully believe that the United States was actually serious about pulling out. Besides, Trump had less than six months left of his first term and would likely be voted out of office before completing the withdrawal. Parasto knew it was possible the Taliban would return to power, but she did not fully believe it would happen. She teased a friend, Ramin, who was convinced the Taliban would come back and said he was being dramatic.

"Imagine, Parasto," he told her. "If the Taliban come, they will burn the doors to the school, and the university. They will say that girls cannot go anywhere. They have to sit inside the house exactly like they did in 1996. Imagine everything that we've built today. None of this is going to remain. You and I won't even be able to sit and have a conversation like this."

She listened, then replied, laughing. "Perhaps we will have to speak over Skype!" she said.

In July, Trump announced the withdrawal of half of the remaining US troops from the country, almost a year before the deadline, further shrinking Khalilzad's leverage and giving the insurgents a massive concession before the United States had even assessed whether they were complying with their side of the deal. In August, Ghani called a *loya jirga*, a consultative assembly of political leaders, which approved the full list of detainees wanted by the Taliban for release.

In September, talks were formally inaugurated between the Taliban and a delegation from Kabul, which consisted of government officials as well as other political figures and civil society members, including a few women. Parasto felt uneasy watching the Kabul delegation meet with the Taliban in Doha. She thought the government delegation and their foreign partners kowtowed to the Taliban in a manner that made her stomach turn. The most visible female member of the delegation was Fawzia Koofi, a seasoned lawmaker from Badakhshan province who had long enjoyed privileged access as one of the first points of call for international media outlets or Western diplomats seeking the opinion of an influential, English-speaking Afghan woman. One of the most prominent women's rights activists in Afghanistan, Koofi was a bold critic of the Taliban and had survived several assassination attempts. When she sat down opposite the Taliban team in Doha, her right arm was still recovering from a bullet wound from the latest attempt on her life days earlier. The camera only filmed her head from behind, apparently pandering to Taliban demands that women's faces not be shown on television. Yet when the delegation, including the women, spoke to rolling cameras afterward, they gave the impression that the Taliban had changed, that they weren't the same extremists that two decades earlier had imposed some of the most misogynist laws in the world. Parasto worried that the female delegates had fallen for the Taliban's platitudes to foreign donors about wanting a peaceful nation for all Afghans.

"They are not listening to you. They think you're not a Muslim,"

Parasto said out loud as she watched Koofi on television. "They don't even look you in the eye when you're talking." She thought the representatives were forgetting about Afghan women back home by failing to stand up for themselves and insisting on being heard.

"If I have chosen you as my representative, I give you the place at that table to be my voice."

She thought back to her trips to the provinces. She had met women there who didn't even know who was in government in Kabul, because they never saw them. That did not give their representatives in Doha carte blanche to do as they pleased.

"If the government wasn't able to go to Uruzgan and speak to the people there, how can they sit in Doha and claim to represent them?" she said. Watching the whole process in Qatar from afar made Parasto fearful of what was to come.

The intra-Afghan talks never really took off. The two sides did not manage to even agree on an agenda. The republic wanted a cease-fire before anything else could be discussed, while the Taliban wanted to discuss Islamic governance. Khalilzad tried different maneuvers to keep things moving. He attempted to reach an agreement on an interim government to temporarily replace Ghani. He sought to get other foreign powers involved by convening a peace summit in Turkey. All of it failed.

In the meantime, in Washington, Joe Biden had defeated President Trump and was preparing to replace him in office. When Biden inherited the war, there were only about 2,500 US troops left in the country, an unsustainable number. Biden was left with a choice: bulk up the troop presence once again, a hard political sell at home, or go ahead with Trump's withdrawal. Biden, who ran for Senate in 1972 as an opponent of the Vietnam War, had always been skeptical of the Afghan war; as vice president, he'd gone so far as to tell President Karzai in 2009 that "Pakistan is fifty times more important to the U.S. than Afghanistan." Biden scrapped Trump's original withdrawal date, but set a new one of only four months later. He chose September 11, 2021, to coincide with the twenty-year anniversary of the terrorist attacks that had brought the United States to Afghanistan in the first place. It was a date bathed in symbolism, and for many Afghans, it was confirmation that their lives for two decades had been defined by the whims of American politicians and generals. Now, the Americans were ready to hand them over to the Taliban according to a timetable that seemed, most of all, designed to serve American sentimentalism and public relations purposes.

19

OMARI

On June 15, 2018, hundreds of armed Taliban fighters walked into government-held towns across Afghanistan. The army and police knew they were coming and let them pass their checkpoints, still armed. Face-to-face, enemies embraced. Soldiers invited turban-clad militants to pray in their ranks. Taliban fighters, some of them seeing these parts of the republic for the first time, handed roses to soldiers. On the highway outside Kabul, Interior Minister Wais Barmak pulled over his car to meet Taliban fighters. Throughout the country, Afghan civilians snapped selfies with Taliban fighters, many of them meeting the insurgents for the first time.

The Afghan government had announced a three-day, unilateral cease-fire to coincide with the end of Ramadan. The Taliban leadership responded by announcing its own cease-fire. This mutual agreement to halt fighting, even if just for three days, was unprecedented. Days before the cease-fire was supposed to take hold, Taliban forces killed scores of soldiers in several districts. But on the day of the cease-fire, fighting stopped. In at least half of the country's provinces, enemy combatants met peacefully, including several government officials and their Taliban shadow counterparts.

Omari, unarmed and wearing a black turban for Eid, greeted civilians, and in the suburb of Kampani walked up to a policeman and hugged him. They both cried. Walking around the city without fear gave him a glimpse of what his country could be.

"I saw that we are brothers, and that we fight because other forces are pitting us against each other," he said.

When the cease-fire ended three days later, fighting flared back up almost immediately. Still, the truce provided a rare flicker of hope. It demonstrated that Taliban commanders had sufficient control of their foot soldiers to stop the fighting if they wanted to, at least temporarily.

Even as the Taliban were negotiating their way to power through talks with the Americans, in reality they had been running shadow states in the countryside for years. The militants controlled large rural areas where they delivered services funded by international donors. The Taliban allowed aid to flow to their areas if they got to co-opt it and take credit, an arrangement the government and foreign donors preferred to cutting off entire swaths of the population. In Sangin in Helmand, the de facto Taliban capital, a young teacher said people in government areas were afraid to send children to school because of incessant fighting, so he had opened a private school for boys where he taught the government curriculum, using materials from public schools. In other instances, the Taliban violently seized infrastructure, kidnapping electricity workers until the government promised not to cut power to areas under their control. When they captured territory, they asked civil servants to stay in their jobs so they could continue to deliver services. The Taliban also created an accessible system of governance and justice in the provinces. They set up local departments of the Ministry for the Propagation of Virtue and the Prevention of Vice to uphold Islamic law, as they had in the late 1990s. Women didn't have the same protections they had in government courts, and justice was delivered according to ultraconservative readings of Islamic scripture, but it was swift and less corrupt than government courts.

One afternoon in Charkh of Logar, a province just south of Kabul where the Taliban had long been strong, a doctor named Abdul followed hundreds of other worshipers from Friday prayer into the bazaar, where the Taliban had told residents to gather. Militants dragged a man in front of the crowd and accused him of stealing motorcycles. A cleric beat the man's back with a rubber whip inscribed with Quranic verses until the captive passed out, Abdul said. With each strike, a second fighter incited the crowd to shout, "God is great." The affair took two hours.

In a different town, Arghistan in Kandahar, Kamaluddin, a twenty-five-year-old shopkeeper said that after the Taliban took control of his area they confiscated his brother's and father's smartphones. Saying they could be used for un-Islamic behavior such as playing music and videos, they forced them to swallow their SIM cards. Kamaluddin told the story during a trip to the government-controlled Kandahar city where he had gone to seek out the illicit pleasure of having his cheeks shaved clean at a barbershop. The Taliban had imposed mandatory beards in the village, and he would wait a week in town for his to grow back before returning home.

"They will put me in prison if they see me like this," he said, stroking his neatly trimmed mustache.

The Taliban raised money through taxation in villages and on highways. It profited from the drug trade through smuggling, protection rackets, and taxing farmers, and taxed the legal and illegal fuel trade with Iran. It used its money to fund a shadow state, seeking to present itself to Afghans as a cleaner, fairer administration-in-waiting than the current government. President Ghani had spent most of his adult life outside Afghanistan, and his government was full of foreign-educated young professionals. Many Afghans saw them as being out of touch with the population. The Taliban argued that, in contrast, they were of the soil. Ignoring the movement's long connections in Pakistan, they claimed to be a truly homegrown movement. Taliban supporters who had spent time abroad and spoke good English carpet-bombed social media with reports in English and Pashto about alleged atrocities committed by government or foreign forces. US drone strikes, night raids, and mistaken bombings of civilians played into the insurgents' hands, creating new enemies among the population.

Yet stories from people living under Taliban rule suggested that the group's governance was as ruthless as ever and, with decades of experience, also appeared more adept. Taliban members did not deny that they still favored corporal punishment. They banned music, forced men to grow beards, limited girls' education, and forbade women from leaving their home without a male relative or burqa. Residents of areas they controlled said beatings and executions of those accused of crimes were commonplace—with bodies of the offenders put on display in public squares as warnings.

In December 2020, Taliban militants chased down a group of robbers who had been preying on buses on a stretch of highway in Wardak under their control. After killing one suspected robber in a shootout, the Taliban left his body dangling from a lamppost by the highway as a warning, according to Hamid, a Taliban fighter, and residents in the area. Hamid recounted that he had kept watch outside a mosque in Sayedabad where the Taliban had apprehended an elderly man accused by one resident of asking other men for sex. The man was taken away and his feet were beaten with thick cherry-tree branches until he could barely stand.

"Our real strength is intelligence," Hamid said. "If you do something, we will find out quickly."

In May 2021, the Taliban in Musa Qala, Helmand, caught two kidnappers who had abducted two women and a man. In a video, the victims, chained and at gunpoint, asked their families to pay for their release. The Taliban freed the hostages and strung the kidnappers up from a tower in the town center. Residents gathered on sidewalks and balconies overlooking the square and watched the Taliban shoot the perpetrators, who were left hanging—eyes blindfolded and blood seeping through their clothes.

Officially, the Taliban did not talk about such incidents, but their fighters readily admitted that they supported this kind of punishment.

Zabiullah Mujahid, the movement's spokesman, said amputations should be reinstated once a sufficiently stable system had been put in place, including healthcare to attend to cut-off limbs. If they were to take power, the Taliban intended to bring back the type of Islamist rule they installed in the 1990s, Hamid said.

"What was wrong in the past? People always say we mistreated women, but it was a necessity at the time," he said. Hamid was sitting in the garden of a restaurant in Kabul during his first visit to the capital in nine years. He waved his hand in the direction of the city outside the walls. "These people, they don't know God." The Taliban were edging closer to the capital and he felt emboldened to spend a day there. Dressed in sandals and a brown shalwar kameez, with curly hair and a scruffy beard, he was distressed to see women in the city's middle-class neighborhoods wearing headscarves instead of all-enveloping burqas. An Afghan pop tune drifted over the wall from a neighbor's house.

"This is haram," forbidden, he said, gesturing at the music.

The Taliban's ability to bring order, however brutal, to much of Afghanistan in the 1990s remained the source of their strength in rural areas where parts of the population shared their values, if not always their violent methods. Locals described how the Taliban settled generations-long land disputes in months, rooted out corruption, and brought trade back to bazaars that had been empty for years. The Taliban were not monolithic and showed flexibility in their application of law depending on local customs of particular areas. In Helmand and Kandahar, they destroyed television antennas and devices that played music or video. In Logar, residents said those items were mostly allowed. Even Taliban fighters themselves watched television.

"We watch Turkish serials, especially *Osman*," a twenty-eight-year-old fighter named Samandan said. The show was a historical television drama called *Kurulus: Osman*, about the Ottoman Empire. "Without it, we can't sleep," Samandar said. He also used the internet to search Google and read news.

"If I can't use the internet, it feels like I'm missing a part of my body," he said.

For some, the quick justice provided a sense of security. Sangin in Helmand enjoyed a population boom as displaced families from more unstable districts in the province returned home after the United States signed the deal with the Taliban in February 2020. Monthly rental prices for a standard house had increased from ten dollars to around a hundred dollars over that period. Many villagers complained of excessive taxation, arbitrary violence, and poor services by the Taliban, particularly in schooling and health. Others said they now avoided mosques in Taliban areas because the insurgents pressured residents to provide tractors, food, and unpaid labor. Yet, as rural residents tried to adjust to their new de facto rulers in government-controlled areas, some influential civil society leaders were openly praising the Taliban's governance in the countryside.

"Most people want the Taliban to come back," said Mahmoud Saeed, a twenty-eight-year-old leader of the Hanafi Masjid Jamia, an influential mosque in Kandahar, the Taliban's birthplace.

"It was better during that time. Now, there is no Islamic rule."

The cleric perhaps wasn't representative of the religious elite at large, but his open praise of the Taliban was a sign that the mood was changing.

Omari had quit university and left Kabul for the provinces. He had tired of the topic of his degree, Pashto literature and linguistics, and wanted to learn skills that were more applicable in life, like engineering or computer science. He had no formal training, but as he gradually withdrew from the battlefield, he looked for other ways to be useful to the movement. In March 2020, he was sent to Helmand to help repair school buildings in Taliban-controlled areas that had been bombed by coalition forces.

"It was a simple task. The buildings were already standing there, and all we had to do was to repair the damaged parts," he said.

Over the next few months, he worked on about fifteen school buildings in villages in the Gereshk, Nawa, Nadali, and Lashkar Gah districts, some of which were surrounded by government troops. His employer was a private company that had cordial relations with the

Taliban, and Omari was able to slip unbothered between government and Taliban areas in Helmand, as he had done traveling from Wardak to Kabul. The construction company paid its taxes to both the insurgents and the government, depending on whose area it operated in. The government turned a blind eye to the company's activities in Taliban territory, and even footed the bill, as it also wanted the schools rebuilt.

"They knew what was going on," Omari said.

This was how the Taliban co-opted government services, whether it was the reconstruction of infrastructure or the distribution of aid from international organizations, who could either hand over food and school materials to the insurgents or watch thousands of children go without.

Omari found that he had a talent for engineering, but after his projects ended in Helmand, his commanders ordered him to Samangan, a remote province between the Hindu Kush mountains and the border with Uzbekistan. His assignment was dangerous and showed the level of trust they now put in him. His task was to establish contact with the district governors hired by the Kabul government, use his newfound knowledge of the building sector to pitch himself as a reconstruction contractor, and offer a bribe in return for a contract. If the governor took the bribe, Omari reported him to the local Taliban commander, who threatened the governor publicly in order for the local community to see that the Taliban were upholding clean financial practices. Omari remembered one district governor who, when discovering that he had been ensnared, broke down in his office in front of Omari and pleaded for forgiveness.

Omari found the intelligence work stressful. When moving across district lines, he always kept multiple SIM cards and avoided making friends. He had no qualms about luring government officials into taking bribes. He believed in the Taliban's interpretation of Islamic law, and trusted his commanders to apply it fairly. But he also knew that without guidance, some Taliban members were prone to petty revenge acts. He had seen Taliban fighters in insurgent-held areas parading thieves through the streets on donkeys. The thieves would face the rear of the donkey, their faces blackened with charcoal or oil, and were forced to shout into a megaphone that they repented.

"A man should not be disgraced in front of everyone. Maybe if he commits a crime several times, despite being given many chances to change his behavior. But I don't like this punishment without trial," he said. "We do have individuals and groups in our ranks who act arbitrarily, without bothering to ask their superiors for guidance or waiting for a court to decide." He believed in harsh punishments, but also in what he saw as due process in Taliban courts. He was worried about the Taliban's reputation. At the same time, he criticized the Afghan and international media for focusing on the Taliban's mistakes and violence and never portraying their governance fairly.

Omari's new role made him more money than he received on the battlefield, where he would often get paid nothing but food and the privilege of carrying a gun. He earned respect, too. Now in his mid-twenties, he was expected to find a wife, but most families were not looking for an insurgent to marry their daughter. They preferred men with actual jobs. He was introduced to the family of a woman who approved of his career when he told them he was an engineer. They never asked about his other activities, though he suspected they must have known. The woman's father asked Omari's father for a hefty dowry of 500,000 afghanis, and an additional 300,000 for the wedding—a total of more than $10,000. After Omari's family members collated all their savings, he still had to borrow half of the amount from shopkeepers and affluent men in the village. He met his wife on the wedding night, and once they were married, he was thrilled.

"I am completely content," he said. "Even if I had handpicked a girl for marriage myself, I could not have found a better wife than her."

Omari tried to pull back from the war, but he couldn't escape it. In early 2020, he went home to his village to visit a childhood friend, Huzaifa. Both men had joined the Taliban in their teens and had kept in touch regularly as they fought on different battlefields. Huzaifa remained committed to the armed struggle. It had been months since the two last spoke, and Omari was eager to catch up. When he pulled up outside Huzaifa's house, a mutual friend came to greet him. Omari was a couple of years older and had taught the two younger boys bits of the Quran. The friend walked with a limp after being injured in an airstrike, he said.

"Where's our friend?" Omari asked.

"Don't you know? He was martyred."

He told Omari how he and Huzaifa had been at the same house one night three months earlier when an aircraft swept in carrying what they assumed were members of the so-called Zero One Unit, a well-trained but brutal part of the Afghan special forces who conducted night raids in Wardak. During the battle, Huzaifah was shot in the head and left paralyzed for days before he passed away. No one had gotten word to Omari because they didn't discuss such matters over the phone. He had missed the funeral.

"This was most painful for me. Going to visit a friend you haven't seen in a long time, only to find out that he's been killed a long time ago is the most painful experience one could ever have," Omari said. Huzaifa had been a nervy kid, fearful of war. The friend who was now injured used to play tricks on him. When they were young teenagers, while a group of boys were talking about operations during a break from religious studies at the madrassa, the friend burst into the room and shouted that the village was being raided. The boys panicked and ran outside in a frenzy. It took them several minutes to realize that he had been joking. Omari and the other boys told him that this was nothing to joke around with. Huzaifa had disappeared. When they found him, he was shivering and crying, still in shock that the madrassa was being raided and that he might get arrested. A few years later, Huzaifa went to Pakistan to deepen his religious studies, spending the spring and summer fighting season in Afghanistan and the colder months across the border.

"When the leaves started to fall, he would go back to Pakistan," Omari said. "He was both a fighter and a maulavi"—a scholar.

The Zero One Units in Wardak were feared not just among the

Taliban but among civilians as well. They were part of the Zero Units, trained by the CIA to conduct risky clandestine operations in the hinterlands, with different provinces corresponding to their numbers. Zero One operated in and around Kabul. The units were now under Afghan control, under the National Directorate of Security, the intelligence agency, but Afghan officials said the CIA still footed the bill. The units were known in the villages for extrajudicial killings, torture, and arbitrary detentions. On the night of July 8, 2019, witnesses in Day Mirdad, an area not far from Omari's family home, heard helicopters circling above and knew a raid was underway. At dawn, members of the local health council went to a medical clinic run by the Swedish Committee for Afghanistan, an NGO, and found the place shattered, marked by a visible crater from a rocket. Staff members told the council members that the clinic had been raided by a Zero One Unit, who had detained all the staff and visiting relatives of injured patients, tied them up, and questioned them about where the Taliban was. They took four men with them, including the clinic's director, and shot them. Their bodies were found in the morning, except that of the director, whom they assumed had been arrested. A relative's body was also found near the clinic. The Swedish Committee called the murders a "shocking violation" of international humanitarian law. It was at least the second time Afghan special forces had visited the clinic in Day Mirdad. Three years earlier, special forces had raided the facility and dragged three people outside, two patients and an eleven-year-old visitor, and shot them dead.

In Omari's village, the Taliban feared the Zero Units.

"They terrified the whole area. People couldn't walk the streets after nightfall. We weren't even able to take patients to the clinics. Farmers couldn't irrigate their fields at night," he said. Their flashlights would attract the attention of the special forces, who shot anything on sight, he said. "They had no mercy. We expected American forces to release civilians who had been mistakenly detained, but we knew the Zero Units would not do the same. Whenever they came, we knew they would take revenge by killing a great number of people, including civilians."

Omari himself evaded the wrath of the Zero Units. But he lost many friends to them, and to the Americans.

"They're countless. I can't give you a number," he said. Grief and fear had ground him down for years. Trauma was not a term he was aware of and not something Afghans usually discussed. According to a European Union survey, 85 percent of Afghans said they had witnessed or experienced at least one traumatic experience. One in five suffered so much from mental health problems that they said they were impaired by them. Four decades of violence had created an epidemic of post-traumatic stress, but it remained mostly hidden. In the absence of better information, Afghans did what they could to help their afflicted family members. It often involved superstition.

In a rural part of Nangarhar, the Mia Ali Baba Shrine had for generations been famous for curing mental illnesses through forced asceticism and spiritual cleansing. The keeper of the holy shrine, a clerical snake-oil salesman who said his name was Mia Saheb, kept his patients in tiny concrete cells, their hands and feet shackled like prisoners. For forty days, he fed them only tea and bread with black pepper.

"We leave everything to God," he said. "The Earth and the sky have been made by God. God takes care of the patients."

The shrine keeper's critics said he was a fraud, and that patients only appeared better because, after more than a month in his hands, they had been completely sedated by hunger and physical restraint, and in the case of drug addicts had gone through a cold turkey withdrawal. But his treatment cost only twenty dollars, cheaper than hospital care. In one cell, a government soldier called Mohammad Qassem had been chained to a wall for thirteen days to rid him of what his family, who brought him there, had said was insanity. Mohammad Qassem said he just had a hashish addiction.

"When I don't smoke, I want to kill all foreigners," he barked, to giggles from a crowd of onlookers who had gathered at the cell entrance. He showed the wounds where the chains had gnawed into his wrists.

"They need to take me to the doctor instead of keeping me here like a prisoner," he said. "They made me crazier by bringing me here."

Omari did not speak about his condition with friends and family, and he was searching for the right words to describe how his mental state had changed.

"I have become forgetful. I forget things quickly. I have a hard time remembering the right words to use when I have a conversation with someone. Usually it takes several minutes to finally uncover the word I wanted to use in the first place. To save myself from embarrassment, I pretend as if I'm busy doing something else. Sometimes, I just stop talking for a while," he said. His temper was still calm but he had become jumpier, and his eyes often darted, unfocused, when others in a group were leading the conversation. He didn't like to stand in the street for more than a couple of minutes at a time.

"Another thing I'm experiencing is insomnia. It is hard for me to fall asleep. I stay up until three a.m. in the morning, thinking about the loss of my friends, life and death and such things." He had more symptoms. "It's causing me a headache. I often feel like my brain freezes."

Even mid-prayer he would occasionally forget parts of the Quran that he had memorized since childhood.

"I have learned three surahs of the Quran by heart but I struggle to recall them when I offer prayers. Sometimes I have to sit and keep quiet and wait in the middle of the prayer until the surah comes back to me and I can continue."

PART IV
EXIT WOUNDS

20

THE FALL

Immediately after the peace deal with the Americans was inked in February 2020, the Taliban went on the offensive. In the forty-five days after signing the deal, the militants conducted 4,500 attacks across the country—an increase of 70 percent compared to the year before. Nearly a thousand Afghan security forces were killed over that period. As September 11, 2021, the deadline for the withdrawal of the remaining US troops, approached, the Pentagon said the level of violence was "unacceptably high," though US troops and contractors were largely unscathed. However, the United States and the Taliban had pledged not to attack each other, and American airstrikes largely ceased. The United States stopped supporting Afghan forces in offensive operations. In return the Taliban would not attack coalition forces on their way out.

Joe Biden, the fourth American president to oversee the Afghan war, came into office determined to finish the withdrawal started by his predecessor.

"I will not send another generation of Americans to war in Afghanistan with no reasonable expectation of achieving a different outcome," he said. Over the summer of 2021, the Taliban advanced rapidly. On May 1, the original withdrawal date set by Donald Trump, the militants went on a lightning offensive. Zalmay Khalilzad, the US negotiator who had signed the deal with the Taliban, stood fast.

"I personally believe that the statements that [the government] forces will disintegrate and the Talibs will take over in short order are mistaken," he told US lawmakers in Washington on May 18. "The choice is between a long war and a negotiated settlement."

With the most vital piece of support for the Afghan government, American airstrikes, out of the equation, the Taliban swept through northern Afghanistan in June, taking dozens of districts and surrounding cities. In their deal with the Americans, the militants had pledged not to attack population centers. Instead, they surrounded them. They severed government bases from supply lines by taking highways and border crossings and occupying swaths of rural areas. Loath to see their country once again under Taliban rule, warlords in the west and the north whose power Ghani had tried to curb rustled up militias comprised of grizzled veterans of past wars. The militias boosted the morale of government forces, but their return sapped Ghani's authority as he sat in his palace surrounded by suit-clad bureaucrats who hadn't yet been born, or had lived abroad, during the Soviet occupation when the strongmen now providing muscle to the anti-Taliban resistance made names for themselves. For years, the Taliban had infiltrated government ministries, military units, and universities, as Omari had done, and even the airport security command center. Now those people got ready for the final battle. The technocrats in the palace had run out of ideas. Omari's superiors asked him to make his way from the north to Kabul.

In early July, the United States vacated Bagram Air Base north of the capital. They turned off the electricity and slipped out during the night without telling the new Afghan commander in charge, who, according to Afghan officials, only found out two hours after the Americans had left. The Pentagon said it had coordinated the handover of Bagram with Afghan political leaders and security forces, but either way, the base was ransacked by looters before Afghan government units managed to get it under control. The relinquishment of the largest US airfield in the country, including a prison holding about five thousand inmates, many of them Taliban, marked a point of no return. In June, the US intelligence community assessed that the Afghan government was likely to collapse six months after the American withdrawal was completed. Only weeks later, on August 6, the Taliban took their first provincial capital, Zaranj in Nimruz. The next day Jowzjan, Sar-e Pul, Kunduz, and Takhar provinces followed. Farah and Samangan were next. In Baghlan, Omari helped launch an assault on government forces, and only two hours later walked into the provincial capital. For the entire war, the Taliban had only ever managed to capture one provincial capital, Kunduz, which they held for a few days in 2015. Now, they had captured nine in four days. On August 10, US officials adjusted their assessment of the government's survival from six months to about ninety days. It would last five.

By August 15, Omari had made it to the western outskirts of Kabul. Word was spreading that Maidan Shahr, the capital of Wardak province, had fallen. There was nothing between the Taliban and the gates of Kabul but fifteen miles of open highway. The elders and the preachers in the mosques said that once the Taliban had taken Kabul, President Ghani would remain in office for up to six months while his government negotiated a surrender and transition with the Taliban. Omari went for a drive. When he returned twenty minutes later, the nearby government checkpoint, which they had planned to seize in the morning, had been ransacked and was now in Taliban hands. Fighters from the nearby town of Paghman had arrived while Omari was away, and they did not want to wait. The government security forces scampered away as soon as the enemy arrived.

"They all thought that if they handed over their gun, they would survive. So everyone had prepared his weapon and everything else to be handed over before the arrival of the Taliban. It was weird," Omari said. Government forces across the country had been surrendering without a fight for the past week, leaving Humvees and other American-supplied equipment to the insurgents. Local politicians and tribal elders negotiated surrender agreements between the Taliban and government forces. In all corners of the country, police officers and soldiers, who often had gone for months without pay, abandoned stockpiles of mortars and heavy machine guns, artillery pieces and convoys of armored vehicles, in exchange for safe passage.

Hours later, Omari and his unit were ordered to enter Kabul in the cover of darkness to stop the looting that had already broken out in some quarters of the city. The Taliban had cast themselves as purveyors of order, and they wanted the ouster of the republic to be as unchaotic as possible. As night fell, Taliban leaders called on the Badri 313 special forces unit to enter Kabul. The Badri force was a highly trusted Haqqani unit, which had already deployed men around the city to disarm government security forces and prevent them from destroying confidential documents when the city fell. Omari stood by the side of the road and watched the special forces roll into the city as the sunset burned the dust in the air orange. They dressed in body armor, which Omari and his fellow fighters had never been issued, and high-quality helmets equipped with night vision goggles. They looked not so different from US Marines, and were similarly secretive, even to Haqqani foot soldiers like Omari.

"At that point, I felt that it was over, that the Taliban were taking power," he said. As he walked around a city under liberation, Omari passed the Mahmoud Khan Bridge, named after a mid-twentieth-century prime minister under the monarchy. Two policemen in uniforms belonging to the republic whose president remained quietly ensconced in the palace sat deflated on the grass beside the road. When they saw Omari, dressed in village garb with his bushy but neatly groomed black beard, they approached him. They held their rifles out.

"Here, Mullah Saheb," one of them said, using an honorific for a scholar. Then they walked off.

For weeks, Parasto and her colleagues at the president's office inside the palace, the Arg, had noticed that Ghani's meeting schedule was busy. They could keep track of whom he met, including a lot of elders from the provinces, particularly from Kandahar and other areas in the south. Then his calendar went dark. Instead, a daily flurry of foreigners from embassies and UN agencies entered the palace. Columns of black cars, their passengers obscured by tinted windows, came and went.

"Nobody knew where the president was. Normally we knew his agenda, who he was meeting with, who was coming and going," Parasto remembered. "There was a lot of activity, but nobody knew anything. Even ministers, the big people around the president, they didn't know what was going on."

From her conversations with officials at the palace, she knew things were bad. Her friend Ramin, who a year earlier had warned her that the Taliban would strip their freedom if they returned to power, pulled her aside.

"Do you remember our conversation?" he asked. "It's here. Everything is finished." Ramin was Parasto's smartest friend, a thinker and poet, and he was often right in his predictions. He urged her to leave the country. To Tajikistan, Uzbekistan, India, Pakistan, Iran, anywhere.

"If you can, leave right now," he said.

On Thursday, August 13, after watching nine provinces and the key cities of Herat, Kandahar, Ghazni, and Lashkar Gah fall to the Taliban in two days without a fight, Parasto stopped going to the office. She had admired Ghani for years, longer than most Afghans who initially supported him. She saw now that he had never been able to save the country. One by one, the provinces had fallen. Military commanders she had spoken to said Ghani had asked them to surrender their weapons. True or not, he had let the military down, she thought. She partly blamed Ghani's inner circle for shielding him from bad news. But he must have known that soldiers were underpaid, underfed, and for years had complained about lack of support from Kabul, all while commanders and politicians in Kabul lived like monarchs. When they stood face-to-face with the enemy, who could blame the soldiers for refusing to die for a government that didn't have their backs?

"He will never be able to convince us that what he did was for our best," she said.

She called as many friends as she could think of and told them to stop going to the university. To stay busy and make herself useful, she and a friend helped a local charity collect clothes and other necessities for people who been displaced to Kabul by the fighting and were now homeless, camped out near her house. Parts of the city center looked like a refugee camp. In Shahr-e Naw Park, hundreds of families were camped out in tents, living off handouts from passersby. They sent their children to beg for bread outside bakeries, contending for space with street kids who had owned the turf their entire lives.

On Sunday, August 15, the first day after the weekend, Parasto went to a bank in the city center to withdraw all her family's money. She was hesitant to take it all out at once. Emptying the family account and bringing all that money home could attract robbers. On the other hand, if the Taliban took power in the morning, who knew what would happen to the banks? Many others with the same idea had queued outside the bank since two in the morning. She thought she would never get inside, so she started making her way back home through a pandemonium of traffic and confusion. Her mother called to ask if she was coming home for breakfast. Parasto hadn't slept properly for days but she had enough clarity of mind to realize that she needed to keep her family close now. Things were getting unpredictable. Yet she was calm, perhaps due to sleep deprivation.

"Where is everybody?" she asked her mother. "Don't let anyone leave the house."

Her father called and suggested that they go to the bank together, perhaps that way they could get their money. He had contacts in the bank. She convinced him to stay at home. When she made it to the house, she packed a small bag with her passport and other documents, two sets of clothes, and a pair of shoes, and put it under her bed, ready to grab.

It slowly dawned on Zahra that this time, the Taliban really were coming. Once Herat fell on Thursday, August 12, she realized this was it. She started preparing for a possible escape. On WhatsApp, she discussed with her sisters and mother what to do. In Herat, they told her, they could hear gunfire. No one slept much that night. Her family worried that the Taliban might single out Shias as they had in the past. They had already secured tourist visas for Iran, and in the morning, they slipped across the border. Before they left, Zahra told them to get rid of any trace of her from their homes, in case the Taliban visited while they were in Iran. Her mother had her election poster on the wall and photos of her around the house.

"What will you do?" they asked her.

"Don't worry. Kabul won't fall so quickly. It's the capital," she replied. The next day, on Saturday, Mazar-e Sharif, the second-biggest city in the north, fell.

The expertise of TLO, the NGO she worked for, was the peace process. They'd expected things to turn bad, but had told Zahra that Kabul would hold for at least two weeks. So on Sunday, August 16, Zahra still thought she had weeks to get out. She imagined the Taliban would force Ghani to resign and then take power. Still, as a precaution, she called an administrator at Green Home, her NGO, and told them to burn the documents of their two thousand beneficiaries.

Jawad had just turned eighteen, and had an appointment that Sunday, August 15, to put in his application for a passport. They went to the passport office at six a.m. After he had his biometrics taken, Zahra left Jawad in another queue and headed toward the office for a meeting. Outside the passport office, she looked at her phone and saw a message from a friend, who said the Taliban had come to Dasht-e Barchi. She jumped in a taxi and once it rounded the corner to Karte

Sakhi, they were stuck in a massive crowd, people shouting that Kabul had fallen. She called her office but no one answered. People left their cars in traffic to walk home. Her phone rang.

"Where are you, Zahra?" It was one of her colleagues, finally. She told them she was in the street.

"Go back," the colleague said. "The staff at the Arg have already left." The president's men had left the palace.

She felt it now, the fear. The security team at TLO had good connections in the palace and always provided reliable information. Through the taxi window she watched a police officer take off his uniform and sprint down the street in his underwear. Jawad called her. "Mom, they say the Taliban have entered the city. What should I do?"

"Take a taxi home immediately," she ordered.

She called Parisa several times but got no answer. Parisa worked as a clerk at a dentist's office in Dasht-e Barchi, but when Zahra called, the receptionist said she hadn't shown up for work that morning. Zahra called the guard at their apartment block. He said he had gone home and hadn't seen Parisa. Zahra's heart raced and her hands got clammy. Things were getting chaotic. What if Parisa ended up in the middle of a crowd of agitated men?

"Sister," the taxi driver said and looked at her in the rearview mirror. "Please get out here. The situation is not good. I want to go home." None of the cars around her were moving. She had dressed up for the office, a habit that made her feel confident and energized. Today she wore white pants with an azure top and high-heeled shoes. She took her shoes off and ran.

August 31. August 31. That's the date Fahim kept hearing when he asked people in the know how long they expected the government to hold out. August 31 was the most recent deadline President Biden had given the Afghan government for the withdrawal of US troops. When he messaged the son of the defense minister, Bismillah Khan, at 7:15 in the morning of August 15, he got the same message.

"He said we are going to be okay. The Americans have said they are staying until August 31," Fahim remembered. Until then, he had been told repeatedly, the Taliban would not storm Kabul. Besides, the government security forces were expected to fend them off for three to six months. The ship was definitely going down, but no one was about to drown just yet. Fahim had a plane ticket to Dubai that evening anyway, so he was good. He had moved his wife and children to the United Arab Emirates a couple of years earlier for security reasons and to put the kids in a good school. He was planning to go for about a week before making a permanent move later in the year. First, he had a tax bill to settle. He shaved, put on a suit and tie, and went to the finance ministry. He would go to the TV station afterward. Shortly after he arrived, officials at the ministry began receiving calls from relatives who lived on the outskirts of the capital. They said the Taliban were there. Police were abandoning their checkpoints.

Everyone Fahim spoke to still remained skeptical that the Taliban would take the city. But he might as well go to the airport early. At 10:30, the streets were already chaotic. He asked his driver to take the back alleyways, and to not bother going home first. He reached Hamid Karzai International Airport, where he met the commander of airport security, who pulled him aside. President Ghani was on his way to the US embassy, he said. Not a good sign. The airport was already full of police commanders, generals, former and current ministers. Many had seats on a Pakistan International Airlines flight to Islamabad that afternoon. Fahim could see the Kam Air plane he had a ticket for sitting idle on the runway. He spent the next few hours in the tiny business-class lounge, waiting for news, while the civilian planes kept getting delayed. Around eight in the evening, things took a turn. Suddenly there was a flurry of military planes, and a lot more people milling in the departure lounge. They were told that all civilian flights were canceled, and it didn't seem likely that they would resume anytime soon. Fahim walked out of the terminal to the VIP parking area, where his driver waited with one car. He usually traveled heavier, but he had sent the other drivers and guards home. Scrolling through his contacts, he texted the Turkish ambassador, a friend. The ambassador told Fahim to get himself to Abbey Gate on the military side of the airport, to the east of the civilian area. This part of the airport had been off-limits for civilians for nearly two decades. Now it was clogged with thousands of people. It was too crowded to drive, so Fahim got out and walked through the scrum. Young men were standing waist-deep in sewage water, clutching papers in plastic folders. At the perimeter before Abbey Gate, a soldier stopped him and asked where he was going. Fahim told them he was an ex-minister, and that he needed to get out of the country. The soldier raised his gun and pointed it at Fahim.

"You're leaving us behind, trying to run away?" he said. Fahim repeated that he was a former minister. He pointed to the people behind him, many of them holders of Special Immigrant Visas to the United States, given to Afghans who had been employed by the US government.

"There are other people, but I'm facing a serious risk here. Would you let me in?"

The soldier didn't budge. He kept his gun aimed at Fahim's face.

"You coward," he said. "You ministers destroyed the country and now you're trying to run away and leave us behind. No, stay there. I'm not going to let you past."

Fahim continued to argue and said diplomats from the Turkish embassy were waiting for him inside.

"Call them, then."

That worked. But even after the Turkish diplomats persuaded the soldier to let Fahim through, he still had to queue to get through Abbey Gate. The collapse of order was a great leveler, even if just for a minute.

"I was the same guy who had fifteen guards and twenty-three cars in the morning, and who could enter the same gates with VIP protocol. Now I had to wait behind the gate with five thousand other people for two hours to get in," he said. "It was humiliating."

Once inside, a bit of his status returned. He was served Turkish kebab, and he was kept in an area of the airport that was quiet and clean. Around four in the morning, he was called on to prepare to board the plane. Fahim noticed many dignitaries around him whom the Turks had helped out, including Sarwar Danish, the second vice president, Hanif Atmar, the foreign minister, and Ahmad Zia Saraj, the intelligence chief. Hours later, as they sat boarded on the tarmac and waited, Fahim looked through the plane window and saw thousands of people flooding onto the runway. The pilot said over the intercom that he was unable to take off. He drove to the periphery of the runway, where he parked the plane. Fahim gazed through the spherical plexiglass window from his seat in business class and watched hundreds of people swarming the wheels of a taxiing US Air Force transport plane. Among the desperate people crowding the wheels of the C-17 Globemaster III Fahim saw a young man whose name he would later come to know: Zaki Anwari, a seventeen-year-old soccer star born two years after the United States invaded his country. In what would become one of the defining images of the chaotic US departure from Afghanistan, Anwari mounted the plane's landing gear and held on as the aircraft accelerated and took off. Then he fell. Fahim saw at least one other person fall with him, but it was Zaki Anwari's death that was captured on cell phone video. The footage was eerily reminiscent of the photos of an unidentified man dropping headfirst from the World Trade Center during the September 11 attacks twenty years earlier, morbid bookends to the war. Anwari became an image of a generation of Afghans so desperate not to live under Taliban rule that they were willing to cling to military planes departing with the last shreds of the political and social order they had brought to the country two decades prior.

The Turkish plane stayed on the tarmac for hours waiting for the runway to clear. When it took off, on August 16, Fahim's thoughts and disappointment turned to the president and his closest circle, who hadn't informed other officials that they were leaving. He thought about the Americans who invested billions in building a new Afghan society only to walk away and watch their political project crumble in hours, and with it, everything *he* had built for himself.

"I was wearing the same suit I had on when I went to the airport from the ministry. I wasn't able to go to my home and take anything, not even my laptop," he said. "It was the worst feeling. To lose your respect, to lose your status, to lose a society, and to lose all your assets," he said. "It was embarrassing."

By the time Zahra reached the hilly park of Bagh-e Bala, most other people around her were running, too. She saw several men without uniforms carrying weapons. Crossing through a group of them, she heard one snigger.

"When the Taliban come," he said and pointed at her. He left the comment hanging in the air. As she ran, while constantly dialing Parisa, she tried to fix her headscarf that kept slipping down. Parisa didn't pick up. At the Bagh-e Bala square, where the road split and traffic went in the direction of her home, she waved down a motorcyclist. She pleaded with him to take her.

"I'll put my purse between us. We'll pretend that I'm your sister," she said, growing desperate. The man said he had his own family to get home to. They noticed a group of armed men watching her.

"Please, my daughter isn't answering her phone," she said, her voice breaking.

"Okay," he relented. "Hop on."

She reached the house at the same time as Jawad. Tears streaming down her face, she got off the bike at the end of the alley and ran. They found Parisa inside, curled up on pillows on the floor, fast asleep. She and Zahra had stayed up late following the news, and Parisa hadn't been able to sleep until early in the morning. Her phone was plugged into the charger but power had been cut, so it had died. She had no idea what was going on in the city. Zahra couldn't stop yelling.

"Why are you mad at me?" Parisa said. "What have I done?" She didn't believe her mother. Power had returned and they switched on the television, which showed that the Taliban had entered the city. The presenter delivered the news: the president had fled the country.

Zahra sat, frozen, for what felt like an hour. What was she supposed to do? Jawad didn't have a passport. The phone rang.

"No, Mom, there's no fighting in Kabul. Stay calm," Zahra replied and hung up. She needed to get off the phone, but it wouldn't stop ringing. The TLO security manager told her to burn all documents related to her work and wipe her phone. A staff member from Green Home called and said they had taken all documents from that office to a colleague's house to be burned in the garden. Zahra paced the house, unable to sit still. In the late afternoon, several friends called from abroad to ask how she was coping. Some of them cried. She was too stressed to engage in small talk, too confused to console anyone.

"What should I do, Shinkai?" she asked one of them. "My mind is frozen."

"Lock the door, and do not open it for anyone," her friend said. "Stay home for now. We will keep looking for a way out." Zahra phoned male colleagues and invited them to come stay at her house, but they said her home wasn't safe. The guard normally stationed on the ground floor of her building had left. Besides, it wouldn't be appropriate to have male visitors. She didn't expect the Taliban to come knocking immediately. She was more afraid of criminals and extremists who might seize an opportune moment in the chaos. She stayed up all night. There were bars on the door in the lobby and on the windows in the hallway. Still, she kept checking all the doors and windows.

At eight in the morning, she still hadn't slept when she looked out the window and saw three Taliban fighters opposite the apartment block, asking neighbors, it appeared, for her landlord. She was seized with dread. No reason to believe they couldn't come for her soon. She called the person she thought had the best contacts abroad and in Kabul, a human rights activist based in the United States named Horia Mosadiq. She told Zahra to find a place to stay as soon as possible, she couldn't stay at the house. In the meantime, Horia would look for a way for her to leave the country.

After the attack on the Mawoud tuition center, Zahra had stayed in touch with two of the injured girls she had assisted, Sima and Shukria. Now their families agreed to let her and the children stay with them. On the morning of Monday, August 16, the second day of the Taliban's new regime, Zahra called a taxi and walked out the door with Parisa and Jawad, carrying small bags containing their documents and a few clothes, so as to not draw attention. That night they stayed at Sima's. The next day they moved to Shukria's. Another human rights activist in the United States, Belquis Ahmadi, called Zahra and asked for personal information for her and the children so they could be added to a list of at-risk activists who needed help.

Horia called and told Zahra someone would be in touch soon. In case anyone was listening, the person would ask how her grandmother was. If Zahra was safe, she should say her grandmother was fine. If Zahra said her grandmother was ill, she was in trouble.

Wednesday morning, three days after Kabul had fallen, Horia Mosadiq called Zahra and told her to hurry home, change clothes, have their small bags ready, and wait for another call. She asked Zahra and the children to wear surgical masks to cover their faces, which many Afghans did anyway because of the ongoing Covid-19 pandemic. Zahra arrived home, got her things ready—then put the kettle on for tea. It made her chuckle to think that even now, there was always time for tea. She threw laundry in the washer. Around 2:30 p.m., she received a message from Horia Mosadiq. The point person who was supposed to pick them up couldn't get through traffic in time, so she needed to hustle to the airport in twenty minutes.

"There is a flight today, and I don't want you to miss it," she said.

Zahra hadn't known that the supposed safe place was the airport. She called a taxi, noticed her tea glass was still half full, the washing machine was still running, then gathered the kids, two backpacks, locked the door, and left the key under the mat.

The night raids started almost immediately. Omari heard from commanders searching the houses of former government officials and military officers to retrieve weapons and armored vehicles. There were many instances of looting. Taliban fighters hounded people in the street, telling them to dress appropriately according to Islam, and harangued taxi drivers for playing music in their cars. The Taliban had not even declared their Islamic emirate yet, but overzealous fighters, fresh off years in the battlefield, many of them seeing the capital for the first time, were adjudicating their personal interpretations of Islamic law already. The official Taliban line was that the robbers and harassers were opportunists who took advantage of the situation.

"They abused the name of the Taliban. They trespassed personal property and took personal revenges. They simply disguised themselves as Taliban by wearing a turban and pulling up their trouser legs," Omari said. He admitted that some of his fellow Taliban from the villages "were not familiar with the city and its culture," and that they would simmer down once the leadership settled in. To what extent the looters were Taliban or, as Omari suggested, imposters, wasn't clear. But after a few days, many possessions, including stolen cars, were returned to their owners. The Taliban leadership seemed intent on preserving their reputation as harsh punishers of crime.

Omari spent the first couple of days under the new regime walking around Kabul for the first time in his life without fear of intelligence agents. He manned checkpoints when needed. The turmoil at the airport continued, and he watched it dispassionately.

"It is natural. If the United States announces that it will take people to their country from Iran, Pakistan, or any other country, you will see everyone rush to be taken away, and create chaos," he said. The Americans could have started the evacuation of people who used to work for them months in advance, instead of calling everyone to the airport when the Taliban were at the gates, he said. (Coincidentally, critics of the Biden administration in Washington, DC, argued roughly the same thing.) Omari believed in amnesty for those who had worked for the former government, even those who worked for foreign forces and embassies. Only spies, Afghans employed by the national intelligence service, were irredeemable. And in the days after the takeover, he believed all Afghans who wanted to stay could do so safely.

"Those who fled Afghanistan were not at risk, unless they were creating problems for us. If they had remained, they would have been able to live here just like other ordinary Afghans," he said. "The people who fled Afghanistan were the people who wanted to do so anyway."

Two days after Fahim's plane had taken off, the airport was still in upheaval. Tens of thousands of people had amassed outside the airport gates and stood crushed against the blast walls. Some had jumped into the gutters, where they stood waist-high in water. A few planes had taken off with evacuees, but most of them had been waiting outside the gates for days. It took Zahra thirty minutes to get to the edge of the crowd. She had been told to go to the northern perimeter of the airport, which was guarded and walled like a medieval fortress, rather than the main gate to the south. Even the back entrance was heaving with people. The first perimeter was controlled by the Taliban's Badri force. Behind them were US Marines and Afghan special forces, who frequently ventured into the crowd, either to disperse it or fetch people for evacuation. Thousands of people waved plastic-sleeved recommendation letters, CVs, diplomas, and other documents proving they had worked for Western forces or embassies, in the hope that the Americans would pick them. Zahra called Belquis Ahmadi to say she had arrived. Promptly she received a photo on her phone of a letter. Show this to the Americans and they'll let you in, Belquis Ahmadi said. It was impossible to move. Zahra tried to approach a couple of Afghan soldiers. They were part of the Zero Units, previously tasked with conducting night raids in suspected Taliban villages but now deployed to secure the airport.

"Move back," one of them barked. Zahra shouted at him that she had a visa, although she didn't know what her letter said.

"Move back or I'll shoot," he shouted.

They were stuck in the middle of the crowd. Whenever someone tried to approach the gate, the crowd would swell forward, nearly lifting Zahra and the children off their feet. The soldiers fired in the air to get people to back off, sending the mob surging in the opposite direction, a wave crushing the air out of Zahra's chest. She tried to shield Parisa and Jawad with her body. She knew from seeing cricket victory celebrations in the streets that bullets fired into the air had to come back down, and this crowd was nothing but a huge, dense mass of flesh. Belquis Ahmadi called again and told Zahra to phone Homeira, an activist who had made it farther ahead in the crowd. When Homeira saw Zahra, she signaled to the soldiers between them to let her through. They were in a group of dozens of women's rights activists. A coalition of Afghans and Americans were working to get hundreds of at-risk women with their families out of Afghanistan. The coalition counted the Georgetown Institute for Women, Peace and Security, the US State Department, and two nonprofits, Mina's List and Vital Voices, the latter cofounded by former secretary of state Hillary Clinton. They were stuck for hours. Some in the queue got ill or were scared off by the crowd swelling and the flying bullets. Behind them, soldiers used tear gas to disperse people. Zahra was tempted to leave but Parisa and Jawad convinced her to stay. The activists had told them this was their one chance to get out.

An American soldier approached Zahra. She didn't speak much English, but she understood that he asked to see her papers. After she showed him the letter on the phone, she understood he said, "Email." She called Belquis Ahmadi, who made another call, and minutes later, an email from the State Department landed in her inbox. The soldier inspected it.

"Go, go, go," he said and waved them inside.

Inside the airport, they had their biometrics taken and were escorted to a container reserved for female activists and lawmakers, about sixty people in total including families. They were supposed to be evacuated to Albania that day, but the flight had been delayed to wait for women who hadn't made it inside yet to catch up. They spent the night on gravel outside the container. Zahra didn't sleep but Parisa and Jawad dozed off on two pieces of cardboard. For two days, they were asked to wait. Everyone was too nervous to eat, and the ready-made military meals they were offered looked foul. Zahra and the kids snacked on fruit and bread. Finally, on August 20, the charter flight arrived, decked out with Canadian flags. The flight still wasn't full, so instead of taking them to Albania, where most of the women who hadn't yet shown up were going to reconvene, it flew them to Bahrain. As the plane took off from Hamid Karzai International Airport, and the crowds of her desperate countrymen below shrank from view, Zahra was too tired to contemplate the magnitude of the turn her life was taking. She was still in a daze when they arrived in Bahrain, where they were placed in a roasting bus on the tarmac while they waited for another plane to arrive. She ate some rice and boiled zucchini placed in front of her. She watched Parisa and Jawad. They were adults now, and just as capable of making this journey as she was. She recognized the feelings of sadness and relief washing over her. She had felt the same when she escaped Herat for Kabul fourteen years earlier. Much like then, she was heading into uncertain territory with only one thing on her mind, safety for her and the children; this time, however, she wasn't fleeing her family, but the Taliban. They boarded a second plane, which touched down in Kuwait in the middle of the night. The heat was suffocating but the officials who dealt with them were friendly. They spent the night in an air-conditioned room with beds. Jawad was ravenous and ate the dinner they were served, while Zahra and Parisa showered and went straight to sleep. In the morning, they had a breakfast of tea, milk, cheese and bread, and chicken and meat skewers. They met with the other women from the plane, and it seemed no one knew where they were headed.

Jawad got the Wi-Fi password from an American soldier so Zahra could text her family. They hadn't spoken since they left the apartment in Kabul more than forty-eight hours earlier. When she turned on her phone, she saw ten missed calls from her mother. She sent her and the sisters a voice message over WhatsApp to tell them where she and the children were. She immediately received one back. Her mother was crying on the phone, terrified that she would never see Zahra again. Fatima was old and suffered from the same blood pressure and heart problems that had killed her husband. Zahra kept her composure enough to send a calming message back, telling her mother not to worry. Then she collapsed in tears.

21

A.J.

For months, American leaders had reassured Afghanistan that even as US soldiers were leaving, its engagement in Afghanistan would persist. To reassure Western aid organizations that it was safe for them to stay, and for financial aid to continue to flow into the country, the United States planned to maintain a 650-strong security force to protect the embassy complex after the last troops left the country on August 31. But as the Taliban were advancing, plans changed. The shadow of the 2012 terrorist attack on the embassy in Benghazi, Libya, that killed four American diplomats still haunted Democrats in Washington, and the White House could not tolerate another calamity of diplomatic personnel getting hurt. On August 12, President Biden ordered the embassy in Kabul to shut down and dispatched 3,000 US soldiers and Marines to Afghanistan. Diplomats shredded classified documents and destroyed hard drives with confidential material as they moved operations to the airport.

Ahmad knew most of the Americans had evacuated when, in the afternoon of August 15, he left his three children and wife at home and drove down to the US embassy. He had no better option. Having watched news of Taliban advances for days, people were scrambling to get out of the country, and he thought he'd try to pull whatever strings he had. He pushed his way through the crowd and told the Afghan guard protecting the entry gate that he had been an interpreter.

"I have to get out of Afghanistan now," he said, but the Afghan soldier rebuffed him and told him to go to the airport. By the time he returned to his home in Macroyan, a neighborhood of Soviet-built apartment complexes, word was spreading that the Taliban had already entered the city. Around 6:30 p.m., news broke that President Ghani had fled the country, escaping in a helicopter from the palace. For Ahmad, Ghani's escape was a shocking act of cowardice. Other leaders, including Ghani's government partner Abdullah Abdullah and former president Karzai, stayed put. Days later, Ghani explained himself on Twitter and said that leaving Kabul had been "the most difficult decision of my life," but that departing the country had been the only way to save Kabul and its six million citizens from a bloodbath. Many Afghans were not convinced. By the time Ghani fled, although the command structure around the capital was crumbling and government forces were deserting, Ghani's own presidential guard was intact. Judging from the Taliban's actions elsewhere in the country, where high-ranking officials had been allowed to defect unharmed, there was no indication that they were going to embark on a massacre in Kabul or harm the president himself.

As they watched the streets outside descend into a frenzy of panic and confusion, Ahmad and his wife, Palwasha, who worked as a midwife at a hospital in Kabul, packed their bags and a couple of blankets, and in the morning set off for the airport. The streets in most of the city were empty. Most people stayed at home, apprehensive about the turban-clad gun-wielding militants who now roamed the neighborhoods. The airport was a different world, it was mayhem. Ahmad and Palwasha with children in tow went to the airport's northern gate, meant to be a low-profile entrance for American citizens and high-priority cases. A crowd of people had already gathered and was growing, pushing its way toward the gate. Afghan special forces and US Marines were positioned along the perimeter to control the crowd.

Nearby, Taliban fighters were present to prevent people from flooding the airstrip. These were the militants that people were fleeing, but their tacit cooperation was also needed to ensure that the evacuation could take place at all. Afghan Zero Units in desert tiger camo declined to look at anyone's papers, focusing only on keeping the crowd at bay. Ahmad caught the attention of a US Marine standing on the wall and waved his plastic folder containing his certificates at the soldier.

"I used to work with your special forces as an interpreter. This is my family," he said, gesturing at Palwasha and his children. "How can I get inside?" The soldier told him to keep his family together and wait to be called forward. The family spent the first night, then the second and third, on the blankets brought from home, and survived on water and snacks handed to them by soldiers. With each day, the crowd grew, even as people were trampled and accidentally shot by guards who fired into the air or threatened with whipping with steel cables when the scrum got too close. In the afternoon of the third day, Ahmad felt a sharp pain in his leg. He bent down and pulled up his trouser leg. A bullet had grazed the flesh enough to cover his calf in blood. He took off his scarf and tied it tightly around his leg to stop the bleeding.

"What happened to your leg?" Palwasha asked when she saw him limping.

"Nothing."

"What happened?"

"Nothing," he repeated. Everyone's nerves were frayed and the last thing they needed was to worry about him.

The Biden administration hailed the mass airlift as an "extraordinary success." After a week outside the airport, Ahmad gave up. Their chances of getting inside were fading, they were all exhausted, and it was getting increasingly dangerous to stay, he thought. Most of the women and children who had been waiting outside had either been let in or gone home. The mood was getting aggressive. After they returned home, Ahmad slept for two days straight. When he ventured outside, one of his neighbors asked him why he and his family hadn't gone to America. The neighbor seemed to think that Ahmad's family, given his previous work experience, could get on the first flight out. Ahmad didn't like that the neighbor seemed to think of him as someone who had curried favor with the Americans, or the nosy manner in which the neighbor had questioned him. Lines of loyalty were shifting fast, and he had a bad feeling of what might come.

As August 31, the date of the American withdrawal, approached, the crowds outside the airport grew increasingly frenzied. On August 26, an Islamic State suicide bomber detonated his vest of explosives in the middle of a crowd near a group of US Marines outside Abbey Gate, on the south side of the airport. Nearly two hundred people were killed in the explosion, including thirteen American troops. It was an extraordinarily high death toll for one suicide bomber. Many were likely trampled to death in the ensuing chaos, but survivors later also said they had seen Afghan forces and Marines firing into the crowd, and at people who in panic tried to climb the walls. Three days later, in retribution, an American drone fired a Hellfire missile at a house inside Kabul. Drones had bombed many corners of the country but never inside the capital. The top US general called the operation a "righteous strike," but it quickly emerged that the drone had errantly killed ten innocent people, several of them children. After dozens of reporters visited the family and unearthed evidence of the civilian casualties, the US military eventually admitted its mistake.

After a few days at home, Ahmad ventured outside to buy groceries. He put on sunglasses, concerned that the Taliban might already be searching for people who had worked with the Americans or the toppled government, and went for a stroll. White Taliban flags emblazoned with the Islamic declaration of faith lined the side of the road. He picked up cookies and soft drinks for the kids, avoiding eye contact with militants as he hurried home.

On August 17, the Taliban gave their first news conference in Kabul. Descending from a marble staircase, Zabiullah Mujahid, the Taliban's longtime spokesman, took his seat in the front of the microphones. Reporters had known Mujahid for years, spoken to him on the phone or traded voice messages over WhatsApp, but had never seen his face. Mujahid's identity had been guarded so zealously that over the years, some had suggested that he might not be real and his name had been a pseudonym for a rotating number of Taliban officials. Yet here he was. In his midforties with a thick black beard and inch-thick eyebrows, Mujahid appeared both mild-mannered and authoritatively smug, beaming with the demeanor of a man who didn't have to answer to anyone in the audience and who perhaps enjoyed the curious eyes of the nation resting on him. From the podium, Mujahid announced a general amnesty for anyone who had worked for the former government, including soldiers and police. No one should fear for their safety, he said. Watching the news conference on television, Ahmad didn't trust the Taliban's promises.

"The Taliban say we helped the invaders, that we killed their friends and dropped bombs on them," he said. Why would the Taliban forgive them? In the days following the collapse of the government, he would occasionally get in a car with Palwasha to escort her for errands. With both their faces covered by scarves, trying to steady their nerves, they watched young Taliban members patrolling traffic, AK-47s in hand with the safeties off. Having a woman in the car seemed to deter the Taliban from stopping them, for now. Days after Kabul had fallen, he was traveling in a friend's car, without his wife, when the Taliban pulled them over. They found Ahmad's passport but didn't ask any questions and let them all go.

Shortly after, the Taliban seized digitalized identity data, such as payroll systems and employment records, containing the personal and biometric information of former security forces and other government employees; they were now in possession of fingerprints and iris scans, photographs, home addresses, plus names and photos of relatives. From then on, Ahmad mostly stayed indoors except to walk his nine-year-old son and six-year-old daughter to primary school, the only type of female education allowed by the Taliban, when Palwasha worked at the hospital in the morning. He was from a Tajik family, and before leaving the house he donned a Kandahari skullcap, to look

Pashtun, and a surgical mask stockpiled during the Covid-19 pandemic. Sometimes he added sunglasses, which made him look more
conspicuous but gave him a sense of safety.

"If they recognize me, they will kill me," he said.

After dropping off the kids, he went straight back home. He considered launching development projects to support women who, like
him, were forced to mostly stay at home, but he had little experience
in the field. Bristling with unspent energy, he washed dishes and
cleaned the house. He watched television: the Saudi-funded Afghanistan International or the BBC's Persian language service. On rare occasions when he did leave the house, he avoided talking about politics,
especially with taxi drivers, who were known to gossip.

Born in Kabul in 1982, he had been a young teenager when the
Taliban took power the first time. His father had a PhD in aircraft
engineering from Ukraine and worked for the Afghan army during the
governments of Zahir Shah and Mohammad Daoud Khan in the 1970s
before retiring as the country fell under Soviet occupation. During
the first Taliban rule, Ahmad watched from his father's fruit and vegetable shop as the Taliban's morality patrol units beat people to force
them to go to the mosque. In school, Ahmad and his friends always got
nervous when the Taliban came to class and asked the pupils to wear
turbans and read the Quran properly.

"We were good Muslims, but we didn't think like them," he said.

At fourteen, Ahmad saw the Taliban string up on a traffic pole in
a central roundabout the dead bodies of two soldiers who had worked
for the previous government. His father covered Ahmad's eyes, but
the boy wanted to see what was going on, even if it frightened him.
Twenty-five years later, weeks after the Taliban had reclaimed control
of Kabul, he saw news footage from Herat where the militants had
hanged the bodies of four alleged kidnappers from cranes.

The sight of the white Taliban flags, now ubiquitous across the city,
unsettled him. Before the militants took the capital, he had only ever
seen the flags in Taliban-occupied villages with the American military.

"It makes me wonder how we could lose all of this," he said.

The treasured Friday picnics were no longer an option. He once went to a park near home with his children but turned around at the gate when he saw a group of young Taliban playing volleyball inside. Sometimes he would take his son to a patch of grass near their apartment block to drink tea and eat cookies.

To get around town, Ahmad called his longtime friend Gul, a taxi driver who kept abreast of where the Taliban erected checkpoints and what kind of control each post conducted: from weapons searches of vehicles to full ID check and body frisking. If the two approached a checkpoint that looked problematic, Gul let Ahmad out of the car and drove alone up to the Taliban officers questioning drivers and passengers. He then collected Ahmad and they passed if it was safe, or took a detour. In the summer of 2023, Ahmad asked Gul to take him to his father's house in northwest Kabul. Driving through a shopping area of high-rises and street stalls, they saw a crowd of Taliban security officers congregating near a traffic incident. Gul told Ahmad to lie down on the back seat and cover his head with a white scarf. When a Taliban officer pulled the taxi over, Gul explained that the man in the back was unwell, and that they were on their way to the hospital. The officer checked Gul's license and registration, asked him to open the glove compartment, and waved them on.

Sheltering inside, Ahmad's days inched by. His wife's monthly $150 salary as a midwife was their sole income. He spent hours in front of the television, watching Taliban officials denounce the past twenty years of Western intervention and the role of people like himself in it.

"They say the Americans spent millions of dollars to bring democracy here and inject Western ideas into people's minds," he said. He used to stay fit by lifting weights in the gym. Now, he grew a paunch. His eyes sunk into his face, cupped by dark circles. He felt like a prisoner, kept in a dark hole with no light.

"I'm like a hostage," he said. "I'm just trying to survive."

Ahmad's work with the Americans began in 2008 when he was hired by a US contractor called Mission Essential Personnel, which supplied the military with interpreters. His primary motivation was money. The salary of about $1,000 per month plus bonuses was much better than any job the Afghan government or military offered. A graduate in English literature from Kabul University, and a native Tajik speaker, he had learned enough Pashto in school to work in all three languages. Based out of Camp Phoenix in Kabul, he worked for the first ten months under a US Navy officer called Tom Banda Jr. Like everyone else, Banda had heard stories of Afghan militants infiltrating bases to kill American soldiers and was always wary at first with new interpreters.

"You have to be on guard about any interpreter that comes into the environment," Banda said. "I wanted them to show me that they were willing to put their lives on the line." Ahmad did. His first mission outside the base was in January 2009, to Kandahar. Banda didn't accompany army units on missions into the field, but said Ahmad was always actively involved in social activities on base, such as barbecues, and participated in volleyball, soccer, and cricket games. He called him A.J. after his initials, and the nickname stuck.

"Everyone knew who A.J. was," Banda said. The two formed a close relationship, he said. Ahmad made a good enough impression to get hired by the special forces in early 2012. On his first night raid, his team went into the Tangi Valley in Wardak, within shouting distance of where the teenage Omari was cutting his teeth with the Taliban insurgency, learning how to handle rocket-propelled grenade launchers and placing improvised explosive devices under bridges. Ahmad followed the soldiers, walking in silence toward a village called Bala Khel. Outside the designated house, Ahmad's team stayed behind while another group breached the gate with an explosive charge. By the time Ahmad entered the compound, the situation was chaotic. Women were screaming at the "infidels" to get out of their house, and children were wailing. The soldiers had put three men they said were Taliban on the floor and confiscated a number of rifles they had found in the house.

"A.J., tell the women to back off!" one of the soldiers shouted. Ahmad was asked to translate questions about the presence of Taliban militants. The men said they didn't know anything. The Americans took the suspected militants back to the base, and Ahmad didn't see them again. He went on numerous similar raids and assisted special forces at the training academy at Camp Morehead south of Kabul.

He was often nervous before entering homes, worried that the people inside, even the women, might shoot at them. The soldiers carried sweets with them to give to children if they made a commotion during the raids, but the kids were too scared to take them. More than once Ahmad saw American soldiers body-search women in their homes and tried to gently tell them it wasn't acceptable.

"Sir," he told the special forces soldiers, "this is not allowed in our culture." This would often be met by suspicious looks, as if raising the issue made him look like a Taliban sympathizer. He didn't push it. His job was to translate and not ask questions. He never knew what happened to villagers brought back to the base, or whether they were actual Taliban. Most villagers kept guns in their homes, so that alone wasn't evidence. Then again, he didn't know much about village culture or the insurgency.

He worked in other provinces, mostly with Navy SEALs, the 173rd Airborne Brigade in Wardak and Logar, and the Combined Special Operations Task Force 10. In the summer of 2012, on an operation near Surobi east of Kabul with a group of French and Afghan national army soldiers, he was caught in an ambush. Ahmad couldn't see where Taliban fire was coming from, but the militants kept up the battle for five hours until the Americans called in two F-16s from Bagram Air Base that circled over the village and scared off the militants without dropping bombs.

His greatest concern was being recognized by villagers who saw him during the raids and always looked him in the eye: a contractor working for the foreign occupiers. Even worse was when villagers were invited to the base. They would promise the Americans to tell them in the future where the Taliban were hiding out in return for electricity, better schools, and paved roads. Ahmad suspected that once they were back in the village, they were willing to cut deals with the militants, and that they would remember his face. A decade later, after the Taliban took Kabul, he feared the memories of these villagers, who might have moved to the city, as much as he feared any individual Taliban fighter.

Ahmad was fired in August 2012 after a dispute over leave. Ahmad had gone home for the Eid holidays, but his superior called him and asked him to report back for duty. Ahmad told him he had promised his family he'd be around, and fighting had broken out on the highway so he couldn't get back in time. The American officer said he had twenty-four hours to report back or else he'd lose his job. That was impossible. After four years with the US military, Ahmad was unemployed. He found office work with various Western NGOs but never anything that could measure up to the thrill and excitement of the military.

In the first six months after the Taliban established their new Islamic emirate, at least five hundred former government officials and members of the Afghan security forces were killed or forcibly disappeared. In the first year, more than six hundred civilians, including former security forces, clerics, and others deemed to be opposition, were killed in Kandahar, Nangarhar, Panjshir, and Sar-e Pol provinces alone. In April 2023, one of Ahmad's friends and former colleagues, Habib, was on the highway to Jalalabad on his way to a picnic with friends when a group of Taliban fighters pulled them over. They forced Habib out of the car and shot him twice, in the chest and in the head.

In late March 2023, Ahmad was watching life pass by below his living room window when he saw two Taliban militants approach the guard at the front of the complex. After a short conversation, they went inside and walked around the blocks, appearing to ask residents questions. Worried they might be looking for him, Ahmad called a trusted taxi driver and asked him to wait downstairs. When the Taliban agents left two hours later, he took Palwasha and the children, locked the doors, and went downstairs and asked the taxi driver to take him across town, to his parents' house in Khair Khana. Since the Taliban took power, his father had returned to the bazaar where he now sold cookies. He barely made any money, and Ahmad's mother was incapacitated with bad knees. Conscious of not imposing on the old man, and keen to make sure the children still went to school, Ahmad returned home two days later. The security guard told him the two Taliban fighters had indeed been asking questions about him, but since no one gave him up, they had left.

Ever since the fall of Kabul and his failure to get evacuated, Ahmad had looked for opportunities to leave Afghanistan. Now he was getting desperate. His oldest sister, who was now fifty, had been living in Leeds in England since 2013, after securing a Schengen visa through her work for a Western embassy. That same year, his youngest brother, who had worked with the US military at Camp Eggers, while he was still employed managed to obtain a Special Immigrant Visa, an SIV, for Afghans. Two months before the fall of Kabul, President Biden announced Operation Allies Refuge, an evacuation plan meant to temporarily relocate eligible SIV applicants to a safe place outside Afghanistan, but the offer was available only to applicants who were already in the final stages of the process.

After Ahmad applied for a visa, he was told that the United States "cannot estimate how long the review will take" in an email from the State Department. His application remains in the first stage, his documents under review at the US embassy in Doha, Qatar.

In the 1960s, the United States fast-tracked permanent residency for Cubans after that country's revolution. A decade later it did the same for Southeast Asians fleeing the Vietnam War. The SIV program was supposed to accelerate visa decisions for people who aided the United States abroad. Yet, the process has been mired in bureaucracy. According to the Afghan Allies Protection Act of 2009, the visa process should be completed no later than nine months after an applicant submitted their documents. Two years after the fall of Kabul, however, roughly 150,000 Afghans who failed to get evacuated were stuck in Kabul awaiting a decision on their SIV application.

Banda said it was up to US Immigration Services to decide on visas, but that he couldn't understand what the holdup was. Afghans who had worked for the United States as interpreters for a couple of years or more should be considered for long service and good conduct, he said, and at least bumped to the front of the queue of visa applicants.

"I think the US owes him a bit of gratitude," Banda said. "One interpreter made sure that ten to fifteen soldiers were safe. There's the value right there." He said that Afghans who had already sacrificed years of their life, time with family, and their safety in service to the Americans had proven their value to the United States.

"If you have any kind of moral compass, you want to help them," he said.

Ahmad was slowly losing confidence that he would get the opportunity to leave.

"There is no good future here for my kids," he said. "Everything is looking dark." Once his daughters reached sixth grade, if the current laws remained in place, he would have to pull them out of school, a dramatic setback for the whole family's future.

"If women are illiterate, the family is illiterate," he said.

Weeks after the Taliban's visit to Macroyan, Ahmad's family marked the end of Ramadan, Eid, at home. As long as he could remember, Ahmad had gone to the mosque for Eid, the most important holiday of the year, but since the Taliban took power, he hadn't had the courage. He resented the Taliban for depriving him of even the smallest moments of pleasure. Before Eid, he had gone to a barbershop within the apartment-block complex, a safe distance from his apartment, and gotten a haircut. The barber knew what he wanted without asking: an American-style buzz cut. He still admired the Americans, although his regard for them was tinged with bitterness.

"I have many questions for the Americans. Why they left us behind? Why they made many promises but weren't honest? But no one is answering our questions," he said.

"The US did a good job in Afghanistan, they did a lot on construction, made a lot of military installations, helped our economy. But why, at the end, did they leave all these achievements behind?" Sheltered in his Soviet-era apartment on the fourth floor, he had no one else to pin his hopes on.

"I love the Americans. I always thought they were my friends," he said. "I am sure one day they will help me."

22

THE EMIRATE

Eighteen years after his bakery was destroyed in an American airstrike, seventy-six-year-old Mohammad Nabi returned to Sangin. Assisted by six younger men, he wrestled a brand-new clay oven off the back of a pickup truck. They placed it gingerly on the ground amid the ruins of his old shop. The houses in the bazaar around him stood scarred, shops and homes shelled into piles of bricks and gravel or disfigured by bullets and mortars into contorted shapes, clustered together like honeycomb.

Sangin in Helmand had probably suffered the heaviest bombardment of any area during the war. It had been the Taliban's de facto capital, with no running water, no electricity, and, after twenty years of war, barely a house left unscathed. The shops in the bazaar sold dust-caked fruits and vegetables, and eggs with tomato deep-fried in two inches of oil, but barely any products that weren't local. The petrol in the gas station was so diluted that it made cars sputter to a halt a few miles down the highway.

The old man had spent the past two decades in Kandahar and was ready to start rebuilding his bakery now that he had finally returned home.

"This is my homeland," he said, flashing a full two-toothed grin.

The return of residents to Sangin had already boosted the area's limited economy. On the banks of the Helmand River, largely dried up by drought, men collected gravel, pebbles, and sand, combined them with water, and stamped the mixture into bricks left to dry in the sun.

"The government is poorer than us," said a fifty-eight-year-old construction worker name Haji Safiullah. He tossed another shovelful of sand on the back of his truck.

"We just pray they won't take anything away from us."

After the Taliban captured Kabul, an unfamiliar calm settled over large swaths of the country that were the most active battlegrounds during the war. In the south, the Taliban's historical cradle, many citizens could now travel for the first time in a generation without having to negotiate their way through checkpoints, roadside bombs, firefights, or airstrikes. There was barely an armed man in sight, partly because most of the insurgents had been sent to the cities to secure them. Highway 1, the ring road connecting Afghanistan's biggest cities, was pockmarked with large holes from explosives, often only a hundred yards apart, a reminder of lives lost and bodies disfigured. Tens of thousands of Afghans returned home after years of displacement in other parts of the country, visiting relatives they hadn't seen in more than a decade. For years, driving the three hours from Kandahar to Lashkar Gah was too dangerous to even contemplate for many Afghans. Now, the road was clogged with traffic, even after dark. At Helmand's hospitals, the war wounded were replaced with casualties of car crashes.

A couple of weeks after the fall of Kabul, in early September 2021, a thirty-three-year-old man named Mohammad Hassan traveled eighteen miles from his home in Sangin for the first time in seventeen years. He traveled with thirty relatives, and they were welcomed by a similar number of uncles, aunts, and cousins when they arrived.

"We weren't even able to go to our relatives' funerals here," he said. "Before, crossing into Sangin was as difficult as going to America."

The safe roads also allowed Afghans to visit national monuments and attractions they had heard about their entire lives but perhaps never seen. In downtown Kandahar, pilgrims converged on a shrine that housed a cloak believed to have been worn by the Prophet Mohammad that Taliban founder Mullah Omar displayed as he proclaimed the Taliban's Islamic emirate in 1996. South of the city, off the highway, families paid tribute to the grave of Malalai, a female Afghan folk resistance hero who was said to have rallied Pashtun forces against the British in 1880 in the Second Anglo-Afghan War.

City and country Afghanistan had been affected by the war in vastly different ways. This much was evident from people's reactions in the early days after the Taliban seized power. In Kabul, the takeover was met with widespread panic. In southern Afghanistan, a more common mood was relief, tinged with profound loss. Since 2001, US airstrikes killed between 4,815 and 6,799 Afghan civilians. Afghan airstrikes killed an untold number as well. The southern region bore the brunt of those strikes. A twenty-seven-year-old resident, Habib Rahman, was asleep one night in 2018 when an airstrike hit his home in Sangin. He thought the plane must have been aiming for a bridge next door, often crossed by Taliban fighters. The strike killed fourteen of his family members, including his parents, four sisters, and six brothers.

"I was the only one who survived," he said. "Every evening when I eat dinner alone, I cry."

Ten years earlier, American soldiers bulldozed an entire tiny hamlet near Sangin after telling villagers repeatedly that they were being shot at from there. A resident, Abdul Razaq, now fifty, said that such disproportionate American punishments had made it impossible for him to support anyone but the Taliban.

"They claimed they came here for humanitarian purposes," he said, and pointed to his flattened village. "Is this humanitarian?"

The final months of the republic had seen fierce fighting in the rural south. In Katar Kalay, a small village of clay houses about twenty miles west of Kandahar, a gray-bearded farmer in his sixties called

Haji Bismillah had spent much of the past nine months before the Taliban takeover hiding in a tunnel under his house, during which his village had been on the front line during the recent battle for Kandahar.

"For nine months, we had to walk like this to water our fields," he said, mimicking crawling on all fours to water his corn and basil plants. He performed his pantomime to a gaggle of laughing grandchildren. To celebrate the arrival of peace when the Taliban took over, Haji Bismillah reassembled an improvised explosive device made from a fuel can that had been recently defused. Then he carried it into a nearby field and detonated it with a massive boom, like fireworks.

In the remote Mizan district of Zabul province, neighboring Kandahar, a pomegranate farmer called Yamatullah said that for the first time since 2005, farmers could now water their fields at night, which saved them loads of water. In the past, using a flashlight at night would get them shot at by the Afghan army or foreign forces looking for Taliban fighters, who'd occupied the village for fifteen years.

"Our children were afraid of shots and bombs at night. It felt like we were living in a prison," he said. Young men in the provincial capital of Qalat said they had started going for overnight picnics in the desert on Friday nights.

This greater freedom of movement did not extend to women. Afghan women had always been a rare sight in public in southern Afghanistan, but the country's new rulers pushed them further into seclusion, telling most of those who worked to stay home.

"I used to travel in the city with a veil over my hair. Now, I have to wear a burqa," said a female English teacher in Lashkar Gah. She hadn't been able to work since the Taliban took power and had no idea how to provide for her seven children, as her husband had also lost his job.

"We'll either stay hungry or beg, send our children to the neighbors, or we'll starve to death," she said.

A female math teacher from Kandahar said the Taliban took over her empty house, which she fled during the fighting, rummaged through her bedroom, tossed her clothes on the floor, and stole personal photographs and belongings. She now lived in hiding.

"I can't live in my home, I don't have the right to work in my own country, I have no salary," she said. "I haven't stepped outside the house in three months. I'm mentally broken."

"Dear Muslim brothers and sisters," a voice shouted through a loudspeaker mounted on the roof of a white pickup truck as the car crawled through a busy street in west Kabul. The truck carried members of the Taliban's religious police, deployed by the Ministry for the Propagation of Virtue and the Prevention of Vice, a much-reviled institution during their regime in the 1990s that the movement had kept alive and fine-tuned as an insurgency and officially reinstated after seizing the capital.

"Hijab and implementation of Shariah law is the duty of every Muslim," the person with the microphone continued. Dressed in white tunics and black turbans, the religious policemen were admonishing the citizens of Kabul, or more accurately, the women of Kabul, reminding them that times had changed.

"You, girl, fix your headscarf. Your hair is showing," one of them scolded a woman during another patrol. "Who are you showing off to?"

It had only been a few months since the Taliban took power, but they wasted no time. They swiftly introduced a raft of draconian social restrictions that in particular curbed the freedoms of women. Most significantly, they banned girls from sixth grade and up from going to school. Months later, they banned female university students, too. The new laws echoed the 1990s when women also weren't allowed to seek education under the Taliban. Live music at weddings was made illegal. Women now had to be accompanied by a male relative when traveling beyond forty-eight miles. In parts of Afghanistan, women had to be accompanied by a male guardian to go to the doctor. In the spring, as streaks of sun cut through the chill of winter, drawing people outside for picnics, the Taliban announced that men and women could no longer mingle in Kabul's parks, but had to use them on alternate days. Not long after, they completely banned women from parks altogether, as well as gyms. On April 1, 2022, the first day of Ramadan, the Taliban enforced segregation at amusement parks, prohibiting parents from taking their children together to ride the carousels. On the last day before the ban went into force, Saeed Jelani, a member of the Taliban's police force, visited an amusement park in Kabul. Was it illegal to have fun in the Taliban's Afghanistan? He insisted it was not—as long as women wore clothing that only revealed their eyes. Families milled around him eating ice cream an hour before the park closed for the last time before genders would be segregated.

"When men and women are close together, it leads to adultery and prostitution," he said confidently. He ignored three young sisters linking arms and eating soft-serve ice cream a few yards away.

"I feel like, from tomorrow, I will be in prison," one of them, Sedarah Afzali, said. A twenty-year-old high school graduate, she wore a tooth gem and a nose stud, nail polish and a bright orange headscarf. She said she had barely seen her girlfriends since the Taliban takeover because her family kept her from moving around the city alone for her safety.

"I begged my brothers today to take us here," she said. Her sisters, Nazi and Neda, age seventeen and twenty-three, nodded. Under the former republic, the country was at war, "but we could enjoy life," she said. "We had freedom."

The country's new rulers were changing the face of the capital. The Taliban's white flag, inscribed with the Islamic declaration of faith in black, was everywhere. For years, the massive red, green, and black tricolored flag of the Afghan republic had flown over Wazir Akbar Khan hill in the heart of the city, visible from miles away. The 97-by-65-foot banner was a gift from India, seen as a symbolic gesture and a sign of changing political winds that no doubt had been noticed in Pakistan. After the Taliban took control of Kabul, they swapped the republic's flag for their own, equally large and of a cheap synthetic material. Street vendors, some of them former soldiers and police officers

desperate to make a buck, sold small versions of the new flag to drivers in the roundabout just outside the former US embassy, whose walls
had been adorned with new pro-Taliban murals. Female faces were
erased from street advertisements. Tailors specializing in slim-fitting
men's suits said their business had nose-dived, and they now had to
go back to cutting traditional tunics. Suits and ties were considered
Western style.

Jarring to many Afghans was the visual presence of morality police, dressed in white lab-style coats that made them look like
doctors, but carrying AK-47s. In the swankiest hotel in town, the Serena, Taliban fighters loafed on the soft furniture of the lobby all hours
of the day, looking intrigued at Western journalists and aid workers.
One afternoon, Anas Haqqani, son of the Haqqani network's founder
and younger brother of its de facto leader Sirajuddin, who had spent
five years in prison before being released in a prisoner exchange in
2019, held court for a small group of Afghan and foreign journalists.
He spoke about the need for the international community to recognize
the Taliban. What he did not discuss as he reclined, dressed in sandals
and black turban, in a lounge chair a few meters from a snooker table
where foreign contractors used to socialize, was the incident in 2008
when a suicide bomber and three gunmen sent by his family's network
attacked the very same hotel and killed six people.

The liberal youth culture that a few months earlier had flourished
across the capital was now confined to small, semi-clandestine cafés.
In a coffee shop in central Kabul, where she and two girlfriends were
guzzling energy drinks and smoking cigarettes, twenty-five-year-old
Fatima Hashemi said her family tried to keep her from going around
town.

"This is the only place we can have a little bit of freedom." Her
friend stubbed out a cigarette on the floor, out of sight. She had been a
journalist under the previous government but now had nothing meaningful to do.

"We are too afraid to even enjoy this moment together," she said.
Until recently, men and women were allowed to mix in the

cafés. Now, women had been relegated to a corner behind bamboo screens. Music had been turned off, the only soundtrack supplied by a customer's iPhone playing a tinny-sounding pop song. When Taliban morality enforcers entered the coffee shop, the usher downstairs sounded an alarm on the upper floors to give female patrons a chance to fix their headscarves or put out cigarettes. Men felt the restrictions, too. The Taliban had ordered male government workers to grow long beards. Female staff had been told not to wear makeup. Basset Zewari, a twenty-three-year-old bitcoin trader wearing blue jeans and a red polo T-shirt to a coffee shop, said he still refused to wear traditional Afghan clothes every day.

"My father told me today, 'Be careful when you go outside in those jeans.'"

When the Taliban came to Kabul, Alex, the dancer, hid at home. He had heard that the Taliban stoned gay people, and that they cut tattoos off with a knife if discovered. He fingered the tribal-style ink on his neck. For the first four months of the Taliban regime, he left the house less than a handful of times. When he did, he dressed in traditional garb instead of jeans, popping the collar of his jacket. He wore a surgical mask to obscure his face, looking straight ahead to avoid people's eyes. His mother did the shopping for the house, while he sat at home in his room. Power outages made it impossible to watch television or rehearse dance videos. Not that he felt like dancing anyway. Most of the time, he sat leaning against the wall and stared into space until he got bored and lay down to rest.

Through contacts, he got in touch with a Canadian case officer who tried to help him win asylum, but so far he'd had no luck. Besides, someone had to look after his older sister, whose husband had died of cancer, and his younger sisters, who had yet to marry. Friends abroad wanted to send him money, but sanctions on Afghanistan's financial system made it impossible to transfer funds. His friends at the presidential palace had all left and it was too dangerous to go to the coffee shops where his friends normally gathered.

"It feels like my hands and feet are cuffed," he said.

For weeks after the Taliban takeover, Omari was in disbelief.

"I can't describe how happy I am. This was something we had never even imagined would happen, even when we were taking provinces one by one," he said. "We never thought we would capture the cities as quickly, especially Kabul."

He had faith the Taliban leaders would impose the Islamic regime they had talked about for decades. Weeks after taking control of the country, Taliban authorities in Herat had shot and killed four alleged kidnappers in a shootout, then strung their bodies up from cranes in a central square to deter others. To Omari, this was a promising sign that the movement was serious about keeping law and order. During the previous government, kidnapping was rife because authorities didn't deal decisively enough with them, he said.

"Now, after they've hung them, everyone is afraid. There was so much fear before in Herat. People now warn each other that if you commit a crime, you'll face the same consequence. The Taliban catch twenty to fifty robbers every day. Some people are suggesting that we should cut off their hands or hang one of them, so that no one will commit the same crime."

Human rights defenders criticized the Taliban's justice system for not providing defendants with fair trials or legal recourse, for discriminating against women, and for imposing inhuman and cruel punishments. Omari believed that as long as the Taliban's Islamic law was applied in an orderly manner, by the official bodies tasked to do so, it was the fairest way to mete out justice. A few weeks into the new reign of the Islamic Emirate of Afghanistan, he was walking a busy street in the city when he saw a man harassing a young woman. She cried out for help, and Omari and a couple of other *mujahed* who were close grabbed the man and dragged him to a police station. The man claimed to be the girl's cousin, Omari remembered, so they brought her in to confirm. She said the man had been harassing her for a while to give him her number. They punished the man by shaving his head and parading him around the city to show people what happens to wrongdoers under the new rule. At the end, they called the man's relatives to pick him up.

Omari moved his family to Kabul, sixteen people living in one small terra-cotta house on the western outskirts, near the highway. Reality slowly set in. At first, the Taliban takeover had a positive impact on many household economies, as travelers and traders no longer had to pay large bribes to cross checkpoints or get their goods cleared in customs. But those benefits were soon eviscerated by a more dramatic economic calamity. The international community responded to the Taliban overthrow of the republic by freezing Afghanistan's entire $9 billion reserves of foreign currency and putting sanctions on the Taliban. Importers could no longer pay for goods through bank transfers. Severing Afghanistan's access to foreign reserves and choking its trade options threatened to cause a total collapse of the economy and exposed just how fragile the economic system was. Afghanistan was deeply dependent on imports. Its trade deficit in 2020 was equal to about a quarter of its GDP. A third of the previous government's revenue had come from taxes on imports. It didn't even have its own money-printing presses, so people stitched together old, disintegrating afghani bills with tape. The new leadership was inexperienced and knew little about running a state. Restricting trade and finance to the country meant the Taliban couldn't service Afghanistan's foreign debt or pay civil servants, including teachers.

Afghanistan shouldn't have been so vulnerable. The United States spent $145 billion over twenty years to rebuild the country, more than it spent on the Marshall Plan to rebuild Europe after World War II, adjusted for inflation. That was on top of the $837 billion in American military spending in Afghanistan since 2001. But the American nation-building project failed. The United States spent $2 billion to improve Afghan farming over two decades, but agricultural input barely increased during that period, a failure also partly due to the war itself and a major problem as two in three Afghans still lived in rural areas. Since the US surge ended in 2012, foreign investment had declined and improvements since 2001 had begun to reverse. In 2008, 34 percent of the Afghan population lived below the poverty line, according to the World Bank. By 2019, the share was 55 percent. In 2021, the United Nations warned that the poverty rate could hit 97 percent of the population. Months after the Taliban seized power, more than half of the Afghan population were facing acute hunger, according to the United Nations. Ninety-five percent didn't have enough to eat. Some got so desperate that they resorted to extreme methods.

One man in Herat, Gul Mohammad, was besieged by people who had lent him money, and agreed with his wife that there was only one way they could pay those people back. They took their fifteen-year-old son, Khalil Ahmad, to the hospital, where doctors put him under anesthesia. Then they removed one of his kidneys. They sold it for $4,500, just enough to cover their debts. Both parents were unsuited for organ donation, as he had kidney stones and she had diabetes, and if they hadn't sold their son's organ, they would have had to sell their daughter in marriage.

"The night I made the decision, I cried so much. It was the last option. No father in the world wants to sell his son's kidney," Gul said.

Money was so short that the government struggled to pay its own loyalists, many of whom had spent years, if not decades, risking their lives on the battlefield to help the movement into power. After the takeover, Omari worked for a couple of months for one of his old commanders from Wardak, seeking out recruits for a new Taliban army academy. When the commander lost his job, so did Omari. He was offered a job as a commander himself, for a unit of twenty people, but his father asked him to turn it down, even though the old man was too old to work himself. He wanted his son to give up war and find a civilian job, and this time he got his way. During the war, as a construction worker, the father had occasionally done jobs for the

Taliban in Wardak, but in the scramble for employment, a man of his age got squeezed out. Omari had a bit of savings that he spent on his own family and the community around it, buying large sacks of rice and gallons of cooking oil. No one else was working, so he shared food with the neighbors, supporting a total of thirty people. He was struggling to pay rent. As winter set in, they could barely pay for firewood to heat the house. Even the local imam started charging worshippers 100 afghanis a month, about a dollar, to keep the stove burning and the place warm, until local Taliban commanders reminded him that the mosque should be a spiritual home even to those who had nothing. Omari mostly blamed the international community. In Doha, the Taliban had promised not to attack cities, a pledge he said they had lived up to when they walked into Kabul peacefully. When the Americans evacuated people from Kabul, the Taliban left them alone and did not attack anyone. They had also assured the West that al-Qaeda and other terrorist groups would no longer operate on Afghan soil.

"We have assured other countries that Afghanistan will not pose a threat to them," he said. In return, the global community of nations should recognize the Taliban and lift sanctions, he said. His was a very liberal interpretation of the Doha agreement, which explicitly said that the United States did not recognize the Taliban's Islamic Emirate of Afghanistan, and committed the Taliban to negotiating with the now-toppled republic, negotiations they had never undertaken in earnest.

Economic hardship was causing the movement to fracture. Throughout the war, the Taliban had remained remarkably cohesive, and now their leaders did what they could to stop foot soldiers and commanders from talking about internal disagreements, threatening to imprison anyone who spoke to journalists. But they couldn't silence everyone.

Sherzad, a twenty-eight-year-old commander of the Haqqani network, left the movement a few months after the takeover because, he said, the leadership hadn't done enough to fix the country's economy and provide for Taliban members.

"A lot of mujahideen have left the Taliban. It should be an alarm for them," he said. "If they don't listen to us, many low-level Taliban will fight against them."

Rival factions were now feuding over the spoils of victory, limited as they might have been. Fighters who dedicated years of their life to the armed struggle expected to be rewarded for their sacrifices with jobs and money. Instead they struggled to buy food.

"I have given martyrs from my family, but I still have no salary," said Qari Abdullah, a forty-year-old former Taliban commander who had left the movement. "I have to feed ten people. When we cook something, everyone fights over the food."

Two groups in particular were feuding over power, and over who deserved credit for toppling the republic. On one side were the Taliban from Kandahar and other southern provinces who were close to Mullah Abdul Ghani Baradar, a cofounder of the Taliban and one of its most important political leaders. Baradar helped negotiate the 2020 deal that paved the way for the US withdrawal. He and his supporters cast the takeover of Afghanistan as a diplomatic victory. On the other side were the Haqqanis, who said the victory was achieved through fighting, and in particular due to the steady supply of suicide bombers from their religious schools in the east of the country. The Haqqanis now complained that the leadership favored southerners and gave them most of the government jobs.

"The Haqqanis made more sacrifices. We gave more suicide bombers," said a former Haqqani commander who left the movement in anger. "But the Kandaharis get all the jobs."

For their part, the southerners complained that all the military power had been too concentrated in the hands of the Haqqanis.

One afternoon in the early days after the Taliban conquest, Omari had gone with his father to the grounds of the presidential palace to see if there were any jobs available. Inside, Baradar was meeting with Khalil Haqqani, brother of the Haqqani group's founder Jalaluddin. During the meeting, the two men disagreed loudly over the formation of an interim government. Baradar, by many tipped for the top job, was appointed deputy prime minister, and apparently felt he had been snubbed. Khalil Haqqani had been appointed minister for refugees, but his nephew Sirajuddin had become interior minister, one of the most powerful positions in the new administration, with oversight of the police and internal security forces. At the meeting, their disagreement escalated into a brawl. Khalil, large, bearded, and broad as a wall, threw a thermos at the bespectacled Baradar. People who had been at the meeting relayed the fight to Omari on their way out. After the scuffle, Baradar flew back to Kandahar and wouldn't be seen in Kabul again for months.

Ideological cracks were appearing, too. The main flashpoint was the leadership's failure to allow girls to go to school. Many Taliban fighters wanted their daughters to get an education. They had seen how Afghan girls under the previous government could go to school without violating Islamic laws, and many opposed the blanket ban on girls' education that had been in place during the first Taliban regime. As long as male and female students were segregated, there was no religious justification for prohibiting girls and women from studying, they said. Most of them seemed to think it was only a matter of time before girls' schools would open. After the Taliban seized Kabul, their leaders assured Afghans that by spring, once the right conditions were in place for schools to reopen, they all would.

Even Taliban government ministers thought the matter was settled when in March, days before the schools were set to reopen, they traveled to Kandahar for what was only the second full meeting of the new government attended by the movement's leader, Mullah Haibatullah. Two ministers gave presentations on the planned school reopening, arguing that it would stabilize the government and boost its domestic legitimacy and its chances of gaining international recognition. They met unexpected opposition from the Taliban's religious council, dominated by ultraconservatives. Mullah Haibatullah listened in silence, according to people with knowledge of the meeting. At the end of the meeting, the supreme leader said the reopening of schools for girls was on hold until further notice. Around the country, teenage girls who showed up to school in their uniforms were turned away in tears. Many Taliban commanders and members were shocked, too. Taliban officials in exile had sent their daughters to schools and universities in Pakistan and Qatar. Some had brought their daughters to Afghanistan on the assumption that they would be allowed to continue their education.

"When I heard about it, I got very upset. If a woman is educated, she can educate the whole community," a Taliban intelligence chief in Kabul who went by the nom de guerre Hakimullah said. "It was a mistake, and they should rethink it . . . This is a decision that concerns all Afghans, not just a few."

Omari, too, was deeply unhappy with the decision. The Haqqani network, which had informed his understanding of Islam and the reasons for the holy war, was generally in favor of girls' education. To many Western observers, it was a paradox that was hard to square. Throughout the war, the Haqqanis had been the most violent wing of the Taliban, exceedingly willing to commit indiscriminate violence, often using teenage suicide bombers. It had also been, comparatively, one of the most moderate factions on social issues. In the eastern tribal areas of the country, where the Haqqanis heralded from and had built madrassas, the network had allowed Western NGOs to run girls' schools for many years. Two months after the contentious meeting in Kandahar, Anas Haqqani still insisted that teenage girls would soon be allowed to go to school, in accordance with Islamic law and cultural values.

"If a matter isn't prohibited by Islam and Shariah law," he said in a televised address, "it should not be banned by an Islamic government."

Some Taliban members said the reason for the divides in the movement was that Mullah Haibatullah was too influenced by hard-liners with a more conservative reading of Islam. Others said proponents of girls' education had only been surprised by the religious leadership's position on education because there was poor communication between the supreme leader's circle in Kandahar and the government in Kabul. Messengers carried written notes between the two main centers of power, a habit they had kept from the insurgency.

"The problem of the education framework was that it was created in Kabul and the leadership wasn't kept in the loop," said one of those messengers, who went by Sharif. "Some of the ministers may get the idea that they are the biggest decision-makers, forgetting about the leadership in Kandahar."

The dispute over girls' education exposed how Taliban leaders were at odds over ideology: how to interpret Islamic law and how strictly to enforce it. Some Taliban members expressed anger publicly over an order by the leadership that all Afghan women should cover their faces in public.

"We shouldn't hide the identity of women in society," complained Jawed Nizami, a thirty-nine-year-old Taliban commander from Paktia province who said he would refuse to work for the government if it continued to impose limits primarily on women.

"It's also a man's responsibility to not look at women he isn't related to," he said. "We shouldn't blame women for everything."

Omari traveled the city, working his contacts and drinking buckets of green tea to position himself for jobs. For a short while, he worked as an administrator at the new Ministry of Defense. Clocking in from nine to five with little to do but browse the internet was a new and, frankly, dull reality. He lived in peace in a city that for his entire life had been a symbol of moral decay, a fortress of invaders, but that was now his home. This was what he had fought for. Yet his fingers itched for the gun. There would come a time when he would have to fight again, he was convinced of that. And he wouldn't mind. There was no other way of putting it: He was bored. War had been harrowing, and it had been fun.

In the coming months, new insurgencies reared their heads— Islamic State cells in the east persisted, and a small band of rebels in the north called the National Resistance Front put up a fight in the Panjshir Valley. Omari tried to pitch himself to the newly established security agency, the General Directorate of Intelligence. The GDI had secret police working to infiltrate enemy groups, which Omari had experience with, but because his tasks in the past had mostly been secret, he didn't have many references and struggled to get a foot in the door. Omari didn't belong to either of the powerful groups. He may have fought for the Haqqani network, but he was not from the east where the group originally heralded from. After the victory, he and other Wardakis found themselves on the bottom rung of the jobs ladder.

"The mujahideen of Wardak fought very well, better than the mujahideen of other provinces. We didn't harm doctors and engineers. We didn't kill these people." He had helped secure the highway between Wardak and Kabul, which had been key to the final victory, he said. "Now, there's no Wardaki in the top positions of the government," he continued. "Even though Wardakis are very educated people. We have religious scholars who have master's degrees, who are sitting at home." At his most frustrated, he said, "They used me to fight their war, but at the end of the day, I'm nothing."

After two nights in Kuwait City, Zahra and the kids were guided onto a small plane and flown from the international airport to an air base where they boarded yet another plane. Because it was just the three of them, it was easier to find space than for other families, which meant they were split up from the larger group of activists. No one told them where they were going until the captain welcomed them on board their flight to Washington, DC. They arrived in the American capital in the early hours of August 23. The airport was mostly empty and their papers were processed quickly. Once through immigration, a bus drove them to a compound set up for the incoming rush of evacuees from Kabul. When Zahra walked through the door, a crowd of American soldiers waiting for them broke into a rapturous applause. She teared up. It felt like she had been crying on and off for days. She felt fortunate to be safe, but at the same time, the warm welcome to America, a strange land, manifested for her that she had left her home country behind. In a matter of days, she had been hurled back into a refugee's existence. She had spent half her life displaced. Now she would have to teach her children how to live that life, too.

"It was very heavy for me. We had left the country in a very horrible situation. I was thinking about the people left behind. I was thinking, why can't I be in my own country, with my own people?" she said.

After a few hours' rest, they were put on a plane to Volk Field Air National Guard Base in Wisconsin, from where they were bused to Fort McCoy, one of eight military installations across the United States designated by the Biden administration to house Afghan evacuees. Zahra, Parisa, and Jawad were put up in a two-story building, seven families to each floor, sharing three toilets and six shower stalls. They quickly agreed to divide the bathroom facilities on each floor by gender. To get some privacy in the sleeping quarters, people made curtains of their bedsheets.

By October, Fort McCoy had become a holding pen for about thirteen thousand Afghan refugees waiting to be settled in various parts of the country. Those who had relatives in the United States left the base quickly. Those who found sponsors who volunteered to help guide them through the American system followed. The less fortunate could spend many months at the base. Zahra did not know anyone in America. All she had was $100 from her apartment in Kabul. At first, Parisa and Jawad were upbeat despite the spartan living conditions. As the weeks dragged on, they began to wither. Jawad became so lethargic that he barely bothered to eat. After two months, Zahra decided she needed to leave the base, even if she had been warned that if she didn't follow the official procedure, she could end up in the street. She called acquaintances back in Afghanistan who gave her the number for a man named Hossein Mahrammi, a fellow Hazara who four years earlier had made the same journey with his wife and two children from Kabul.

"My name is Zahra Yagana," she said when she called him up. In Kabul, she had made a name for herself among Hazaras, especially since her run for Parliament. "You probably know who I am."

Hossein Mahrammi had never heard of her. Nonetheless, he agreed to lend her money for the flight from Wisconsin to Washington, DC, and her first month's rent once she had found a place. Afghans looked after each other abroad, he said. On October 22, she landed back in Washington, two months after she had first arrived. Mahrammi then got to work and facilitated a fundraising campaign for her. Zahra watched as other Afghans came together, this time for her.

"Mahrammi did exactly for me what I had done for others in Afghanistan," she said. In the end, he fundraised $10,000 for her. This, to Zahra, was evidence of a God she wanted to believe in, one who did not punish arbitrarily but rewarded people for doing their best.

"God is kind, and sees our hearts and good deeds. If you're honest, he will reward you," she said. About a month later, she received authorization to work.

Many Afghans faced more obstacles after arriving in the United States. In the first four months after Kabul fell, about seventy-five thousand Afghans were given permission to live in the United States temporarily. Tens of thousands lived for months in US camps, waiting for work authorizations and resettlement. US officials and former ambassadors to Kabul conceded that the system was unprepared.

Zahra was relieved to see Parisa and Jawad settle quickly into their new lives. She had left Afghanistan partly because she wouldn't have felt safe under the new regime, but also because she wanted to make sure that her children would be able to shape their own futures. After everything she had been through, she knew she didn't want them to have to make a life under the Taliban.

"I had fought so much for my personal freedom," she said.

Parisa took to the American way of life instantaneously. She dyed her hair green, then red. She walked around the capital's parks, speaking and laughing loudly. She claimed space in a way that could have been dangerous in Afghanistan. Zahra wanted her daughter, now in her early twenties, to grow up as unburdened as possible by the pain that had tainted her own life. There was also discrimination in the United States, and Zahra firmly believed that women everywhere suffered due to their gender. But here, at least, Parisa could plan a future with many opportunities. She eventually enrolled in college to study dental hygiene. Zahra wanted Jawad to become a man who was friendly and respectful toward women. She would like him to get rich, too, she would say with a laugh. Mostly, though, she wanted him to be a gentleman. At eighteen, he behaved almost too modestly with women. He avoided their gazes and spoke to them with deference. He said he knew that men tended to make women uncomfortable. Jawad began a degree in graphic design and got a job running the teleprompter at an Iranian news channel. Life in America forced him to adjust his view of others' lifestyles, even as he guarded his own faith. When they first arrived, it upset him to see Americans drink alcohol. Zahra asked him to be less judgmental.

"It's their culture," she said. "They drink wine like we drink tea." Some of the most lauded Persian poets, Hafez and Saadi, were practicing Muslims but also wrote extensively about wine, she reminded him.

It was Hafez who wrote in the fourteenth century: "O Beloved, upon this river of wine, launch our boat-shaped cup / And into this river throw those weeping with envy / Wine-bringer, throw a cask of wine into my boat / For without that, for forty days and nights on the open sea, I will die of thirst."

Like Saadi a century before him, he was a native of the Iranian city of Shiraz, famous for its namesake grapes.

"Even though I am drunk and worthless, be kind to me / And on this dark heart shine the light of your smile," Hafez wrote.

During her first year in America, Zahra tried alcohol three times. Once, she had wine for Thanksgiving at an American friend's house. The second time she had a wine-colored substance that tasted different and made her nauseous and dizzy. On a third occasion, she drank a couple of shots of some clear alcohol with an Afghan friend. They went for a walk in the cold night air, and she felt light and happy.

Zahra focused on fundraising campaigns for Afghans, especially widows, and she got involved with organizations advising newly resettled Afghans. She kept as busy as she had been in Afghanistan.

"Time in the US passes really quickly. I haven't had time to take care of myself," she said. Yet her longing for her home country had not diminished as other refugees had told her it gradually would. In

Afghanistan, her mother's health was deteriorating, but she refused to live with her remaining daughters. In her older age, she often justified her tough child-rearing by pointing out that it had made her daughter tough. Now that she herself was ailing, she didn't want to burden her daughters. It was up to her sons to take care of her, she said, but they were too busy. Zahra and her sisters hired a housekeeper who could care for her. Parisa helped out, too, insisting on sending some of her own money to Fatima. Zahra frequently spoke to her mother on video calls, and Fatima said she was happy to see her daughter gain a little weight in America. Zahra stopped wearing her hijab in public, which she had never liked anyway. Zahra's God was not one who needed to be impressed by what women wore. This had been a source of tension with her mother. But even her sister Tahera, who was more conservative and taught at a theological institute in Herat, had taken Zahra's side and always said that women should primarily wear the hijab for their own safety. Zahra thought back to a visit to her mother's house a few years earlier when she had sat on the floor wearing a loose headscarf and rolled-up sleeves that drew attention to her crimson-red fingernails. She had conversed loudly with the guests, spreading a cackling laughter through the house. Her mother had pulled Tahera aside and asked her to tell Zahra that her dress was immodest and her manners too bold. But Tahera told her mother that as long as Zahra did not feel harassed, it was not up to them to tell her, an adult woman, what to wear. Zahra still wore a headscarf during Skype calls with colleagues in Kabul who had stayed behind. Her coworkers knew her as a Muslim woman, and many of their parents saw her as a role model, someone they wanted their children to aspire to emulate. But America was becoming home. If life here had taught her one thing already, it was that you didn't have to care what people thought of you. She often reminded herself of the saying her mother used to describe her. It hadn't been meant as a compliment, but Zahra took it as one: "A thorn, no matter how beautiful the rose, will always be sharp."

23

PARASTO

Parasto didn't flee. During the first chaotic days after the Taliban's conquest of the capital, she left her bag under the bed untouched. If someone had offered her a seat on a flight out, she might have taken it, but no one did. One by one, her former colleagues from the palace were airlifted out of Kabul. Many of her friends left, too. No one provided Parasto with guidance on how to get out.

Stories soon began circulating about Taliban fighters killing and raping former government employees. Parasto was terrified of going outside. For weeks, she barely left the house. Initially, she allowed herself, cautiously, to believe what the Afghan government negotiators and the Americans had told the Afghan population after meeting with the Taliban—that the Taliban had changed. A month after taking power, when the new government announced that girls were no longer allowed to attend school after sixth grade, she fell into depression. She kept her curtains drawn and never knew the hour of day. She lost her appetite and forgot to eat. The only person she spoke to regularly was a male friend who had also stayed behind. They spoke once a day, and she often cried on the phone with him.

One day, her friend asked if she wanted to help out as a translator for some foreign journalists he had been in touch with, a welcome distraction. When she met with the reporters, they took her along to a meeting at the house of a senior Haqqani commander. It was the first time Parasto stood face-to-face with a Taliban member. The Haqqani commander was different from what she had imagined. Instead of a hate-spewing, wild-eyed warrior from the mountains, she met an elegantly dressed, eloquent man in a crisp tunic and well-tended beard. In the presence of foreign journalists, he was charming, joked around, and even looked Parasto in the eye when answering questions for her to translate, something she imagined most male Taliban wouldn't do.

After the interview, the journalists kept asking her if she knew about any secret schools for girls, like there had been during the previous Taliban regime. She didn't, but their questions set her mind working.

Over the next few days, Parasto called dozens of people, searching for a teacher willing to defy the Taliban's edict. Officially, the Taliban had stated that girls from sixth grade would be able to return to school once school uniforms, gender-segregated classrooms, and other undefined conditions had been brought into accordance with Sharia law and "Afghan culture." Parasto knew from a CNN documentary from the 1990s that the Taliban had said the exact same thing back then, without ever allowing girls' education to resume. Some Western observers, as well as Afghans, seemed to hold out hope that the Taliban would eventually relent, but Parasto felt certain they wouldn't.

"I am one hundred percent sure they are never going to reopen the schools," she said.

Through a university friend, she met a secondary school teacher named Rahela who invited her to her house. Before the Taliban, Rahela had taught twenty girls in a school in Kabul, and now she said she'd be willing to set up a classroom in her own house. Parasto said she would fundraise for books and other materials, or if she failed, pay out of her own pocket. They put a four-by-two-foot whiteboard on the wall and filled a cupboard with copies of the Quran. If the Taliban came knocking while students were there, Rahela would tell them she ran a madrassa, which they had declared were legal. Her husband agreed to maintain the ruse.

Days later, groups of girls started arriving, climbing over the back wall of Rahela's compound to avoid the Taliban patrolling the main street. Twenty girls spread out on the floor in front of the whiteboard. Parasto was astonished.

"If they hadn't been this motivated, even while they were afraid, it would have been hard for us to do," she said. "Don't make them forget what they have learned," Parasto told Rahela. "Let us at least help them finish the semester."

It took only a few days before other teachers heard about the home school in Rahela's house and approached Parasto to ask if they could help. Days later, with the addition of several teachers, about sixty-five girls came to Rahela's house in one afternoon, and Parasto realized they had outgrown the space. She found a landlord in Dasht-e Barchi who was willing to rent them a house for 4,000 afghanis a month, about fifty dollars. They decked it out with rugs on the floor and Qurans in the cabinet. Parasto decided to expand the school to include adult women who hadn't received an education during the first Taliban regime. She called the program Second Chance and enrolled fifteen women who came to the school for afternoon shifts, after the morning classes for children had ended. Parasto spent the days at home, working the phones to find more teachers and emailing friends and contacts abroad to find funding. Weeks later, she opened two more schools, in the neighborhoods of Khoshal Khan and Arzan Qimat.

When the inevitable happened and a group of armed Taliban one day came to Rahela's school and asked the landlord who his visitors were, the landlord replied that he didn't know but that the women and girls used the house as a madrassa, and that he always left the house before they arrived. The Taliban commander asked him to call the manager of the school and waited while the landlord pretended to call Parasto, punching the wrong number. The commander lost patience and asked for Parasto's number so he could contact her himself. Minutes later, she received a text.

"Hi, how are you?" The next message only contained a photo of a Taliban flag. She blocked the number.

The unannounced visit had spooked the landlord, who asked Parasto to move the school somewhere else. Another teacher had been stopped in the street by Taliban fighters who said they saw her every day and asked where she was going. Parasto and the teachers decided to suspend classes for ten days to let things cool down. It was December 2021 by the time they reopened in a new house, this one owned by a teacher and her husband. The girls huddled around a woodstove to keep warm.

The Americans had justified their withdrawal from Afghanistan by saying they had extracted peace guarantees from the Taliban. But when they walked away, they silently abandoned one of the fundamental pillars meant to ensure that peace. Twenty years earlier, President George W. Bush had said that there would be no peace without education for all Afghans: "Peace will be achieved by helping Afghanistan develop its own stable government. Peace will be achieved by helping Afghanistan train and develop its own national army. And peace will be achieved through an education system for boys and girls which works."

Most Muslim scholars agreed that there was no religious justification for banning girls' education. The Taliban's prohibition seemed designed for political purposes, as a building block in a new totalitarian system.

There were historical precedents for banning education as a way to suppress a people and keep them from revolting. In the antebellum United States, most southern states made it illegal to educate enslaved African Americans beyond religious instruction, primarily to prevent them from rising up against their masters. Even so, activists, teachers, religious figures, and even some owners of enslaved people ran secret schools for African Americans. American enslaved people hid their books, but were whipped, mutilated, and sold for seeking education. The girls who attended Parasto's home schools under the Taliban's violent theocracy stuffed books in the bottoms of backpacks and hid their homework on notes slipped inside Qurans. In reality, Parasto suspected that the Taliban knew about the schools, and that many of their officials in the capital silently allowed them to exist in a legal gray zone, perhaps because they secretly supported girls' education, or because confronting the schools with force was a battle they didn't need to pick right now. Many senior Taliban officials sent their daughters to school in Doha and Pakistan. They monitored the schools, she thought, to show Afghan women, in particular, that they were being watched and intimidate them from claiming any more freedoms. She thought parents were safe to send their children to school. Her own safety, as her profile among teachers and the Taliban who watched them grew, was a different matter.

The Taliban were right to fear education. Schools and universities exposed Afghans to secular ideas and notions of human rights and equality—values that the Taliban saw as Western despite the strong dedication to those ideals among many of their fellow Afghans. As such, schools were potential cradles of insurrection. At the very least, Parasto thought, education would make the Afghan population immune to Taliban propaganda.

"A literate woman will never allow her children to join the Taliban, or to marry a Talib," she said.

Parasto doubted that the Taliban even believed their own religious justification for the new rules. An important verse in the Quran says, "La ikraha fiddin," or "There is no compulsion in religion." To be a true Muslim, you have to be a Muslim at heart. Parasto thought the Taliban were simply trying to prevent women from socializing, inspiring each other, and hatching plans.

"It all comes from the fact that they don't want women to meet each other and unite," she said. "If a woman who is in a bad situation, or who is married to a Talib, goes out and meets other women, she will see that their life is better, and expect a better life of her own," she said. "If women are united, they can change the world.

"If even one woman shares a video online, everybody will talk about her, and it will go viral. They cannot deny the power of women. This is why they don't want women to go out. They want to silence them, and make sure they don't sit together and plot a revolution."

Case in point, in Iran, nationwide protests erupted in September of 2022 after a twenty-two-year-old woman, Mahsa Amini, died in the hospital after being arrested and mistreated by Iran's morality police, allegedly for violating the country's strict Islamic dress code. Iranians across the country rose up in anger. Some of the biggest and most enduring protests emanated from the country's universities. In high schools, girls filmed each other stomping on pictures of the Islamic republic's founder, Ayatollah Ruhollah Khomeini, and the current supreme leader, Ayatollah Ali Khamenei. High school girls banded together to forcefully evict government officials who visited their schools.

Such scenes must have worried the Taliban. For an Islamist movement trying to build a durable totalitarian regime in the twenty-first century, the Islamic Republic of Iran, having survived forty years of war and waves of unrest, provided a playbook. The greatest threat to the clerical rule came from educated women. The only street protests against the Taliban in the early days of their new reign were also orchestrated by women. The militants struck down hard, beating women in public and arresting multiple protesters in the following days. Banning women from parks, gyms, and most offices made public socializing and organizing for women exceptionally difficult.

Parasto knew the Quran did not ban women from education. On the contrary, the Hadiths—accounts of Prophet Mohammad's thoughts and actions—stipulated that seeking knowledge was a religious duty for all. The Quran said that knowledge was power, and that "good guidance" was necessary in life for all, regardless of gender. She decided to take her schools beyond Kabul.

Afghan women had created lives for themselves under oppressive self-proclaimed Islamic rule before, and they would do so again. Women from other cities were asking Parasto to help them set up home schools as well. Parasto was slightly concerned that her phone number was circulating among strangers, but there was nothing she could do about it. To standardize the schools, she required that the teachers find at least twenty girls from sixth to twelfth grade, and ten illiterate adult women who wanted to study as well, plus a house with cheap rent that could operate as a dedicated classroom. If they did, she'd make them part of her network and find funding for them.

Over the coming weeks, she opened schools in Mazar-e Sharif, Herat, Kandahar, and Uruzgan, followed by an eighth school in Kunduz. They were filled to capacity immediately, and the total number of girls in Parasto's schools grew to about three hundred. She had friends in all the cities who helped check in on schools. She made regular video calls with the teachers so she could see the classrooms for herself and make sure the schools followed the national curriculum, which she knew from her time in government.

"I was the minister," she said, laughing.

She founded an NGO, through which she administered the schools and fundraised from foreign benefactors; the organization was called Srak, Pashto for the first light at dawn. She would occasionally visit all the schools in Kabul but left the management and teaching to other women. The schools ran largely on their own. She visited the first school that she and Rahela had opened in Dasht-e Barchi and asked the girls there what they wanted to be in life. Astronaut, teacher, president, they said. A girl in sixth grade made Parasto choke up.

"I just don't want to be like my mother," the girl said. Her mother had grown up during the Taliban regime in the 1990s and could not read or write.

"Everywhere in the world, if you ask a child in sixth grade who they want to be like, they will say my mother or my father, because they are their heroes," Parasto said. "In Afghanistan, children don't want to be like their mother. That was really brutal to hear."

As spring surrendered to summer, Parasto resumed an old habit of starting her day walking in the hills to escape the warming dust bowl of the Afghan capital. One morning, she was hiking above Kabul with two female friends and her brother Inayat, snapping photos of each other overlooking the city, when they were approached by a couple of Taliban fighters.

"What are you doing up here in this outfit?" one of them asked. Parasto and her friends were dressed in long-sleeved coats covering their legs to the knees, but because of the heat, they had pushed their headscarves slightly back.

"Pray. Recite the Quran for us," the Taliban fighter said. All four knew their scripture and complied.

"So why are you on the wrong path?" the fighter said, unimpressed. "Is this what democracy is?" In Taliban rhetoric, "democracy" was synonymous with the Western-backed political order they had fought for twenty years. He addressed one of the other girls: "Where is your father?"

"He is dead." That was true.

"So you're a bastard," he said. The Talib turned to Inayat.

"Do you call yourself a man? You take your sister to the mountains when no one is around to take her picture?" he said. Inayat was the only male in the group, seventeen years old, and as Parasto's brother, her chaperone. It was clear that the two other girls had come without one. The Taliban led Inayat away from the group. Parasto was seized with fear. They asked him to define his relationship to the two other girls.

"They are like sisters to me," he remembered saying.

"But are they your sisters?" Inayat admitted they were not.

"This is Afghanistan. You can't just do whatever you want," the Talib told him. They brought Inayat back to the group and told the other girls to leave and Parasto and Inayat to stay. The girls walked off. As they turned around to look back at her, Parasto saw they were crying. There was no one else on the hill at this hour. Parasto recited the shahada, the Islamic declaration of faith, to herself.

"Listen to me carefully," the Talib said. "If I ever see you two around here again, I will kill you. I won't hesitate." They stood up to leave.

"Hey," the fighter said. Parasto turned around, careful not to look him in the eye.

"I was talking to you." He held out his AK-47. "Do you see this gun? I will kill you if I see you here again," he repeated. "I am letting you go only because you are Pashtun." Shaking, Parasto promised never to wear that outfit again, and to never return to the hill. As she and Inayat walked off, the Taliban fighter fired two shots into the air. At the bottom of the hill, they found the two other girls sitting on the ground, crying. They had heard the shots and thought the worst. They kept walking down into the city until they could no longer see the Taliban fighters following them.

If the Taliban wanted to unsettle Parasto, they had succeeded. Her experience on the hill convinced her that the militants were willing to use violence at random, and that their efforts to squeeze women out of public life had only just begun.

"In six months, you won't see any women in the streets of Kabul," she predicted in the late summer of 2022. She became fatalistic, expecting to be kidnapped or worse at any time.

"So many before me have been killed or hurt," she said in her most despondent moments. "I have a strong feeling that my time has come."

Her mood clouded.

"I hope I will be remembered as a kind and gentle girl," she said. She was twenty-four.

The Taliban came to the school in Dasht-e Barchi again. They were different gunmen this time, and they had followed two of the girls there. The teacher's husband invited the gunmen inside to see for themselves. Twenty girls sat in a room, Qurans in their laps. The man explained they were running a religious madrassa, and they were all his daughters and nieces and children of his cousins. The schools are closed and the girls need somewhere to be, so my wife teaches them the Quran, he said. I don't even come in here. The gunmen said they'd confer with their commanders and get back to them.

When she heard about the incidents, Parasto asked all the schools in Kabul to close for a while to see if they would receive more visits. When the Taliban hadn't returned after a week, the schools reopened.

In late December 2022, the Taliban instituted new restrictions on women. Afghan women were no longer allowed to work for nongovernmental organizations, neither local nor international. The new rule further curbed women's ability to participate in public life, but also eroded the livelihoods of thousands of Afghan families who depended on women as breadwinners. Widows and wives of men who weren't able to work were suddenly left without means to provide for their children. The decision threatened to deepen Afghanistan's already dire humanitarian crisis. Jobs had dwindled with the exit of international organizations, embassies, and militaries. According to the UN, 90 percent of Afghans did not eat enough, and half the population faced acute hunger. Former middle-class citizens lined up for sacks of rice and beans and bottles of vegetable oil. Malnutrition caused children to be born early, imposing further costs on families. And now winter set in, forcing families to find money not just for food but heating as well when the highland temperatures dropped well below zero for months at a time. The Biden administration had responded to the Taliban's ouster of the republic by seizing roughly $7 billion in foreign exchange reserves of the Afghan central bank held on US soil. Another approximately $2 billion in foreign reserves held in other banks abroad were also frozen. Humanitarian donors and Afghans across the political spectrum said freezing Afghanistan's funds did not hurt the Taliban but the Afghan people, and called on the United States to release some of the funds, but the Biden administration refused, saying that the Taliban had abandoned a peace process meant to lead to an end to sanctions targeting the movement. By the end of 2022, two-thirds of the country's population of forty million people depended on humanitarian aid, and international organizations faced the dilemma of accepting the Taliban's draconian rules that violated fundamental principles of international humanitarian assistance or halting their operations. Some organizations did the latter, temporarily. Many others continued on.

On December 20, 2022, the Taliban also officially banned women from attending university, closing the last remaining avenue for female education beyond the age of twelve. Parasto's sister Forozan, who was twenty-three, worked with a local television station—one of the few places women were still allowed to work, though they could only do so under tough scrutiny. Her other sister, Tamana, who was seventeen, had been at university but was now forced to sit at home. Their father, Abdulhakim, was distressed to see his daughters' lives constrained.

"Tamana cries, she is depressed, she can't see her friends," he said. "Women make up half of society. I want to find a way for my daughters to get an education."

Parasto and some friends started a group on WhatsApp, asking university teachers they knew to share a link for female university students who'd like to continue their studies online. Four hours after they created the group, nearly eight hundred girls had joined. Sixty students attended the first online class. Parasto instructed the university teachers to use the old curriculum of the republic, but she also wanted to teach the students about the current situation of the country.

"In Afghanistan, we have gender apartheid. We wanted to make that clear for them," she said. "We need to protest peacefully. We want to put peaceful thoughts in the minds of people."

Six months earlier, Parasto had predicted that by now, women would not be seen in the streets of Kabul. That premonition was coming closer to reality. One of her friends was detained by the Taliban and asked specifically about her activities. In moments of perhaps foolhardy defiance, Parasto had given a couple of interviews to international media about her schools. The Taliban asked her friend to tell her to be quiet.

When he was released, Parasto's friend came to see her.

"Don't leave the house," he said. She protested that if they already knew who she was, they could come for her regardless of where she was. Her friend said it would create more of a scene if they arrested her at home.

"Please don't go anywhere, and keep your phone off," he urged her. Parasto did as he suggested. For the next couple of months, she only left the house once, to bring winter clothes to the schools, relying on her father to bring food home for the family. She managed to keep her phone turned off for about a week.

On January 15, unknown gunmen entered the house of a female former lawmaker in the middle of the night. Twenty-nine-year-old Mursal Nabizada was one of only a handful of female members of Parliament who had chosen to stay in Afghanistan, hoping, according to her former colleagues, that the Taliban had changed and she would be able to do some kind of work in the country. She was one of the few public female voices in the country, and a vocal critic of the Taliban. The gunmen shot her to death, alongside one of her bodyguards. It was one of the highest-profile killings since the Taliban had taken power. Taliban authorities pledged to investigate. However, of the several hundred civilians killed in targeted attacks since the Taliban takeover, not a single one had been properly investigated.

Secluded at home, Parasto watched the curtains draw around her country. She thought she was still in shock.

"I cannot cry," she said. "I cannot laugh, but I cannot cry either. It feels like a dream, unrealistic."

In this waking nightmare, she pictured herself standing as if in a circus, the star attraction, in the middle of several circles of spectators. The first was made up of Taliban, the second of women in burqas, their eyes barely visible. The third circle in her dream was made up of Afghan citizens who had helped the Taliban come to power. She felt as if something wasn't right with her face or the way she was dressed, but she was unable to see anything but grinning faces. All she could hear was them laughing at her.

The growing dangers put pressure on her family. If she was detained, even if she returned unharmed, her father would be known as the man who couldn't prevent his daughter from getting taken by the Taliban. No men would marry their daughters off to the sons of a man like that.

"It's all about their dignity," Parasto said. She knew her parents were proud of her, even if she didn't tell them everything about what she did.

"Every second, every minute, we worry about her," her brother Inayat said. He had seen the messages Parasto received from Taliban members who let her know they were watching her. He and Parasto had not told their parents about the incident on the hill, and Parasto downplayed the extent of her work so as to not worry them. Abdulhakim was concerned, he said, but did not want to prevent Parasto from running the schools.

"She is the pride of our family," he said. To keep her safe, Abdulhakim and Sofia tried to convince Parasto to get married.

"I'm afraid they will push me to marry someone, and I can see why," she said. "They want someone else to be responsible for me, and remove the danger from them."

She did want a husband at some point. But she didn't want to marry a cousin or a stranger in an arranged marriage. She still believed in romantic love.

She knew the schoolgirls saw her as a role model, and she had received letters from several of them who said they wanted to grow up to be like her, although they had never seen her in person. She went to the schools and told the girls not to idolize someone they had never even met. She did not fancy herself a hero. A hero was someone great, someone an entire people could unite around.

"We have never had a hero who could unite the nation. First, when Ghani came, we had hope," she said, but Ghani had ended up a villain. "He ruled like a dictator."

Afghanistan had only ever had men who thought too highly of themselves.

"If you consider yourself a hero, no one will accept you," she said.

The Taliban came to Rahela's school again, this time in a Ford Ranger seized from the previous government. They forced their way into the home, where they asked the students for personal details about the teachers and Parasto specifically. The students didn't know Parasto's address, but the visit rattled her. The Taliban's patience was clearly running out. When Rahela called to relay what had happened, Parasto told her to immediately pack up all the school materials and move them to a house in a different part of town. Rahela should stay at home for a while, Parasto said. The phone calls intensified, all from unknown numbers, with men on the other end saying nothing but "Hello."

Parasto and the university teachers discovered that their online classes appeared to have been infiltrated by Taliban members. On the WhatsApp group, where Parasto shared the link for upcoming classes and discussed teaching plans with hundreds of students, some students used photos of women as their profile picture, but on Google Meet, where the classes took place, their voices would be gruff and unmistakably male. They shared excerpts from the Quran on the WhatsApp group and proclaimed that all true Muslims should feel fortunate that Afghanistan was now under Sharia law. They texted some of the girls directly, saying that they should not listen to the infidel Western ideas taught in class. When they were identified, the imposters were kicked off the platforms, but even though the students were anonymous on the apps, several of them were spooked.

Parasto had insisted that she did not want to leave Afghanistan but she realized she had to reassess. Some foreign activists who helped Afghan women out of Afghanistan had introduced Parasto to employees at the French embassy, and worked on getting her a visa, just in case. In February, she was told the visa was coming through. Parasto wavered but knew that she would be of no use if she was arrested. She was not too proud to admit that the Taliban scared her. She packed three suitcases, one of which she filled with books, reserved a seat on a flight to Islamabad, and went to the airport with her brother Inayat chaperoning her. On February 17, seventeen months after the Taliban had returned to power, she settled into a hard plastic chair in the departure lounge of the Kabul airport, her brother by her side. She felt no relief, only guilt and a sense that her identity was already coming apart.

"I feel like I have been burned. All I am is ashes. I walk very cautiously so that I don't break down. With every step, a little bit of my ashes are falling off," she said. She wanted to cry but didn't allow herself to break down in front of her brother.

In Islamabad, she and Inayat stayed in a hotel paid for by her foreign contacts while waiting for her French visa. Once it was ready, Inayat went back to Kabul, where the family needed him, while she flew on to Dubai. On the plane she sat next to a young Pakistani man who worked in IT, who asked if she was Moroccan. He told her he was happy the Taliban had taken power and beaten the Americans. She looked out of the window for the rest of the journey.

The Dubai airport gave her the first taste of life as a refugee. As she handed over her documents to the Emirati passport officer, he got up to have a conversation with his colleagues. She saw them laughing and whispering, clearly about her.

"I wished the earth would open and I would disappear," she said, tearing up. The humiliation cut deep. It dawned on her that she had really left her home country behind.

She landed in Paris early in the morning. At Charles de Gaulle Airport, a retired French diplomat and his Indian wife helped her through passport control and escorted her to the luggage carousel. In the arrivals hall a team of government employees received her and took her to an asylum reception center in Créteil, a southern suburb of Paris. Her room was small, with a single bed, a sink, a mirror, a fridge, and a closet, where she stored her three suitcases and her books. Next to the window, there was a desk where she could eat and write, with a view through the window of a massive leafless tree with branches stretching from its trunk toward her. Outside the door, kids ran up and down the hallways, bouncing off the walls. "I didn't know that rooms in Europe are so small," she said. She thought it looked like a mental asylum.

"I just broke down. I could not take it," she said. The women who had picked her up asked if they could help.

"Just leave me alone," she said.

In the afternoon, her phone rang, still operating with her Afghan WhatsApp number. It was a young Afghan man who had recently moved to Paris himself, and whom she had been introduced to before arriving. He said he'd pick her up that evening. She declined, saying she didn't feel like doing anything.

"If you stay in tonight, you'll never want to go out," he said. He picked her up and took her to a social gathering of Afghans, where she was served Afghan food and briefed by other Afghan refugees about the asylum process that she was about to embark upon. They told her stories about their own journeys to Europe, many of which had been more arduous and dangerous than her own.

She spent her first days in Paris, her introduction to Europe, walking for hours through the city streets brimming with history. Her photographic memory helped her and she quickly learned to navigate her way with the metro from Créteil to the center. She did some sightseeing. She found the Eiffel Tower old and rusty but enjoyed the Parisian cafés, such as Café République, with its tricolored marquee and round tables where she could face the sidewalk and watch people walk past. She realized, with a faint tinge of embarrassment, that French fries were French. She spent hours in libraries, for free, reading about French history and that most famous "French warlord," as she called him: Napoleon. She read *Crime and Punishment* and thought it was beautiful.

On the metro and in the streets, she saw Ukrainian refugees, newly arrived like her, but thought they looked more scared than she felt—perhaps, she thought, because war to them was a relatively new phenomenon. To her surprise, she missed Kabul's putrid smells of city life, dust, and smoke. Before getting on the plane at home, she had collected a handful of soil, which she carried with her now. When she

had the chance, she wanted to use it to plant a cactus. An ugly, resilient plant.

Every day she returned to the center in Créteil, where the smell
of stewed food from the kitchen greeted her long before she reached
the front door. The stench reminded her of rotten eggs. In a rushed
purchase, she had picked up a pair of boots in size 37, because they
didn't have a size 39, and within days, she was taping up her heels with
Band-Aids. She slept badly, without rest. Life in exile provided no relief, even though she knew, rationally, that she was safe, and she didn't
want to appear ungrateful. She ate, but didn't feel hungry. She slept,
but always felt tired. She wanted to go for walks, but was exhausted.
When she sat down, she immediately became too restless to sit still.

The French were polite and helpful, but she found it difficult to
make sincere connections.

"No one really wants to be your friend, because they think you
need help, and they can't help you," she said. "It makes you hate
yourself."

One afternoon in late February, she pulled herself out of her stu-
por and decided to take advantage of some of Paris's cultural offer-
ings. She had always wanted to see modern art but had never been to
a museum. She went to the Pompidou Centre, the industrial-looking
complex in the 4th arrondissement, built to look like it'd been turned
inside out, with color-coded water pipes and air-conditioning ducts
and mechanical systems placed on the building's exterior, escalators
snaking like water slides on the facades. Parasto was drawn to darker
works in the museum's collection, often made in times of war. She
spent several minutes in front of Marc Chagall's *Newspaper Seller*,
painted during the first year of the First World War, which would
prevent the painter from returning to France from Russia for years.
The painting depicted the newspaper vendor with a somber face, in
front of a red sky and a sad representation of a town. An allegory for
the misfortunes of war. Parasto had studied the history of the Soviet
Union's invasion of Afghanistan and did not agree with the prevailing
historical interpretation in her country that the Afghans had won.

"We didn't beat anyone. They just got tired of fighting and then left. They call Afghanistan the graveyard of empires. It is not," she said.

She paused in awe in front of a work by the French American sculptor Niki de Saint Phalle called *La mariée*, or *The Bride*, which showed a large, sad-looking doll in a wedding dress, as if burdened by duty. Saint Phalle called the bride "a total failure of individuality."

Parasto was equally fascinated by the geometric work of Marcel Breuer, depicting sharp angular structures, unwelcoming reminders that we humans often don't fit into the shapes made for us by our circumstances, she said.

"In any corner of the world, if you see a refugee, or a person who comes from a developing country, they will never enjoy peace. They will never be happy," she said. "You don't feel like yourself anymore. You have to change, but you don't want to change."

A few weeks later, she was offered an apartment in Plaisir, a commune west of Paris, with two other asylum seekers, a girl from Iraqi Kurdistan and a girl from Syria. She could stay at the apartment while her asylum case was being reviewed. She taught her new housemates the Afghan traditional *attan* dance. She listened to patriotic songs by Farhad Darya, whose pathos-laden odes to his homeland were standard fare among the Afghan diaspora, including one set to lyrics by the late poet Qahar Asi. His declaration of love for his home country as his "seventh heaven" gave her solace. But the next lines no longer rang true for her.

"What rebellious people," Darya sang, "what a proud nation, what a proud people."

"Our men are no longer brave, courageous, and revolutionary. They are cowards," Parasto said. Afghan men had failed to rise up against the Taliban when the Islamists entered the homes of families, closed schools to women, and mocked Afghans in front of the world. The bravest of them complained on social media, from the safety of their homes.

"They humiliated us all, they made fun of our beliefs and called us non-Muslims," she said. "And all our men do is post tweets."

For a long time, her mind at night had been a blank slate, but she, too, had started dreaming again. Her new apartment was near a lake, where she ran six miles every day and was pleasantly exhausted when she went to bed. Her dreams were intense and literal: in one she helped her family climb a mountain; in others she was stuck in a roaring river or hiding from Taliban militants. A therapist she had started seeing told her the dreams would get better with time. She practiced painting and singing and studied four hours of French four days a week. Generations of Afghans before her had made a life in exile. She always thought she would have a different fate. As the weeks and months went by, her country receded in her mind into a rhyme of history, subjugated once again by forces that robbed its people of their dignity. She resigned to the reality that she, too, would have to search outside her own land for a home that accepted her. She would have to wait.

When she needed solitude, or a cry, she went to the lake and watched schools of fish swim in circles. As far as she could tell, they had no hierarchy, no categories. They swam without purpose.

She was not free, but she was safe. That alone made life, every day, a little easier.

A NOTE ON REPORTING AND SOURCES

This book is a work of nonfiction. It is the result of reporting conducted over the course of nine years, including three years when I lived in Afghanistan, and regular, lengthy trips since. I was present for some scenes in the book, including events taking place in Kabul, in the provinces, and in Paris. Other scenes were recounted to me. There are no conflated events or composite characters in the book, and no dialogue or scene has been fabricated. When I describe the inner life, thoughts, or dreams of a person, the individual has relayed those thoughts to me.

Memory, though, is volatile. I have sought wherever possible to corroborate individual accounts by speaking to other sources—family members, friends, acquaintances—or by use of articles, reports, video footage, photos, and other archival material. When corroboration wasn't possible, I included details according to my best journalistic judgment, especially avoiding claims that stretched credulity or involved allegations against specific individuals. Throughout I have strived to be accurate and fair. Any mistake or misunderstanding is my responsibility alone.

Writing a book based partly on people's recollections of events entails working with different realities. There are indisputable facts, which are all-important. There are also the stories we carry, the stories that help form our outlook on the world, the actions we take, and the people we become. These stories are real insofar as they shape us. As such, this is a book about the facts of what happened, and a book about memory, about the perceptions people have of the world and their place in it.

The main protagonists in the book all appear under their real names, although Omari's last name is omitted for the sake of his security. The name of Parasto's mother has been changed and her father's last name left out at their request. I have known Zahra and Omari since 2015 and 2016, respectively, and have interviewed each of them on more than a dozen occasions, for hours at a time, since then. I have watched Zahra's children grow from puberty to adulthood, and I witnessed her rise in public prominence, from an unknown first-time author to parliamentary candidate. I have seen Omari transform from hardened jihadist fighting foreign occupiers to a member of the winning side who's increasingly nagged by doubts about the people who sent him into holy war. Our first meetings took place in his home province, in hiding from government intelligence agents. Our last interviews were conducted around Kabul, in empty houses or abandoned restaurants during the fasting month of Ramadan, in secret because the Taliban commanders had banned their fighters from speaking to media.

I have known Fahim since years before the fall of Kabul. I met Parasto shortly after the fall, in 2021, and interviewed her at length several times during subsequent trips to Taliban-controlled Afghanistan and later in Paris.

The book also draws on books, newspaper articles, and other literature.

Edward Said's quotation on the experience of exile is taken from *Reflections on Exile and Other Essays* (Cambridge, MA: Harvard University Press, 2000), p. 180.

The Quran passage referred to in chapter 1 is chapter 4 of the

Quran, verse 34, which describes a good woman as being obedient to her husband, and says he is allowed to "strike" her if she repeatedly disobeys him. The passage is disputed, particularly regarding what is meant by "strike," and some scholars argue that misinterpreting the verse can wrongly justify domestic violence.

Ahmed Rashid's *Descent into Chaos: The U.S. and the Disaster in Pakistan, Afghanistan, and Central Asia* (New York: Penguin, 2008) provided source material for the history about ISI's double game after 2001, helping both the American military and the Taliban. Rashid's *Taliban: Islam, Oil, and the New Great Game in Central Asia* (London: I.B. Tauris, 2000) is a great resource on the militant movement's place in Afghan history.

For details on how US units were ordered to capture and kill suspected terrorists regardless of the cost (chapter 3), see Carter Malkasian, *The American War in Afghanistan: A History* (New York: Oxford University Press, 2021). Australian commandos can be heard joking about meeting their "quota" in a video broadcast by the Australian Broadcasting Corporation on September 20, 2022: https://www.abc.net.au/news/2022-09-20/australian-commandos-in-afghanistan-filmed-discussing-quota/101432000.

Steve Coll's *Directorate S: The C.I.A. and America's Secret Wars in Afghanistan and Pakistan* (New York: Penguin Press, 2018) is an eminent work on Afghanistan's modern history. It served specifically as source material for passages on the Taliban's offers to surrender following 9/11 (chapter 3); details about building the Afghan security forces (chapter 5); internal disputes in the Obama administration, such as that between Gen. David Petraeus and Richard Holbrooke; the interference of Holbrooke and others in the 2009 election (chapter 6); and the profile of young Afghan suicide bombers (chapter 9), which in turn draws on research by Brian Glyn Williams of the University of Massachusetts. Coll's earlier book *Ghost Wars: The Secret History of the CIA, Afghanistan, and bin Laden, from the Soviet Invasion to September 10, 2001* (New York: Penguin, 2005) is an equally excellent account of Afghanistan's history before the 2001 invasion.

The idea of the collective as the basic unit of Afghan society (chapter 4) is well explained in Huma Ahmed-Ghosh, "A History of Women in Afghanistan," *Journal of International Women's Studies* 4, no. 3 (May 2003).

Statistics on divorce rates in Afghanistan (chapter 4) are hard to come by. According to the Afghanistan Independent Human Rights Commission, 600 couples got divorced in 2017. The number would likely have been even lower when Zahra and Hussein got divorced. For comparison, around 150,000 couples were divorced in Iran in 2010, according to official figures, equaling roughly one in seven marriages. In Saudi Arabia, nearly 46,000 divorce cases were filed in 2015, according to the Saudi General Authority for Statistics.

For data on casualties as a result of American drone warfare (chapter 5), see the Bureau of Investigative Journalism's database "Drone Warfare": https://www.thebureauinvestigates.com/projects/drone-war. For data on casualties from US airstrikes (chapter 22), see Airwars.org.

The life and career of Hamid Karzai and his family are recounted best in *A Kingdom of Their Own: The Family Karzai and the Afghan Disaster* (New York: Vintage, 2016) by Joshua Partlow. This is also the source for the story of Ruhollah Popalzai, aka the Butcher, including the assertion that he was released from prison due to his relations with the Karzai family, and the story of the cousins Rashed and Rateb Popal (chapter 6). Bette Dam's *A Man and a Motorcycle: How Hamid Karzai Came to Power* (Utrecht: Ipso Facto, 2014) is also a great work on Karzai's life.

Much has been written about American "black sites" and the allegations of torture taking place there. In chapter 6, I drew on Adrian Levy and Cathy Scott-Clark, "One Huge US Jail," in *The Guardian*, March 19, 2005.

Data in chapter 7 on corruption and how US military funds primarily benefited American contractors is taken from a February 2021 report by the Special Inspector General for Afghanistan Reconstruction, or SIGAR, "SIGAR 21-20 Evaluation Report: U.S.-Funded Capital

Assets in Afghanistan: The U.S. Government Spent More Than $2.4 Billion on Capital Assets That Were Unused or Abandoned, Were Not Used for Their Intended Purposes, Had Deteriorated, or Were Destroyed." It is worth noting that there is a significant margin of uncertainty here, as 49 percent of the funds reviewed by SIGAR ($3.8 billion) went toward assets that were not yet fully constructed or procured at the time of the report's publication. An additional 9 percent ($733 million) was directed to assets whose fate could not be determined. SIGAR in general is a rich and authoritative source on military and reconstruction spending.

On the observation in chapter 7 that much of the military aid ended up back in the US economy as a result of Pentagon outsourcing to private contractors, see William D. Hartung, "Profits of War: Corporate Beneficiaries of the Post-9/11 Pentagon Spending Surge," Watson Institute for International and Public Affairs at Brown University and Center for International Policy, September 13, 2021, as well as Jon Schwarz, "$10,000 Invested in Defense Stocks When Afghanistan War Began Now Worth Almost $100,000," *The Intercept*, August 16, 2021.

Kate Bateman with the United States Institute of Peace provided valuable insight into the debates in Washington, DC, and inside the US military over the war effort, and the limited ability of external experts to influence strategic planning in Western capitals (chapter 7). She and her colleague Dipali Mukhopadhyay kindly let me read their paper on the topic, with a working title of "Knowledge Production and Policymaking in America's Longest War," United States Institute of Peace, before publication in a forthcoming anthology on the war. The idea that underdeveloped states cannot absorb an excess of aid is laid out in Paolo de Renzio, "Increased Aid vs Absorptive Capacity: Challenges and Opportunities Toward 2015," *Institute of Development Studies Bulletin* 36, no. 3 (September 2005).

A note on the claim in chapter 8 that of the estimated $2.3 trillion spent on the war through 2020, less than 6 percent went to reconstruction projects: According to the US Department of Defense, the total US military expenditure reached $824.9 billion from 2001 to 2020, while $131 billion was spent on reconstruction. The nongovernmental study "Human and Budgetary Costs to Date of the U.S. War in Afghanistan 2001–2022" by researchers at the Watson Institute at Brown University put the total cost of the US war much higher, at $2.31 trillion. The higher estimate included interest on debt used to finance the war, expenses such as veterans' care, and spending in Pakistan, which the United States used as a base for operations related to the Afghan conflict—all of which can fairly be considered part of the costs of the Afghan war.

The research on teenage suicide bombers and the Dadullah Lang interview referenced in chapter 9 can be found in Brian Glyn William, "Mullah Omar's Missiles: A Field Report on Suicide Bombers in Afghanistan," *Middle East Policy* 15, no. 4 (2008).

For a good account of the Kandahar massacre perpetrated by US Army S.Sgt. Robert Bales (chapter 9), see Brendan Vaughan, "Robert Bales Speaks: Confessions of America's Most Notorious War Criminal," *GQ*, October 21, 2015.

The account in chapter 10 of the killing of US general Harold Greene is based on reporting I did for an article in *Harper's Magazine* called "Death of a General," published in July 2016, for which I spoke to family members of the general's killer, Sefidullah. A copy of the American military's investigation into the incident was previously accessed at http://apps.washingtonpost.com/g/documents/local/the-militarys-narrative-overview-of-the-attack/1694. A summary of the report can be found at: https://www.armytimes.com/news/pentagon-congress/2014/12/04/report-general-s-killer-fired-30-rounds.

A lot has been written about the phenomenon of *bacha bazi* and the child abuse sometimes associated with it. For the claim in chapter 11 that US commanders told their soldiers not to intervene when they witnessed such abuse on bases, see Joseph Goldstein, "U.S. Soldiers Told to Ignore Sexual Abuse of Boys by Afghan Allies," *The New York Times*, September 20, 2015.

For details on how the United States continued to pay Afghan governors to eradicate poppy cultivation after abandoning such efforts itself (chapter 12), see the Afghan National Drug Action Plan 2015–2019, published by the Afghan Ministry of Counter Narcotics, October 14, 2015.

The official statistics showing that 40 percent of soldiers in Helmand did not exist, referred to in chapter 12, are from a confidential study commissioned by the Afghan government that I obtained. Read more in Sune Engel Rasmussen, "Afghanistan's 'Ghost Soldiers': Thousands Enlisted to Fight Taliban Don't Exist," *The Guardian*, May 17, 2016.

Data related to Iran's funding and arming of Shia militias in Syria (chapter 14) is disputed. I relied on Tobias Schneider, "The Fatemiyoun Division: Afghan Fighters in the Syrian Civil War," Middle East Institute, October 15, 2018.

My description in chapter 15 of how Islamist groups had a following among Afghan university students, and the views among university students of democracy and liberal values, draws on two studies: Borhan Osman, "Beyond Jihad and Traditionalism: Afghanistan's New Generation of Islamic Activists," Afghanistan Analysts Network, June 23, 2015; and Robert Zaman and Abdul Ahad Mohammadi, "Trends in Student Radicalization Across University Campuses in Afghanistan," Afghan Institute for Strategic Studies, 2014.

Descriptions of Ashraf Ghani's character, behavior, and politics draw on my own reporting and several meetings with the president. See also Emma Graham-Harrison, "Ashraf Ghani: The Intellectual President Who Can Now Put Theory into Practice," *The Guardian*, September 26, 2014; Mujib Mashal, "The President, the Envoy and the Talib: 3 Lives Shaped by War and Study Abroad," *The New York Times*, February 16, 2019; Adam Nossiter, "As Afghan Forces Crumble, an Air of Unreality Grips the Capital," *The New York Times*, July 2, 2021; and "SIGAR 23-05-IP Evaluation Report: Why the Afghan Government Collapsed," Special Inspector General for Afghanistan Reconstruction, November 2022.

A good blow-by-blow of the peace negotiations between the United States and the Taliban is found in Steve Coll and Adam Entous, "The

Secret History of the U.S. Diplomatic Failure in Afghanistan," *The New Yorker*, December 10, 2021. The best critical account of the process is Steve Brooking, "Why Was a Negotiated Peace Always Out of Reach in Afghanistan? Opportunities and Obstacles, 2001–21," United States Institute of Peace, August 30, 2022.

Reports of the Taliban summary executions of alleged criminals in chapter 19 are based on eyewitness statements and photos and video material. I wrote about them for *The Wall Street Journal* in "The Taliban Say They've Changed. On the Ground, They're Just as Brutal," May 31, 2021.

Abuses and unlawful killings by Afghanistan's special forces Zero Units (chapter 19) are described in Lynzy Billing, "The Night Raids," *ProPublica*, December 15, 2022, and in "'They've Shot Many Like This': Abusive Night Raids by CIA-Backed Afghan Strike Forces," Human Rights Watch, October 31, 2019.

I found statistics on trauma and mental health issues among Afghans (chapter 19) in Meera Thoompail and Jake Tacchi, "The Impact of the Conflict in Afghanistan on Civilian Mental Health," Action on Armed Violence, October 1, 2020, and "Afghanistan: Little Help for Conflict-Linked Trauma," Human Rights Watch, October 7, 2019.

The account of the fall of Kabul is compiled from my own reporting, as well as detailed reports by colleagues. See in particular: Andrew Quilty, *August in Kabul: America's Last Days in Afghanistan* (New York: Bloomsbury Academic, 2023); Yaroslav Trofimov and Margherita Stancati, "Taliban Covert Operatives Seized Kabul, Other Afghan Cities from Within," *The Wall Street Journal*, November 28, 2021; Gordon Lubold and Yaroslav Trofimov, "Afghan Government Could Collapse Six Months After U.S. Withdrawal, New Intelligence Assessment Says," *The Wall Street Journal*, June 23, 2021; Kathy Gannon, "US Left Afghan Airfield at Night, Didn't Tell New Commander," Associated Press, July 6, 2021; and Matthieu Aikins, "Inside the Fall of Kabul," *The New York Times Magazine*, December 10, 2021.

The number of former government officials and members of the Afghan security forces who were killed or forcibly disappeared under the Taliban (chapter 21) is documented by the human rights organization Rawadari and in Barbara Marcolini, Sanjar Sohail, and Alexander Stockton, "The Taliban Promised Them Amnesty. Then They Executed Them," *The New York Times*, April 12, 2022.

The details on the internal divisions within the Taliban are all based on reporting I did in the country at the time, including numerous interviews with Taliban insiders and officials.

For additional reading, I highly recommend the following books: Alex Strick van Linschoten and Felix Kuehn's *An Enemy We Created: The Myth of the Taliban/Al-Qaeda Merger in Afghanistan, 1970–2010* (London: Hurst, 2012) is an authoritative work on the relationship and differences between the two militant groups. Anand Gopal's *No Good Men Among the Living: America, the Taliban, and the War Through Afghan Eyes* (New York: Henry Holt, 2014) was an early inspiration for its perspective on the war from an Afghan point of view. Thomas Barfield's *Afghanistan: A Cultural and Political History* (Princeton, NJ: Princeton University Press, 2012) is compulsory reading in the genre. Graeme Smith's *The Dogs Are Eating Them Now: Our War in Afghanistan* (Toronto: Random House Canada, 2013) is an exemplary account of the missteps and atrocities committed by Western forces. Read Matthieu Aikins, *The Naked Don't Fear the Water: An Underground Journey with Afghan Refugees* (New York: HarperCollins, 2022) for an excellent narrative account of the refugee experience, and for the war's endgame from the perspective of US soldiers, read Jessica Donati, *Eagle Down: The Last Special Forces Fighting the Forever War* (New York: PublicAffairs, 2021).

ACKNOWLEDGMENTS

I am indebted to a small army of people who provided help, inspiration, and critique during the writing process. I owe immense gratitude to the people whose stories constitute the heart of this book. They were exceedingly generous with their time and gracious in their response to my incessant and detailed questions. Having people trust me to tell their stories, sometimes at great risk to their own safety, is a huge privilege I don't take for granted.

Much of the reporting would not have been possible without the help and advice of Qari Shahab, Aziz Tassal, Mokhtar Amiri, and Rauf Mehrpoor. All of them are impeccable journalists and dear friends whom I entrusted with my life on multiple occasions. I would do so again in a heartbeat. Early readers of the manuscript provided wise feedback that made the book stronger in many ways: Shaharzad Akbar, who was kinder than she needed to be when checking my interpretations of Afghan culture and politics; Tommy Wide, one of the smartest foreigners I know on all things Afghanistan, whose incisive reading I was lucky to benefit from; Emma Graham-Harrison, whose deep knowledge of Afghanistan continues to impress me, and whose generous reading during a hectic schedule strengthened the final text;

and Tshepo Mokoena, indefatigable hype woman whose surgical editorial eye was invaluable as I scrambled to finish. Zahra Nader might have forgotten that she was the one who initially introduced me to her namesake in the book, but I have not, and I remain grateful for that.

Sahar Fetrat and Rada Akbar taught me a lot over the years about the lives of progressive young women in Afghanistan, and were extremely useful interpreters of interviews and of Afghan culture. Both deserve to have books written about them, and had they not been my good friends, they would have appeared in this one. Mahdi Omaidi was a valuable conduit on the ground at times when I couldn't be in Afghanistan myself. Zamir Saar provided much-needed reporting and transcription help. Andrew Quilty was a treasured and frequent travel partner and housemate in Kabul whom I consider family, and a source of much-needed levity in dire situations as well as professional inspiration. Joel van Houdt is another close friend and companion I never tire of being on the road with. Matthieu Aikins and Graeme Smith taught me the ropes early on in Kabul and have been dear friends for nearly a decade since. Nagieb Khaja continues to be a source of insight, ideas, contacts, and brotherhood.

Over the years, countless people in Afghanistan made me significantly smarter and offered friendship I still treasure: Andrew Watkins, Kate Clark, Timor Sharan, Mujib Mashal, David Gill, Victor Blue, Steve Brooking, Jelena Bjelica, Lenny Linke, Rahmatullah Amiri, Chris Fitzgerald, Jasmine Bhatia, Kate Carey, Stephen Carter, Liza Schuster, and Mark Bowden. Outside Afghanistan, my parents, Pia and Torben, and my brother, Janus, were always supportive of my choice to live in various conflict zones, oceans away, for more than a decade, which I will always be grateful for. Jason Rezaian was an early mentor and remains a true friend and counsel. My editors at *The Wall Street Journal* were supportive in allowing me space to finish the book at an extremely busy time for world news, and have helped sharpen my work and enabled me to make a career of sorts. I'm in particular grateful to Gordon Fairclough, Michael Amon, Karen Pensiero, Nikhil Lohade, and Peter Wonacott. My *Journal* colleagues on the Afghanistan beat made me a better reporter and provided friendship along the way: Ehsanullah Amiri, Habib Totakhil, Jessica Donati, Margherita Stancati, Yaroslav Trofimov, and Saeed Shah. Stevo Stephen and Nathan Puffer have put up with an unfair amount of my bullshit while trying to keep me safe and still believing in the journalistic mission. Also thank you to my former foreign editor at *The Guardian*, Jamie Wilson, for his support as I traveled to many of the places from which substantial chunks of the book were reported.

I could not have asked for a better agent than Elias Altman, who was driven from day one and an invaluable help in both conceptualizing the book and getting it going. At Farrar, Straus and Giroux, my editor, Alex Star, believed in the project from the beginning, gave every sentence his undivided attention, and wrung a better book out of me. Thank you also to the rest of the FSG team: Ian Van Wye, Susan VanHecke, Nancy Elgin, and Brian Gittis.

My biggest thanks, of course, to Danielle, my heart and ally who makes everything possible. My most honest and inquisitive reader, this book would not have existed without you. It was your idea to move to Afghanistan in the first place, and you have never stopped championing and pushing me. I hope I have made you proud.